P9-AQD-941

Betty Crocker's

ANNUAL RECIPES

2·0·0·3

Bac-Os, Basic 4, BETTY CROCKER, Bisquick, Corn Chex, Country, Gold Medal, Honey Nut Clusters, Lloyd's, SuperMoist, and Yoplait are registered trademarks and Harmony is a trademark of General Mills, Inc. This edition published by arrangement with Wiley, Inc.

General Mills, Inc.

Betty Crocker Kitchens

Manager, Publishing: Lois Tlusty

Recipe Development: Betty Crocker Kitchens Home Economists

Food Stylists: Betty Crocker Kitchens Food Stylists

Photography: Photographic Services Department

Editor: Kathy Everleth

Book Designer: Leanne Coppola

For consistent baking results, the Betty Crocker Kitchens recommend Gold Medal Flour.

ISBN 1–57954–642–0

Printed in the United States of America

10 9 8 7 6 5 4 3 2 1   hardcover

Cover: Chocolate Turtle Cake (page 215)

For more great ideas, visit www.bettycrocker.com.

C O N T E N T S

Asian Pork and Noodle Soup (page 75)

Introduction

It's time to celebrate another year of delicious recipes! In this second edition of *Betty Crocker's Annual Recipes*, we've once again collected your favorites from the past year of *Betty Crocker* magazine into one convenient volume of easy, great-tasting dishes. With more than 240 recipes to choose from, you'll never run out of ideas for pleasing your family!

Make breakfast extra-special with Apricot French Toast with Pineapple Apricot Topping or Denver Eggs Frittata. Dinner's a snap with 30-minute pasta dishes like Spring Vegetable Fettuccine or Penne with Spicy Sauce. Pair savory one-pot dishes like Tomato Lentil Soup with cozy homestyle breads like Triple-Cheese Flatbread. And hot-from-the-oven dishes like Zesty Italian Chicken and Gruyère Vegetable Bake are lifesavers on a busy weeknight.

There's no shortage of creative serving suggestions and kitchen tips for making your life easier and more fun: making a shortcut flan, creating a beautiful fan out of Parmesan cheese, decorating an appetizer table, even baking cupcakes in ice cream cones!

And speaking of sweets, there's a great selection of desserts to satisfy your every craving. Try Chocolate Turtle Cake, Praline Puffs, or Hot Buttered Rum Cheesecake for sheer decadence. And bites like Key Lime Mini-Tarts, Rocky Road Bars, and Luscious Chocolate Truffles simply melt in your mouth.

For those who enjoy cooking for company, we've included recipes and tips to make every occasion special. Serve impressive appetizers like Baked Coconut Shrimp or Brie in Puff Pastry with Cranberry Sauce. If the whole gang is coming for dinner, turn to "Crowd Pleasers" to find big-batch dishes like Sausage Chili Bake and Sweet and Spicy Rubbed Ham. Plus, the menus in "Company's Coming!" will give you ideas for entertaining no matter what the occasion—from a fun summer supper to a movie night with friends. To create your own menus, turn to "Celebrate the Seasons," an easy way for you to find just the right recipes for your special occasion any time of year.

For speedy dishes, look for the "Quick" label to find recipes that can be ready in 30 minutes or less. If you want dishes with less fat, the "Low-Fat" label helps you find them. Main dishes with this label have 6 grams of fat or less per serving, while side dishes and desserts have 3 grams or less.

And finally, don't forget the beautiful photographs—there's one for every recipe! One look will tell you that these are recipes your family will love.

It's a delicious celebration, and we're so glad you're joining us!

Betty Crocker

Celebrate the Seasons

Want the perfect entrée for a winter weeknight? Or maybe just the right dessert for a hot summer evening? Use this handy list of recipes categorized by season to select dishes for any occasion, any time of year.

Spring

Summer

Fall

Winter

Any Time of Year

Morning Glories

Elegant Entrées for Breakfast or Brunch

Apricot French Toast with Pineapple Apricot Topping (page 8)

Blueberry Pancakes with Maple Cranberry Syrup (page 7)

Easy Caramel Sticky Rolls

Prep: 10 min   Bake: 25 min

½ cup packed brown sugar
½ cup whipping (heavy) cream
¼ cup chopped pecans
2 tablespoons granulated sugar
1 teaspoon ground cinnamon
1 can (11 ounces) refrigerated soft breadsticks

1. Heat oven to 350°. Mix brown sugar and whipping cream in ungreased round pan, 8 × 1½ inches. Sprinkle with pecans.

2. Mix granulated sugar and cinnamon. Unroll breadstick dough, but do not separate into breadsticks. Sprinkle cinnamon-sugar mixture over dough. Roll up dough from short end; separate at perforations. Place coiled dough in pan.

3. Bake 20 to 25 minutes or until golden brown. Cool 1 minute. Turn pan upside down onto heatproof tray or serving plate. Let stand 1 minute so caramel will drizzle over rolls.

6 rolls.

1 Roll: Calories 310 (Calories from Fat 100); Fat 11g (Saturated 5g); Cholesterol 20mg; Sodium 320mg; Carbohydrate 50g (Dietary Fiber 2g); Protein 5g
% Daily Value: Vitamin A 4%; Vitamin C 0%; Calcium 8%; Iron 12%
Diet Exchanges: Not Recommended

BETTY'S TIPS

☺ Serve-With
Serve these gooey rolls with a platter of fresh fruit, Canadian bacon slices and a pot of fresh-brewed coffee for a fast and fabulous holiday breakfast.

☺ Variation
For **Easy Caramel Apple Sticky Rolls,** omit the cinnamon-sugar mixture and spread ⅓ cup cinnamon-flavored applesauce over dough.

Apple Kuchen Coffee Cake

Prep: 15 min   Bake: 50 min   Cool: 10 min

½ cup sugar
⅓ cup butter or margarine, softened
1 egg
2 cups Original Bisquick®
½ cup vanilla yogurt
1 egg
1 large cooking apple, peeled and thinly sliced (1½ cups)
¼ cup sugar
¼ teaspoon ground cinnamon

1. Heat oven to 350°. Grease bottom and side of springform pan, 9 × 2 inches, or round pan, 9 × 1½ inches, with shortening.

2. Beat ½ cup sugar, the butter and egg in medium bowl with electric mixer on low speed about 30 seconds or until smooth. Beat in Bisquick. Spread over bottom and 1 inch up side of pan.

3. Mix yogurt and egg in small bowl until smooth. Stir in apple; spoon over batter in pan. Mix ¼ cup sugar and the cinnamon; sprinkle over apple mixture.

4. Bake 45 to 50 minutes or until center is set and crust is deep golden brown. Cool 10 minutes; remove side of pan. Serve warm.

8 servings.

1 Serving: Calories 305 (Calories from Fat 115); Fat 13g (Saturated 6g); Cholesterol 75mg; Sodium 500mg; Carbohydrate 44g (Dietary Fiber 1g); Protein 4g
% Daily Value: Vitamin A 8%; Vitamin C 0%; Calcium 8%; Iron 6%
Diet Exchanges: 1½ Starch, 1½ Fruit, 2 Fat

BETTY'S TIPS

☺ Extra Special
Drizzle with a glaze made by mixing ½ cup powdered sugar and 1 to 2 tablespoons milk until smooth and thin enough to drizzle.

☺ Did You Know?
A kuchen is a fruit- or cheese-filled yeast-raised cake, usually served for breakfast but also enjoyed as a dessert. It originated in Germany. We've simplified the traditional yeast-raised kuchen by using Bisquick to make a delicious crust.

Easy Caramel Sticky Rolls

Apple Kuchen Coffee Cake

Golden Carrot Spice Scones

Prep: 15 min   Bake: 18 min

2 cups Gold Medal® all-purpose flour
¼ cup sugar
2½ teaspoons baking powder
1 teaspoon pumpkin pie spice
½ teaspoon salt
⅓ cup firm butter or margarine
⅓ cup whipping (heavy) cream
1 cup finely shredded carrots (1½ medium)
½ cup golden raisins
1 egg
   Spice Glaze (right)

1. Heat oven to 400°. Mix flour, sugar, baking powder, pumpkin pie spice and salt in large bowl. Cut in butter, using pastry blender or crisscrossing 2 knives, until mixture looks like fine crumbs. Stir in whipping cream, carrots, raisins and egg until dough leaves side of bowl and forms a ball.

2. Drop dough by heaping tablespoons 2 inches apart onto ungreased cookie sheet; press slightly.

3. Bake 15 to 18 minutes or until light golden brown. Immediately remove from cookie sheet to wire rack. Drizzle with Spice Glaze. Serve warm.

8 scones.

Spice Glaze
½ cup powdered sugar
2 tablespoons whipping (heavy) cream or milk
⅛ teaspoon pumpkin pie spice or ground cinnamon

Mix all ingredients until smooth.

1 Scone: Calories 320 (Calories from Fat 115); Fat 13g (Saturated 8g); Cholesterol 60mg; Sodium 370mg; Carbohydrate 48g (Dietary Fiber 2g); Protein 5g
% Daily Value: Vitamin A 60%; Vitamin C 0%; Calcium 10%; Iron 10%
Diet Exchanges: Not Recommended

BETTY'S TIPS

✪ Substitution
If you don't have any pumpkin pie spice on hand, make your own by mixing ½ teaspoon ground cinnamon, ¼ teaspoon ground ginger, ⅛ teaspoon ground nutmeg and ⅛ teaspoon ground cloves.

✪ Variation
Make wedge-shaped scones by patting dough into a circle and cutting into wedges before baking.

Golden Carrot Spice Scones

Breakfast Wraps

Prep: 20 min   Cook: 25 min

- 3 cups sliced strawberries (about 1½ pints)
- ½ cup sugar
- 1½ cups Gold Medal all-purpose flour
- 1 tablespoon sugar
- ½ teaspoon baking powder
- ½ teaspoon salt
- 2 cups milk
- 2 tablespoons butter or margarine, melted
- 1 teaspoon finely shredded lime peel
- 2 tablespoons lime juice
- 2 eggs
  Lime Cream Filling (below)

1. Toss strawberries and ½ cup sugar in bowl; let stand at room temperature at least 20 minutes. Meanwhile, mix flour, 1 tablespoon sugar, the baking powder and salt in medium bowl. Stir in milk, butter, lime peel, lime juice and eggs. Beat with hand beater until smooth.

2. Lightly grease 6- to 8-inch skillet with butter. Heat over medium heat until bubbly. Pour batter by slightly less than ¼ cupfuls into skillet. Immediately rotate skillet until thin layer of batter covers bottom. Cook until light golden brown. Run wide spatula around edge to loosen; turn and cook other side until light brown. Repeat with remaining batter, greasing skillet as needed. Stack wraps, placing waxed paper between each; cool.

3. Make Lime Cream Filling. Spoon about 2 tablespoons of the filling down center of each wrap; fold sides over filling. To serve, place 2 wraps on each of 6 plates. Spoon strawberries over wraps.

6 servings.

Lime Cream Filling

- ⅔ cup whipping (heavy) cream
- 1 package (8 ounces) cream cheese, softened
- ½ cup sugar
- 1 tablespoon finely shredded lime peel

Beat whipping cream in chilled small bowl with electric mixer on high speed until stiff; set aside. Beat cream cheese in medium bowl on high speed until fluffy; stir in sugar and lime peel. Gently stir in whipped cream.

1 Serving: Calories 515 (Calories from Fat 260); Fat 29g (Saturated 17g); Cholesterol 160mg; Sodium 450mg; Carbohydrate 53g (Dietary Fiber 2g); Protein 12g
% Daily Value: Vitamin A 24%; Vitamin C 28%; Calcium 18%; Iron 14%
Diet Exchanges: 1 Starch, 1 Medium-Fat Meat, 2 Fruit, 4 Fat

BETTY'S TIPS

⊙ **Do-Ahead**
Unfilled wraps can be tightly wrapped with aluminum foil and refrigerated up to 48 hours.

⊙ **Extra Special**
Garnish with thin strips of lime peel and a dollop of whipped cream.

Breakfast Wraps

Waffles with Honey Chestnut Spread

Prep: 15 min   Rise: 1 hr 30 min   Chill: 8 hr   Bake: 15 min

1   package active dry yeast

¼   cup warm water (105° to 115°)

2   cups Gold Medal all-purpose flour

¼   cup butter or margarine, softened

1¾   cups lukewarm milk (scalded then cooled)

2   tablespoons sugar

1   teaspoon salt

3   eggs

Honey Chestnut Spread (below)

1. Dissolve yeast in warm water in large bowl. Add remaining ingredients except Honey Chestnut Spread. Beat with electric mixer on medium speed until smooth.

2. Cover and let rise in warm place 1 hour 30 minutes. Stir down batter. Cover and refrigerate 8 to 12 hours. Make Honey Chestnut Spread.

3. Heat waffle iron; grease with shortening if necessary (or spray with cooking spray before heating). Stir down batter. For each waffle, pour about ½ cup batter from cup or pitcher onto center of hot waffle iron. (Waffle irons vary in size; check manufacturer's directions for recommended amount of batter.) Close lid of waffle iron.

4. Bake about 5 minutes or until steaming stops. Carefully remove waffle. Serve with spread.

12 four-inch waffle squares.

Honey Chestnut Spread

½   cup creamy honey spread

1   can (10 ounces) whole chestnuts in water (not water chestnuts), drained

Place spread and chestnuts in blender or food processor. Cover and blend on medium speed, stopping blender often to scrape down sides, until smooth. Store covered in refrigerator.

1 Waffle: Calories 220 (Calories from Fat 55); Fat 6g (Saturated 3g); Cholesterol 65mg; Sodium 260mg; Carbohydrate 37g (Dietary Fiber 2g); Protein 6g
% Daily Value: Vitamin A 6%; Vitamin C 0%; Calcium 6%; Iron 8%
Diet Exchanges: 2 Starch, ½ Fruit, 1 Fat

BETTY'S TIPS

✪ Do-Ahead
You can make the Honey Chestnut Spread up to a week ahead of time and keep it tightly covered in the refrigerator.

✪ Extra Special
Serve these waffles with a dollop of whipped cream and a generous sprinkling of ground cinnamon or nutmeg.

Waffles with Honey Chestnut Spread

— Quick & Low-Fat —

Blueberry Pancakes with Maple Cranberry Syrup

Prep: 10 min   Cook: 20 min

Maple Cranberry Syrup (right)
2 eggs
2 cups Gold Medal all-purpose flour
1½ cups milk
2 tablespoons sugar
¼ cup vegetable oil
3 teaspoons baking powder
½ teaspoon salt
1 cup fresh or frozen (thawed and well drained) blueberries

1. Make Maple Cranberry Syrup; keep warm. Heat griddle or skillet; grease with shortening if necessary (or spray with cooking spray before heating).

2. Beat eggs in medium bowl with hand beater until fluffy. Beat in remaining ingredients except blueberries just until smooth. Stir in blueberries.

3. Pour batter by slightly less than ¼ cupfuls onto hot griddle. Cook until bubbly on top, puffed and dry around edges. Turn; cook until golden brown. Serve with syrup.

18 four-inch pancakes.

Maple Cranberry Syrup
1 cup maple-flavored syrup
½ cup whole berry cranberry sauce

Heat ingredients in 1-quart saucepan over medium heat, stirring occasionally, until cranberry sauce is melted.

1 Pancake: Calories 170 (Calories from Fat 35); Fat 4g (Saturated 1g); Cholesterol 25mg; Sodium 190mg; Carbohydrate 31g (Dietary Fiber 1g); Protein 3g
% Daily Value: Vitamin A 2%; Vitamin C 0%; Calcium 8%; Iron 4%
Diet Exchanges: 1 Starch, 1 Fruit, ½ Fat

BETTY'S TIPS

☺ **Success Hint**
Consider mixing the batter in a 4- or 8-cup glass measuring cup with a handle and spout. Then pouring the batter onto the griddle will be easy.

☺ **Variation**
If you love the combination of cranberry and orange, add 1 to 2 teaspoons grated orange peel and 1 tablespoon orange juice to the syrup ingredients; heat as directed.

Blueberry Pancakes with Maple Cranberry Syrup

Apricot French Toast with Pineapple Apricot Topping

Prep: 20 min   Chill: 30 min   Bake: 25 min
Photo on page 1

16   slices French bread, 1 inch thick
½   cup apricot preserves
6   eggs
1½   cups half-and-half
¼   cup sugar
¼   teaspoon ground nutmeg
2   teaspoons vanilla
¼   cup butter or margarine, melted
    Pineapple Apricot Topping (below)
    Fresh mint leaves, if desired

1. Heat oven to 425°. Spray jelly roll pan, 15½ × 10½ × 1 inch, with cooking spray. Cut lengthwise slit in side of each bread slice, cutting to but not through other edge. Spread preserves inside slit. Place in pan.

2. Beat eggs, half-and-half, sugar, nutmeg and vanilla until well blended. Pour over bread; turn slices carefully to coat. Cover and refrigerate at least 30 minutes or overnight.

3. Uncover French toast. Drizzle with melted butter. Bake 20 to 25 minutes or until golden brown. Make Pineapple Apricot Topping. Serve topping with French toast. Sprinkle with mint.

16 slices.

Pineapple Apricot Topping

1   can (8 ounces) crushed pineapple in juice, undrained
2   ounces dried apricots, cut into fourths (¼ cup)
2   tablespoons water
1   cup sugar
¼   cup maraschino cherries (from 6-ounce jar), drained and chopped
2   tablespoons lemon juice

Heat pineapple, apricots and water to boiling in 1-quart saucepan, stirring occasionally; reduce heat. Cover and simmer about 10 minutes, stirring occasionally, until apricots are tender. Stir in remaining ingredients. Heat to boiling over high heat, stirring occasionally. Boil and stir 1 minute; remove from heat and keep warm.

1 Slice: Calories 255 (Calories from Fat 70); Fat 8g (Saturated 4g); Cholesterol 95mg; Sodium 200mg; Carbohydrate 41g (Dietary Fiber 1g); Protein 6g
% Daily Value: Vitamin A 6%; Vitamin C 4%; Calcium 6%; Iron 6%
Diet Exchanges: 2 Starch, ½ Fruit, 1½ Fat

BETTY'S TIPS

✪ **Success Hint**
Day-old bread makes fabulous French toast.

✪ **Simplify**
Skip the topping and serve this make-ahead brunch-time favorite with purchased strawberry or maple syrup.

Or sprinkle French toast slices with powdered sugar and serve with creamy honey butter.

✪ **Extra Special**
Sprinkle toasted coconut over topped French toast. To toast coconut, bake uncovered in an ungreased shallow pan in 350° oven for 5 to 7 minutes, stirring occasionally, until golden brown.

Egg Burrito Grande

Prep: 10 min   Cook: 10 min

- 1 medium potato, diced (1 cup)
- 1 medium green bell pepper, chopped (1 cup)
- 1 small onion, chopped (1/4 cup)
- 1/2 teaspoon chili powder
- 1 teaspoon butter or margarine
- 5 eggs, slightly beaten
- 1 cup canned vegetarian refried beans, heated
- 1/2 cup shredded reduced-fat Cheddar cheese (2 ounces)
- 1 small tomato, seeded and chopped (1/2 cup)
- 1/2 cup salsa
- 8 flour tortillas (8 to 10 inches in diameter)

1. Spray 10-inch skillet with cooking spray. Cook potato, bell pepper and onion in skillet over medium heat, stirring occasionally, until tender. Stir in chili powder. Remove from skillet; keep warm.

2. Melt butter in same skillet over medium heat. Cook eggs in butter, stirring frequently, until set but still moist.

3. For each burrito, spread about 2 tablespoons beans, 2 tablespoons potato mixture, 1 tablespoon cheese, 2 tablespoons eggs, 1 tablespoon tomato and 1 table-spoon salsa in center of each tortilla. Fold tortilla around filling.

4 servings.

1 Serving: Calories 495 (Calories from Fat 145); Fat 16g (Saturated 5g); Cholesterol 275mg; Sodium 920mg; Carbohydrate 73g (Dietary Fiber 9g); Protein 24g
% Daily Value: Vitamin A 20%; Vitamin C 36%; Calcium 24%; Iron 32%
Diet Exchanges: 4 Starch, 1 1/2 High-Fat Meat, 2 Vegetable

BETTY'S TIPS

✪ Substitution
You can use regular refried beans instead of vegetarian and regular cheese instead of reduced-fat.

✪ Success Hint
Warm the tortillas quickly in the microwave oven before filling.

Egg Burrito Grande

Betty...
MAKES IT EASY

Country Egg Scramble

Prep: 15 min   Cook: 10 min

1	pound small red potatoes (6 or 7), cubed
6	eggs
⅓	cup milk
¼	teaspoon salt
⅛	teaspoon pepper
2	tablespoons butter or margarine
8	medium green onions, sliced (½ cup)
8	slices bacon, crisply cooked and crumbled

1. Heat 1 inch water to boiling in 2-quart saucepan. Add potatoes. Cover and heat to boiling; reduce heat to medium-low. Cover and cook 6 to 8 minutes or until potatoes are tender; drain.

2. Beat eggs, milk, salt and pepper with fork or wire whisk until a uniform yellow color; set aside.

3. Melt butter in 10-inch skillet over medium-high heat. Cook potatoes in butter 3 to 5 minutes, turning occasionally, until light brown. Stir in onions. Cook 1 minute, stirring constantly.

4. Pour egg mixture into skillet. As mixture begins to set at bottom and side, gently lift cooked portions with spatula so that thin, uncooked portion can flow to bottom. Avoid constant stirring. Cook 3 to 4 minutes or until eggs are thickened throughout but still moist. Sprinkle with bacon.

4 servings.

1 Serving: Calories 335 (Calories from Fat 180); Fat 20g (Saturated 8g); Cholesterol 340mg; Sodium 500mg; Carbohydrate 26g (Dietary Fiber 3g); Protein 16g
% Daily Value: Vitamin A 16%; Vitamin C 12%; Calcium 8%; Iron 14%
Diet Exchanges: 2 Starch, 2 Medium-Fat Meat, 1 Fat

Country Egg Scramble

Smoked Salmon and Cream Cheese Omelet

Vegetable Cheese Strata

Smoked Salmon and Cream Cheese Omelet

Prep: 5 min   Cook: 10 min   Stand: 2 min

4	teaspoons butter or margarine
8	eggs, beaten
½	cup soft cream cheese with chives and onion
1	cup flaked smoked salmon
	Chopped fresh chives, if desired

1. Heat 2 teaspoons of the butter in 8-inch omelet pan or skillet over medium-high heat until butter is hot and sizzling.

2. Pour half of the beaten eggs (about 1 cup) into pan. As mixture begins to set at bottom and side, gently lift cooked portions with spatula so that thin, uncooked portion can flow to bottom. Avoid constant stirring. Cook 3 to 4 minutes or until eggs are thickened throughout but still moist.

3. Spoon ¼ cup of the cream cheese in dollops evenly over omelet; sprinkle with ½ cup of the salmon. Tilt skillet and slip pancake turner under omelet to loosen. Remove from heat. Fold omelet in half; let stand 2 minutes. Repeat with remaining ingredients. Cut each omelet crosswise in half to serve; sprinkle with chives.

4 servings.

1 Serving: Calories 290 (Calories from Fat 200); Fat 22g (Saturated 10g); Cholesterol 460mg; Sodium 470mg; Carbohydrate 2g (Dietary Fiber 0g); Protein 20g
% Daily Value: Vitamin A 20%; Vitamin C 0%; Calcium 6%; Iron 10%
Diet Exchanges: 3 High-Fat Meat

BETTY'S TIPS

⚙ **Success Hint**
Omelets cook quickly, so always have your filling ingredients ready before you begin cooking the eggs. The butter should be sizzling before the egg mixture is added.

⚙ **Serve-With**
Omelets aren't just for breakfast or brunch. They're also great dinner entrées, accompanied by biscuits and a salad or fresh fruit.

Vegetable Cheese Strata

*Prep: 13 min   Chill: 2 hr   Bake: 1 hr 28 min
Cool: 45 min   Stand: 10 min*

1⅔	cups Original Bisquick
3	tablespoons Italian dressing
3	tablespoons milk
1	bag (1 pound) frozen broccoli, green beans, pearl onions and red peppers, thawed and drained
3	cups milk
1	teaspoon yellow mustard
½	teaspoon seasoned salt
¼	teaspoon pepper
8	eggs
2	cups shredded Cheddar cheese (8 ounces)

1. Heat oven to 450°. Generously grease bottom and sides of rectangular baking dish, 13 × 9 × 2 inches, with shortening. Stir Bisquick, Italian dressing and 3 tablespoons milk in medium bowl until soft dough forms. Pat dough on bottom of baking dish. Bake 8 minutes. Cool completely, about 45 minutes.

2. Sprinkle vegetables over baked crust. Beat remaining ingredients except cheese in medium bowl with wire whisk or fork until blended. Pour over vegetables. Sprinkle with cheese. Cover and refrigerate at least 2 hours.

3. Heat oven to 350°. Cover and bake 30 minutes. Uncover and bake 40 to 50 minutes longer or until knife inserted in center comes out clean. Let stand 10 minutes before cutting.

8 servings.

1 Serving: Calories 365 (Calories from Fat 200); Fat 22g (Saturated 10g); Cholesterol 250mg; Sodium 790mg; Carbohydrate 25g (Dietary Fiber 2g); Protein 19g
% Daily Value: Vitamin A 22%; Vitamin C 16%; Calcium 36%; Iron 10%
Diet Exchanges: 1 Starch, 1 High-Fat Meat, 1 Skim Milk, 2 Fat

BETTY'S TIPS

⚙ **Substitution**
You can use French, ranch or honey-mustard dressing in place of the Italian dressing. Vegetable oil could also be substituted, but the strata will be a little less flavorful.

⚙ **Do-Ahead**
This easy strata can be refrigerated up to 24 hours before baking. The strata will still bake in about the same amount of time.

Fresh Spinach and New Potato Frittata

Prep: 15 min   Cook: 20 min

6	eggs
2	tablespoons milk
¼	teaspoon dried marjoram leaves
¼	teaspoon salt
2	tablespoons butter or margarine
6 or 7	small red potatoes, thinly sliced (2 cups)
¼	teaspoon salt
1	cup firmly packed bite-size pieces spinach
¼	cup oil-packed sun-dried tomatoes, drained and sliced
3	medium green onions, cut into ¼-inch pieces
½	cup shredded Swiss cheese (2 ounces)

1. Beat eggs, milk, marjoram and ¼ teaspoon salt; set aside.

2. Melt butter in 10-inch nonstick skillet over medium heat. Add potatoes to skillet; sprinkle with ¼ teaspoon salt. Cover and cook 8 to 10 minutes, stirring occasionally, until potatoes are tender.

3. Stir in spinach, tomatoes and onions. Cook, stirring occasionally, just until spinach is wilted; reduce heat to low.

4. Carefully pour egg mixture over potato mixture. Cover and cook 6 to 8 minutes or just until top is set. Sprinkle with cheese. Cover and cook about 1 minute or until cheese is melted.

4 servings.

1 Serving: Calories 305 (Calories from Fat 170); Fat 19g (Saturated 9g); Cholesterol 345mg; Sodium 500mg; Carbohydrate 20g (Dietary Fiber 2g); Protein 16g
% Daily Value: Vitamin A 32%; Vitamin C 16%; Calcium 20%; Iron 12%
Diet Exchanges: 1 Starch, 1½ High-Fat Meat, 1 Vegetable, 1 Fat

BETTY'S TIPS

☺ Simplify
Purchase spinach that has already been washed to speed preparation for this tasty breakfast or brunch dish.

☺ Serve-With
Serve with Easy Caramel Sticky Rolls (page 2), bacon slices or sausage links and a bowl of fresh fruit or berries.

Quick

Denver Eggs Frittata

Prep: 6 min   Cook: 16 min   Stand: 2 min

8	eggs
½	teaspoon salt
2	tablespoons vegetable oil
½	medium green bell pepper, cut into 1-inch strips
½	medium red bell pepper, cut into 1-inch strips
1	medium onion, sliced
1	can (1.7 ounces) shoestring potatoes
½	cup shredded Cheddar cheese (2 ounces)

1. Beat eggs and salt with fork or wire whisk; set aside. Heat oil in 12-inch nonstick skillet over medium-high heat. Cook bell peppers and onion in oil about 5 minutes, stirring occasionally, until tender. Spread vegetables evenly in skillet.

2. Pour eggs over vegetables; reduce heat to low. Cover and cook 7 to 9 minutes or until eggs are set; remove from heat.

3. Sprinkle with potatoes and cheese. Cover and let stand about 2 minutes or until cheese is melted. Cut into wedges.

4 servings.

1 Serving: Calories 325 (Calories from Fat 215); Fat 24g (Saturated 8g); Cholesterol 440mg; Sodium 530mg; Carbohydrate 11g (Dietary Fiber 1g); Protein 17g
% Daily Value: Vitamin A 32%; Vitamin C 40%; Calcium 12%; Iron 10%
Diet Exchanges: 2 High-Fat Meat, 2 Vegetable, 1½ Fat

BETTY'S TIPS

☺ Did You Know?
Frittata is the Italian word for "omelet," but it differs from a classic French omelet in several ways. The ingredients are cooked with the eggs instead of being folded inside the omelet. Also, frittatas are cooked over a lower heat for a longer period of time than regular omelets. The traditional way to serve a frittata is to cut it into wedges.

Fresh Spinach and New Potato Frittata

Denver Eggs Frittata

Mediterranean Breakfast Bake

Prep: 10 min   Cook: 15 min   Broil: 2 min

8	eggs
½	cup milk
¼	teaspoon salt
¼	teaspoon pepper
½	cup finely crumbled feta cheese
1	tablespoon vegetable oil
1	cup frozen hash brown potatoes with onions and peppers
1	tablespoon chopped fresh or 1 teaspoon dried oregano leaves
1½	cups bite-size pieces spinach

1. Beat eggs, milk, salt and pepper with fork or wire whisk until a uniform yellow color. Stir in cheese; set aside.

2. Heat oil in 10-inch ovenproof skillet over medium heat. Cook potatoes and oregano in oil 3 minutes, stirring frequently. Stir in spinach. Cook about 1 minute, stirring frequently, until potatoes are tender and spinach starts to wilt. Reduce heat to medium-low.

3. Pour eggs over potato mixture. Cover and cook 7 to 10 minutes or until eggs are set almost to center and are light brown on bottom.

4. Set oven control to broil. Broil frittata with top about 5 inches from heat about 2 minutes or until top just starts to brown.

4 servings.

1 Serving: Calories 290 (Calories from Fat 170); Fat 19g (Saturated 7g); Cholesterol 440mg; Sodium 520mg; Carbohydrate 14g (Dietary Fiber 1g); Protein 17g
% Daily Value: Vitamin A 34%; Vitamin C 6%; Calcium 18%; Iron 10%
Diet Exchanges: 1 Starch, 2 High-Fat Meat

BETTY'S TIPS

⊙ **Substitution**
No feta cheese on hand? Grated Parmesan cheese or shredded Cheddar cheese can be substituted for equally delicious results.

⊙ **Time-Saver**
Speed up preparation by picking up a bag of prewashed spinach, available in the produce section of your supermarket.

Mediterranean Breakfast Bake

Hash Brown Potato Brunch Bake

Prep: 15 min   Bake: 50 min

1   can (10¾ ounces) condensed cream of mushroom soup

1   can (10¾ ounces) condensed cream of chicken soup

1   container (8 ounces) sour cream

½   cup milk

¼   teaspoon pepper

1   bag (30 ounces) frozen shredded hash brown potatoes, partially thawed

8   medium green onions, sliced (½ cup)

1   cup shredded Cheddar cheese (4 ounces)

1. Heat oven to 350°. Grease bottom and sides of rectangular baking dish, 13 × 9 × 2 inches, with shortening.

2. Mix soups, sour cream, milk and pepper in very large bowl. Stir in potatoes and onions. Spoon into baking dish.

3. Bake uncovered 30 minutes. Sprinkle with cheese. Bake 15 to 20 minutes longer or until golden brown on top and bubbly around edges.

8 servings.

1 Serving: Calories 325 (Calories from Fat 135); Fat 15g (Saturated 8g); Cholesterol 40mg; Sodium 1,060mg; Carbohydrate 39g (Dietary Fiber 3g); Protein 9g
% Daily Value: Vitamin A 12%; Vitamin C 12%; Calcium 16%; Iron 6%
Diet Exchanges: 2 Starch, 2 Vegetable, 3 Fat

BETTY'S TIPS

✪ Variation
For a **Southwest Brunch Bake,** use southern-style hash brown potatoes and shredded Colby-Monterey Jack cheese instead of the regular hash browns and Cheddar cheese.

✪ Do-Ahead
To make this the night before, assemble the recipe in the baking dish, cover and refrigerate overnight. Bake uncovered at 350° for 40 minutes. Sprinkle with cheese, and bake 15 to 20 minutes longer as directed.

Hash Brown Potato Brunch Bake

Easy-Bake Breads

Country-Style Favorites, Fresh from the Oven

Savory Sweet Potato Pan Bread (page 34)

Pine Tree Parmesan Breadsticks (page 30)

Banana Gingerbread Muffins

Prep: 5 min   Bake: 20 min

1 package Betty Crocker gingerbread cake and cookie mix
1 cup mashed very ripe bananas (2 medium)
¾ cup quick-cooking or old-fashioned oats
¾ cup water
2 eggs

1. Heat oven to 375°. Grease bottoms only of 16 medium muffin cups, 2½ × 1¼ inches, with shortening, or line with foil or paper baking cups.

2. Mix gingerbread mix (dry) and remaining ingredients in large bowl until well blended. Divide batter evenly among muffin cups.

3. Bake 15 to 20 minutes or until toothpick inserted in center comes out clean. Immediately remove from pan to wire rack. Serve warm or cool.

16 muffins.

1 Muffin: Calories 150 (Calories from Fat 35); Fat 4g (Saturated 1g); Cholesterol 25mg; Sodium 180mg; Carbohydrate 27g (Dietary Fiber 1g); Protein 3g
% Daily Value: Vitamin A 0%; Vitamin C 0%; Calcium 0%; Iron 4%
Diet Exchanges: 1 Starch, 1 Fruit

BETTY'S TIPS

❂ Do-Ahead
You can bake these muffins in greased or paper-lined muffin cups and freeze them. To reheat, place 6 frozen muffins on a microwavable plate or napkin-lined basket. Microwave uncovered on Medium (50%) 1 minute to 1 minute 30 seconds.

❂ Extra Special
For a dazzling holiday finish, drizzle muffin tops with melted white baking chips and sprinkle with sugar.

Banana Gingerbread Muffins

Quick

Apple Cheddar Muffins

Prep: 11 min   Bake: 19 min

1   egg
2   cups Original Bisquick
¾   cup coarsely chopped peeled cooking apple
⅔   cup shredded Cheddar cheese
⅓   cup sugar
⅔   cup milk
2   tablespoons vegetable oil
1   teaspoon ground cinnamon

1. Heat oven to 400°. Grease bottoms only of 12 medium muffin cups, 2½ × 1¼ inches, with shortening, or line with paper baking cups.

2. Beat egg slightly in medium bowl. Stir in remaining ingredients just until moistened. Divide batter evenly among cups.

3. Bake 17 to 19 minutes or until golden brown. Serve warm.

12 muffins.

1 Muffin: Calories 170 (Calories from Fat 70); Fat 8g (Saturated 3g); Cholesterol 25mg; Sodium 330mg; Carbohydrate 20g (Dietary Fiber 0g); Protein 4g
% Daily Value: Vitamin A 2%; Vitamin C 0%; Calcium 8%; Iron 4%
Diet Exchanges: 1 Starch, 2 Fat

BETTY'S TIPS

☺ Success Hint
Here are a couple of hints so your muffins will be rounded on top instead of peaked. Don't overmix the batter. Mix only until the dry ingredients are moistened and the batter is slightly lumpy. Also, be sure that your oven isn't too hot. If the oven heats unevenly or is too hot, the muffins will be peaked.

☺ Do-Ahead
Rewarm leftover muffins in the microwave to serve with another meal. Place muffins on a microwavable plate. Microwave uncovered on High 10 to 15 seconds for 2 muffins or 20 to 30 seconds for 4 muffins.

Apple Cheddar Muffins

Lemon Basil Muffins

Praline Pumpkin Date Bread

Lemon Basil Muffins

Prep: 14 min   Bake: 18 min

2 eggs
2 cups Original Bisquick
⅓ cup sugar
1 teaspoon grated lemon peel
¼ cup lemon juice
¼ cup water
2 tablespoons vegetable oil
½ teaspoon dried basil leaves, crumbled

1. Heat oven to 400°. Place paper baking cup in each of 12 medium muffin cups, 2½ × 1¼ inches, or grease bottoms only of cups with shortening.

2. Beat eggs slightly in medium bowl. Stir in remaining ingredients just until moistened. Divide batter evenly among cups.

3. Bake 15 to 18 minutes or until tops are golden brown. Serve warm.

12 muffins.

1 Muffin: Calories 135 (Calories from Fat 55); Fat 6g (Saturated 1g); Cholesterol 35mg; Sodium 300mg; Carbohydrate 18g (Dietary Fiber 0g); Protein 2g
% Daily Value: Vitamin A 0%; Vitamin C 0%; Calcium 4%; Iron 4%
Diet Exchanges: 1 Starch, 1 Fat

BETTY'S TIPS

❂ Success Hint
After filling the cups, be sure to wipe up any batter that spills onto the edge of the pan so it won't stick and burn.

Bake muffins for the shortest time stated in the recipe, then check for doneness. If the muffin tops aren't golden brown or they don't spring back when touched lightly in the center, bake a minute or two longer, then check again.

❂ Special Touch
Sprinkle tops of muffins with ¼ cup white coarse sugar crystals before baking.

Praline Pumpkin Date Bread

Prep: 15 min   Bake: 1 hr   Cool: 1 hr 10 min

Praline Topping (below)
1⅔ cups sugar
⅔ cup vegetable oil
2 teaspoons vanilla
4 eggs
1 can (15 ounces) pumpkin (not pumpkin pie mix)
3 cups Gold Medal all-purpose flour
2 teaspoons baking soda
1 teaspoon ground cinnamon
¾ teaspoon salt
½ teaspoon baking powder
½ teaspoon ground cloves
1 cup chopped dates

1. Move oven rack to low position so that tops of pans will be in center of oven. Heat oven to 350°. Grease bottoms only of 2 loaf pans, 8½ × 4½ × 2½ inches, or 1 loaf pan, 9 × 5 × 3 inches, with shortening. Make Praline Topping; set aside.

2. Mix sugar, oil, vanilla, eggs and pumpkin in large bowl. Stir in remaining ingredients except dates until well blended. Stir in dates. Pour batter into pans. Sprinkle with topping.

3. Bake 8-inch loaves 50 to 60 minutes, 9-inch loaf 1 hour 10 minutes to 1 hour 20 minutes, or until tooth-pick inserted in center comes out clean. Cool 10 minutes. Loosen sides of loaves from pans; remove from pans to wire rack. Cool completely, about 1 hour, before slicing.

2 loaves (24 slices each).

Praline Topping
⅓ cup packed brown sugar
⅓ cup chopped pecans
1 tablespoon butter or margarine, softened

Mix all ingredients until crumbly.

1 Slice: Calories 110 (Calories from Fat 35); Fat 4g (Saturated 1g); Cholesterol 20mg; Sodium 100mg; Carbohydrate 18g (Dietary Fiber 1g); Protein 2g
% Daily Value: Vitamin A 28%; Vitamin C 0%; Calcium 0%; Iron 4%
Diet Exchanges: 1 Starch, ½ Fat

Betty...
MAKES IT EASY

— *Low Fat* —

Sugar 'n' Spice Wreath

Prep: 30 min   Dough Cycle: 1 hr 30 min   Rest: 10 min
Rise: 50 min   Bake: 30 min

- ¼ cup water
- ¾ cup sour cream
- 1 egg
- 3 cups Gold Medal Better for Bread™ flour
- 3 tablespoons granulated sugar
- 1 teaspoon salt
- 2 teaspoons bread machine or quick active dry yeast
- 1 egg, beaten
- 3 tablespoons white coarse sugar crystals (decorating sugar) or granulated sugar
- ¼ teaspoon ground cinnamon
- ¼ teaspoon ground cloves
- ¼ teaspoon ground nutmeg

Starting at middle, braid together gently and loosely.

Shape braid into circle and pinch ends together.

1. Place water, sour cream, egg, flour, granulated sugar, salt and yeast in bread machine pan in order recommended by manufacturer. Select Dough/Manual cycle. Do not use delay cycles.

2. Remove dough from pan, using lightly floured hands. Cover and let rest 10 minutes on lightly floured surface.

3. Grease large cookie sheet with shortening. Divide dough into thirds. Roll each third into a 26-inch rope; place ropes side by side. Starting at middle, braid one end gently and loosely; repeat with other end. Pinch ends to fasten. Shape into circle on cookie sheet; pinch ends together. (Wreath can be covered with plastic wrap and refrigerated up to 48 hours. Before baking, remove from refrigerator and remove plastic wrap. Cover with a towel and let rise in warm place 2 hours or until double.) Cover and let rise in warm place 45 to 50 minutes or until double. (Dough is ready if indentation remains when touched.)

4. Heat oven to 350°. Brush beaten egg over dough. Mix sugar crystals, cinnamon, cloves and nutmeg; sprinkle over dough. Bake 25 to 30 minutes or until golden brown.

24 servings.

1 Serving: Calories 80 (Calories from Fat 20); Fat 2g (Saturated 1g); Cholesterol 20mg; Sodium 105mg; Carbohydrate 16g (Dietary Fiber 1g); Protein 2g
% Daily Value: Vitamin A 6%; Vitamin C 0%; Calcium 8%; Iron 10%
Diet Exchanges: 1 Starch

Sugar 'n' Spice Wreath

Quick French Onion Biscuits

Quick French Onion Biscuits

Prep: 4 min   Bake: 12 min

2   cups Original Bisquick
¼   cup milk
1   container (8 ounces) French onion dip

1. Heat oven to 450°.

2. Stir all ingredients until soft dough forms. Drop dough into 6 mounds onto ungreased cookie sheet.

3. Bake 10 to 12 minutes or until light golden brown. Serve warm.

6 biscuits.

1 Biscuit: Calories 240 (Calories from Fat 110); Fat 12g (Saturated 5g); Cholesterol 15mg; Sodium 850mg; Carbohydrate 27g (Dietary Fiber 1g); Protein 5g
% Daily Value: Vitamin A 4%; Vitamin C 0%; Calcium 12%; Iron 6%
Diet Exchanges: 2 Starch, 2 Fat

BETTY'S TIPS

✿ Substitution
Refrigerated dips are available in several flavors. Substitute one of your favorite flavors for the onion dip.

✿ Success Hint
Bisquick reacts to the environment just like other flour-based products do. If the weather is hot and humid, you may find that doughs and batters are more sticky, soft or wet. You can add small amounts of Bisquick to make the dough or batter easier to work with.

Sweet Potato Biscuits

Prep: 10 min   Bake: 12 min

2½   cups Original Bisquick
⅓   cup butter or margarine, softened
1   cup mashed cooked sweet potatoes
½   cup milk

1. Heat oven to 450°. Stir all ingredients until soft dough forms.

2. Place dough on surface dusted with Bisquick; roll in Bisquick to coat. Shape into a ball; knead 3 or 4 times. Roll ½ inch thick. Cut with 2½-inch cutter dipped in Bisquick. Place with edges touching on ungreased cookie sheet.

3. Bake 10 to 12 minutes or until golden brown. Serve warm.

16 to 18 biscuits.

1 Biscuit: Calories 130 (Calories from Fat 65); Fat 7g (Saturated 4g); Cholesterol 10mg; Sodium 290mg; Carbohydrate 16g (Dietary Fiber 1g); Protein 2g
% Daily Value: Vitamin A 44%; Vitamin C 2%; Calcium 4%; Iron 2%
Diet Exchanges: 1 Starch, 1 Fat

BETTY'S TIPS

✿ Success Hint
Here's a tip for making nicely shaped biscuits. Push the cutter straight down through the biscuit dough. If you twist as you cut, the biscuits may be uneven.

✿ Variation
Biscuits don't have to be round! You can use a 2-inch cookie cutter in any shape. Or cut the dough into smaller squares, rectangles or triangles with a sharp knife that has been dipped in Bisquick to prevent sticking.

Mini Rosemary Garlic Breads

Prep: 15 min   Bake: 10 min

2¼ cups Original Bisquick
⅔ cup milk
2 teaspoons olive or vegetable oil
½ teaspoon dried rosemary leaves, crumbled
½ teaspoon garlic powder

1. Heat oven to 450°. Mix Bisquick and milk until soft dough forms; beat 30 seconds. If dough is too sticky, gradually mix in enough Bisquick (up to ¼ cup) to make dough easy to handle.

2. Place dough on surface generously dusted with Bisquick; gently roll in Bisquick to coat. Shape into a ball; knead 10 times. Roll ¼ inch thick. Cut with 2-inch cutter dipped in Bisquick. Place about 2 inches apart on ungreased cookie sheet. Brush with oil. Sprinkle with rosemary and garlic powder.

3. Bake 8 to 10 minutes or until golden brown. Serve warm.

24 biscuits.

1 Biscuit: Calories 55 (Calories from Fat 20); Fat 2g (Saturated 1g); Cholesterol 0mg; Sodium 160mg; Carbohydrate 7g (Dietary Fiber 0g); Protein 1g
% Daily Value: Vitamin A 0%; Vitamin C 0%; Calcium 0%; Iron 0%
Diet Exchanges: ½ Starch, ½ Fat

BETTY'S TIPS

⚙ **Success Hint**

Shiny aluminum cookie sheets of good quality produce the best biscuits. If the cookie sheet is brown, black or darkened from a buildup of fat, the bottoms of the biscuits will be darker in color. Reducing the oven temperature to 400° may help. Also, be sure to place the cookie sheet on the center oven rack. That way, the biscuits will brown evenly on both the top and bottom.

⚙ **Serve-With**

Serve these miniature focaccia biscuits with any Italian meal.

Mini Rosemary Garlic Breads

Quick Corn Breadsticks

Prep: 10 min   Bake: 15 min

2 eggs
1 cup Original Bisquick
1 cup yellow cornmeal
1½ cups buttermilk
2 tablespoons vegetable oil
  Yellow cornmeal

1. Heat oven to 450°. Grease bottom and sides of 2 loaf pans, 9 × 5 × 3 inches, with shortening.

2. Beat eggs in large bowl with hand beater until fluffy. Beat in Bisquick, 1 cup cornmeal, the buttermilk and oil just until smooth (do not overbeat). Pour into pans. Sprinkle lightly with cornmeal.

3. Bake about 15 minutes or until toothpick inserted in center comes out clean. Remove from pans. Cut each loaf crosswise into 8 sticks. Serve warm.

16 breadsticks.

1 Breadstick: Calories 70 (Calories from Fat 35); Fat 4g (Saturated 1g); Cholesterol 30mg; Sodium 130mg; Carbohydrate 6g (Dietary Fiber 0g); Protein 2g
% Daily Value: Vitamin A 0%; Vitamin C 0%; Calcium 4%; Iron 2%
Diet Exchanges: 1 Starch

BETTY'S TIPS

☺ **Substitution**
No buttermilk on hand? Use 1½ tablespoons lemon juice or white vinegar plus enough milk to equal 1½ cups; let stand a few minutes.

☺ **Serve-With**
These hearty corn sticks are simply superb spread with honey butter or drizzled with maple syrup. They also make dynamite dunkers for bowls of steaming chili.

Quick Corn Breadsticks

Pine Tree Parmesan Breadsticks

Prep: 15 min   Rise: 30 min   Bake: 15 min

Cornmeal, if desired

12 frozen white bread dough rolls (from 48-ounce package), thawed

2 tablespoons olive or vegetable oil

3 or 4 long fresh rosemary sprigs

1 tablespoon grated Parmesan cheese

1. Brush 2 cookie sheets with olive oil; sprinkle with cornmeal. Roll each ball of dough into a 9-inch rope. Place ropes about ½ inch apart on cookie sheets.

2. Brush 2 tablespoons oil over dough. Break 36 small clusters of rosemary leaves off rosemary sprigs. Using 3 clusters for each breadstick, insert stem end of each cluster ¼ inch deep into top of breadstick. Sprinkle cheese over dough. Cover loosely with plastic wrap and let rise in warm place about 30 minutes or until almost double.

3. Heat oven to 350°. Bake 12 to 15 minutes or until light golden brown.

12 breadsticks.

1 Breadstick: Calories 125 (Calories from Fat 65); Fat 7g (Saturated 1g); Cholesterol 0mg; Sodium 350mg; Carbohydrate 13g (Dietary Fiber 0g); Protein 2g
% Daily Value: Vitamin A 0%; Vitamin C 0%; Calcium 0%; Iron 4%
Diet Exchanges: 1 Starch, 1 Fat

Pine Tree Parmesan Breadsticks

Triple-Cheese Flatbread

Prep: 10 min   Stand: 10 min   Bake: 12 min

- 2 cups Original Bisquick
- ½ cup hot water
- 2 tablespoons butter or margarine, melted
- ¼ cup shredded Cheddar cheese (1 ounce)
- ¼ cup shredded Monterey Jack cheese (1 ounce)
- ¼ cup grated Parmesan cheese
- ½ teaspoon garlic powder
- ½ teaspoon Italian seasoning, if desired

1. Heat oven to 450°. Stir Bisquick and water until stiff dough forms. Let stand 10 minutes. Place dough on surface sprinkled with Bisquick; gently roll in Bisquick to coat. Shape into a ball; knead 60 times.

2. Pat or roll dough into 12-inch square on ungreased cookie sheet. Brush butter over dough. Mix remaining ingredients; sprinkle over dough.

3. Bake 10 to 12 minutes or until edges are golden brown. Serve warm.

16 servings.

1 Serving: Calories 90 (Calories from Fat 45); Fat 5g (Saturated 2g); Cholesterol 5mg; Sodium 280mg; Carbohydrate 9g (Dietary Fiber 0g); Protein 3g
% Daily Value: Vitamin A 2%; Vitamin C 0%; Calcium 6%; Iron 2%
Diet Exchanges: ½ Starch, 1 Fat

BETTY'S TIPS

✿ Substitution
Instead of Parmesan cheese, use the shredded three-cheese blend of Parmesan, Romano and Asiago cheeses.

✿ Success Hint
To make the dough easier to pat onto the cookie sheet, dip your fingers into Bisquick.

✿ Variation
For additional color in this flavorful flatbread, mix 2 teaspoons parsley flakes with the cheese mixture.

Triple-Cheese Flatbread

Nacho Pinwheels

Prep: 15 min   Bake: 13 min

- 3 cups Original Bisquick
- ¾ teaspoon chili powder
- ½ teaspoon dried oregano leaves
- ⅔ cup water
- 2 tablespoons butter or margarine, melted
- 1 cup shredded Cheddar cheese (4 ounces)
  Salsa, if desired
  Sour cream, if desired

1. Heat oven to 425°. Grease cookie sheet with shortening. Stir Bisquick, chili powder, oregano and water until soft dough forms. Place dough on surface sprinkled with Bisquick; gently roll in Bisquick to coat. Shape into a ball; knead 10 times.

2. Roll dough into 18 × 10-inch rectangle. Brush butter over dough. Sprinkle with cheese. Roll up rectangle tightly, beginning at 18-inch side. Pinch edge into roll to seal. Cut into 18 slices. Place on cookie sheet.

3. Bake 11 to 13 minutes or until golden brown. Serve warm with salsa and sour cream.

6 servings (3 pinwheels each).

1 Serving: Calories 325 (Calories from Fat 145); Fat 16g (Saturated 6g); Cholesterol 20mg; Sodium 990mg; Carbohydrate 37g (Dietary Fiber 1g); Protein 9g
% Daily Value: Vitamin A 6%; Vitamin C 0%; Calcium 20%; Iron 10%
Diet Exchanges: 2½ Starch, 3 Fat

BETTY'S TIPS

○ **Substitution**
For added zip, use Monterey Jack cheese with jalapeño peppers instead of the Cheddar.

○ **Serve-With**
These flavorful pinwheels are a great accompaniment to taco salad. Pop the pinwheels in the oven, then assemble the salad while the pinwheels bake. It's a quick and satisfying meal for either lunch or dinner.

Nacho Pinwheels

Savory Sweet Potato Pan Bread

Prep: 15 min   Bake: 30 min
Photo on page 19

1½ cups uncooked shredded sweet potato (about ½ potato)
½ cup sugar
⅓ cup vegetable oil
2 eggs
1 cup Gold Medal all-purpose flour
½ cup Gold Medal whole wheat flour
2 teaspoons instant minced onion
1 teaspoon dried rosemary leaves, crumbled
1 teaspoon baking soda
½ teaspoon salt
¼ teaspoon baking powder
1 tablespoon sesame seed

1. Heat oven to 350°. Grease bottom only of round pan, 9 × 1½ inches, with shortening.

2. Mix sweet potato, sugar, oil and eggs in large bowl. Stir in remaining ingredients except sesame seed. Spread in pan. Sprinkle sesame seed over batter.

3. Bake 25 to 30 minutes or until toothpick inserted in center comes out clean. Serve warm.

8 servings.

1 Serving: Calories 245 (Calories from Fat 100); Fat 11g (Saturated 2g); Cholesterol 55mg; Sodium 340mg; Carbohydrate 33g (Dietary Fiber 2g); Protein 5g
% Daily Value: Vitamin A 34%; Vitamin C 2%; Calcium 2%; Iron 6%
Diet Exchanges: 2 Starch, 2 Fat

BETTY'S TIPS

☺ Variation
If you don't have a round pan, you can bake the bread in an 8 × 8 × 2-inch square pan.

☺ Extra Special
Top off warm wedges of this savory bread with **Orange Butter.** To make, beat together ½ cup softened butter, 1 teaspoon grated orange peel and 1 tablespoon orange juice. If desired, chill about 1 hour to blend flavors.

Spinach Cheese Bread

Prep: 19 min   Bake: 1 hr 5 min   Cool: 20 min

3 cups Original Bisquick
¼ cup vegetable oil
1 tablespoon caraway seed
3 eggs
1 can (11 ounces) condensed Cheddar cheese soup
1 package (10 ounces) frozen chopped spinach, thawed and squeezed to drain

1. Heat oven to 350°. Grease bottom and sides of loaf pan, 9 × 5 × 3 inches, with shortening.

2. Stir together all ingredients except spinach thoroughly; beat with spoon 1 minute. Stir in spinach. Pour into pan.

3. Bake 55 to 65 minutes or until toothpick inserted in center comes out clean. Cool 20 minutes; remove from pan to wire rack.

1 loaf (16 slices).

1 Slice: Calories 155 (Calories from Fat 80); Fat 9g (Saturated 2g); Cholesterol 40mg; Sodium 510mg; Carbohydrate 16g (Dietary Fiber 1g); Protein 4g
% Daily Value: Vitamin A 28%; Vitamin C 0%; Calcium 8%; Iron 6%
Diet Exchanges: 1 Starch, 1½ Fat

BETTY'S TIPS

☺ Success Hint
Most quick breads are removed from their pans to a wire rack. This produces a drier, crispier surface. If left in the pan, the bread would steam and become soft.

Drain the thawed spinach in a strainer, then squeeze out the excess moisture using paper towels or a clean kitchen towel until the spinach is dry.

☺ Variation
Instead of caraway seed, use 1 tablespoon of instant minced onion to add a subtle onion flavor to the bread.

Spinach Cheese Bread

Betty... ON WHAT'S NEW

Sweet Spices
for Any Season

For centuries, spices have been used to enhance the flavor of foods. Sweet spices, although by themselves not sweet, are at their best when combined with complementary flavors. Although they're used extensively for holiday cooking and baking, these sweet spices are very popular any time of year.

SPICEOLOGY

Whole Spices have been cleaned and chosen for appearance. They can be used as a garnish and as a flavoring agent.

Ground Spices have been ground up to release their flavor more quickly and easily into food. The coarser the spice, the more gradually the flavor will be released.

Seasoning Blends are spices that have been preblended and then packaged as a combination. Pumpkin pie spice, for example, is a mixture of cinnamon, cloves, ginger and nutmeg.

SPICE STORAGE

Keep spices at their peak of freshness and flavor so they are at their best when you want to use them.

Store spices away from heat. It may seem more convenient to keep them over or near the stove, but they won't last as long. For optimum flavor, keep them in a cool, dry place and, if possible, a dark place.

Dried whole spices can be kept for years. Ground spices, on the other hand, are more fragile and have a shelf life of about six months if properly stored.

ALLSPICE

Allspice comes from the berry of an evergreen tree. When dried, it resembles dark brown peppercorns. Its taste, pungent with hints of cinnamon, clove and nutmeg, is reminiscent of its name "all spice." Whole allspice is typically used in marinades, in soups and stews and with roasts. Ground allspice is often used in baked goods and desserts.

ANISE SEED

Anise seed is a small crescent-shaped seed harvested from a plant in the parsley family. It has an earthy brown color and unique sweet, licorice flavor. Anise seed is a common spice used in Middle Eastern and Indian cuisines.

CARDAMOM

Cardamom comes from the seed of a tropical fruit in the ginger family. It has a pungent flavor with a subtle sweetness and can be purchased as whole pods, seeds or ground. Cardamom is used in many Scandinavian baked goods and to flavor coffee and tea, cakes, breads and fruit pies.

CLOVES

Cloves are the dried unopened flower buds of an evergreen tree. Dark brown and rich in aroma, cloves have a strong, pungent flavor. Simmer whole cloves in beverages, soups, stews and sauces. Ground cloves add a unique spiciness to cakes, cookies and breads.

CINNAMON

Cinnamon, with its sweet-spicy taste, is one of the most common baking spices. True cinnamon is native to Sri Lanka; the kind we commonly use is from the cassia tree grown in Central America and Southeast Asia. Cinnamon is available both whole (as sticks) and ground.

STAR ANISE

Star anise is a small, star-shaped pod with a cocoa brown color. Its flavor is similar to anise seed but is more bitter. Star anise, used frequently in Asian cuisine, comes from a plant related to the magnolia family. Star anise can be ground or used whole as a garnish.

MACE

Mace and nutmeg both come from the small seed of an evergreen tree. Mace, the lacy, scarlet outer membrane of the seed, has a flavor and aroma similar to nutmeg.

NUTMEG

Nutmeg, the inner brown seed, has a warm, sweet flavor. Nutmeg and mace are both used in a wide variety of savory foods. You'll also find nutmeg and mace in sweets such as puddings and pies.

Pear and Rosemary Focaccia with Fontina Cheese

Prep: 15 min   Rise: 30 min   Bake: 25 min

1 package (16 ounces) white bread mix with yeast

1¼ cups very warm water (120° to 130°)

⅓ cup olive or vegetable oil

1 tablespoon chopped fresh or 1 teaspoon dried rosemary leaves, crumbled

1 medium unpeeled red or green pear, thinly sliced

16 slices Fontina cheese, cut in half

Fresh rosemary sprigs, if desired

1. Mix contents of flour pouch and yeast packet in large bowl. Stir in water and 2 tablespoons of the oil until dough is soft and leaves side of bowl.

2. Place dough on lightly floured surface. Knead about 5 minutes or until dough is smooth and springy, sprinkling with additional flour as necessary if sticky. Cover with large bowl; let rest 5 minutes.

3. Grease large cookie sheet or 12-inch pizza pan with small amount of oil. Press dough into 12-inch circle on cookie sheet. Cover loosely with plastic wrap lightly sprayed with cooking spray and let rise in warm place about 30 minutes or until double.

4. Heat oven to 375°. Gently make depressions in dough about 1 inch apart with fingers or handle of wooden spoon. Carefully brush with remaining oil. Sprinkle with rosemary. Arrange pear slices on dough.

5. Bake 15 to 25 minutes or until golden brown. Serve warm or cool. To serve, cut focaccia into 16 wedges. Alternate focaccia wedges with slices of cheese on serving platter. Garnish with rosemary sprigs.

16 appetizers.

1 Appetizer: Calories 185 (Calories from Fat 100); Fat 11g (Saturated 5g); Cholesterol 20mg; Sodium 290mg; Carbohydrate 16g (Dietary Fiber 1g); Protein 7g
% Daily Value: Vitamin A 4%; Vitamin C 0%; Calcium 18%; Iron 4%
Diet Exchanges: 1 Starch, ½ High-Fat Meat, 1 Fat

BETTY'S TIPS

☻ Substitution
We love the flavor of Fontina cheese with the focaccia, but you can also use 8 slices of provolone cheese, cut in half.

☻ Success Hint
Use your hands to press the dough into a circle, or use a rolling pin.

Pear and Rosemary Focaccia with Fontina Cheese

Cheesy Roasted Red Pepper Bread

Prep: 20 min   Bake: 20 min

1 loaf (1 pound) French bread
1 cup shredded mozzarella cheese (4 ounces)
½ cup mayonnaise or salad dressing
¼ cup finely chopped roasted red bell peppers (from 7-ounce jar), well drained
1 tablespoon chopped fresh cilantro, if desired
½ teaspoon ground cumin
1 small onion, finely chopped (¼ cup)

1. Heat oven to 400°. Cut bread loaf horizontally into 3 layers. Mix remaining ingredients.

2. Spread half of the cheese mixture over bottom layer. Top with second layer; spread with remaining cheese mixture. Top with third layer; press firmly.

3. Wrap loaf securely in heavy-duty aluminum foil. Bake 15 to 20 minutes or until hot. Serve warm.

12 slices.

1 Slice: Calories 190 (Calories from Fat 90); Fat 10g (Saturated 2g); Cholesterol 10mg; Sodium 320mg; Carbohydrate 20g (Dietary Fiber 1g); Protein 6g
% Daily Value: Vitamin A 62%; Vitamin C 6%; Calcium 10%; Iron 6%
Diet Exchanges: 1 Starch, ½ High-Fat Meat, 1 Fat

BETTY'S TIPS

✪ Substitution
You can substitute finely chopped fresh red bell pepper for the roasted red bell peppers in this recipe.

✪ Variation
Preparing your dinner on the grill? You can heat this bread on the grill over medium heat for 15 to 20 minutes.

Cheesy Roasted Red Pepper Bread

Savory Pull-Apart Bread

Prep: 30 min   Bake: 20 min

10 sun-dried tomato halves (not packed in oil)

 2 cups Original Bisquick

 1 package (8 ounces) feta cheese, coarsely crumbled

¾ cup milk

¾ cup roasted red bell peppers (from 7-ounce jar), drained and finely chopped

 1 tablespoon chopped fresh or 1 teaspoon dried oregano leaves

 1 tablespoon chopped fresh or 1 teaspoon dried basil leaves

 1 clove garlic, finely chopped

 2 tablespoons olive or vegetable oil

1. Heat oven to 425°. Grease bottom and sides of square pan, 9 X 9 X 2 inches, with shortening. Cover dried tomatoes with boiling water. Let stand 10 minutes; drain. Finely chop tomatoes.

2. Stir Bisquick, tomatoes, half of the cheese and the milk in medium bowl until dough forms. Mix remaining cheese, the bell peppers, oregano, basil, garlic and oil in small bowl. Drop half of the dough by tablespoonfuls closely together in an irregular pattern in pan. Spoon half of the cheese mixture over dough. Drop remaining dough over cheese mixture. Top with remaining cheese mixture.

3. Bake about 20 minutes or until golden brown. Serve warm.

6 servings.

1 Serving: Calories 325 (Calories from Fat 170); Fat 19g (Saturated 8g); Cholesterol 35mg; Sodium 1060mg; Carbohydrate 30g (Dietary Fiber 1g); Protein 10g
% Daily Value: Vitamin A 32%; Vitamin C 34%; Calcium 30%; Iron 10%
Diet Exchanges: 1½ Starch, 1 Vegetable, 4 Fat

BETTY'S TIPS

☺ Success Hint
Using kitchen scissors makes the task of chopping dried tomatoes much easier. Try cutting them before soaking in boiling water.

☺ Time-Saver
A jar of chopped garlic, available in the produce section of the grocery store, is convenient to keep on hand for saving a step when quickly getting a main dish together.

Savory Pull-Apart Bread

Super Starters

Super Starters

Delicious Dips, Spreads, and Tidbits

Fresh Vegetable Appetizer Pizzas (page 68)

Olive Tapenade on Cucumber Stars (page 49)

Ginger Peanut Butter Dip

Prep: 10 min   Cook: 5 min

2	teaspoons olive or vegetable oil
8	medium green onions, sliced (½ cup)
2	teaspoons finely chopped gingerroot
2	cloves garlic, finely chopped
½	cup peanut butter
½	cup chicken broth
1	tablespoon packed brown sugar
¼ to ½	teaspoon ground red pepper (cayenne)
1	package (3 ounces) cream cheese, softened
	Assorted raw vegetables and crackers, if desired

1. Heat oil in 10-inch skillet over medium-high heat. Cook onions, gingerroot and garlic in oil about 2 minutes, stirring frequently, until tender.

2. Stir in remaining ingredients except vegetables. Cook about 2 minutes, stirring constantly, until hot.

3. Serve hot dip with vegetables.

12 servings (2 tablespoons each).

1 Serving: Calories 115 (Calories from Fat 80); Fat 9g (Saturated 3g); Cholesterol 10mg; Sodium 115mg; Carbohydrate 4g (Dietary Fiber 1g); Protein 4g
% Daily Value: Vitamin A 2%; Vitamin C 2%; Calcium 2%; Iron 2%
Diet Exchanges: ½ High-Fat Meat, 1½ Fat

BETTY'S TIPS

◎ **Success Hint**
If the mixture thickens after standing, stir in a few tablespoons of chicken broth.

◎ **Serve-With**
Serve this creamy dip with cooked frozen breaded chicken tenders. Look for them in the frozen foods section, and heat according to package directions.

◎ **Do-Ahead**
Prepare the dip up to 12 hours ahead; cover and refrigerate. Reheat just before serving.

Ginger Peanut Butter Dip

Chipotle Black Bean Dip

Prep: 20 min   Stand: 10 min   Bake: 15 min

2 large dried chipotle chilies
1 cup thick-and-chunky salsa
½ cup jalapeño black bean dip
2 tablespoons chopped fresh cilantro
1 cup shredded Colby-Monterey Jack cheese (4 ounces)
2 medium green onions, chopped (2 tablespoons)
  Sweet red cherry chili half, if desired
  Tortilla chips, if desired

1. Heat oven to 350°. Cover chilies with boiling water; let stand 10 minutes. Drain chilies and remove seeds. Chop chilies.

2. Mix chilies, salsa and bean dip; stir in cilantro. (If making ahead, cover and refrigerate up to 24 hours.) Spoon into shallow 1-quart ovenproof serving dish. Sprinkle with cheese.

3. Bake about 15 minutes or until mixture is hot and cheese is melted. Sprinkle with onions. Garnish with chili half. Serve with tortilla chips.

15 servings (2 tablespoons each).

1 Serving: Calories 45 (Calories from Fat 30); Fat 3g (Saturated 2g); Cholesterol 10mg; Sodium 150mg; Carbohydrate 2g (Dietary Fiber 1g); Protein 2g
% Daily Value: Vitamin A 6%; Vitamin C 2%; Calcium 6%; Iron 2%
Diet Exchanges: 1 Vegetable, ½ Fat

BETTY'S TIPS

⚙ **Special Touch**
When serving foods with unusual ingredients, write out a place card with the recipe name and place it next to the serving plate to let your guests know what they are eating. Also, consider labeling any foods with nuts or shellfish, because these are common allergens.

⚙ **Did You Know?**
Chipotle chilies are actually dried, smoked jalapeño chilies. They have a wrinkled, dark brown skin and a smoky, sweet flavor. In addition to dried, chipotle chilies can be found canned in adobo sauce.

Chipotle Black Bean Dip

Spinach Artichoke Dip

Roasted-Garlic Hummus

Spinach Artichoke Dip

Prep: 10 min   Cook: 1 hr 15 min

- 1   cup mayonnaise or salad dressing
- 1   cup freshly grated Parmesan cheese
- 1   can (14 ounces) artichoke hearts, drained and coarsely chopped
- 1   package (10 ounces) frozen chopped spinach, thawed and squeezed to drain
- ½   cup chopped red bell pepper
- ¼   cup shredded Monterey Jack or mozzarella cheese (1 ounce)

    Toasted baguette slices, assorted crackers or pita chips, if desired

1. Spray inside of 1- to 2½-quart slow cooker with cooking spray. Mix mayonnaise and Parmesan cheese in medium bowl. Stir in artichoke hearts, spinach and bell pepper. Spoon into slow cooker. Sprinkle with Monterey Jack cheese.

2. Cover and cook on low heat setting 1 hour to 1 hour 15 minutes or until cheese is melted. Serve warm with baguette slices. Dip will hold up to 3 hours.

24 servings (2 tablespoons each).

1 Serving: Calories 100 (Calories from Fat 80); Fat 9g (Saturated 2g); Cholesterol 10mg; Sodium 190mg; Carbohydrate 3g (Dietary Fiber 1g); Protein 3g
% Daily Value: Vitamin A 18%; Vitamin C 6%; Calcium 8%; Iron 2%
Diet Exchanges: 1 Vegetable, 2 Fat

BETTY'S TIPS

❂ Substitution
One cup of loosely packed, coarsely chopped spinach leaves can be substituted for the frozen spinach.

❂ Health Twist
To reduce the fat to 2 grams and the calories to 40 per serving in this crowd-pleasin' dip, use ½ cup fat-free mayonnaise or salad dressing and ½ cup plain fat-free yogurt instead of the mayonnaise.

Low Fat

Roasted-Garlic Hummus

Prep: 10 min   Bake: 1 hr

- 1   bulb garlic, unpeeled
- 2   teaspoons olive or vegetable oil
- 1   can (15 to 16 ounces) great northern beans, drained and 2 tablespoons liquid reserved
- 3   tablespoons lemon juice
- ½   teaspoon salt

    Chopped fresh parsley

    Pita bread wedges, crackers or raw vegetables, if desired

1. Heat oven to 350°. Cut ½-inch slice off top of garlic bulb. Drizzle oil over garlic bulb. Wrap garlic in aluminum foil. Bake 50 to 60 minutes or until garlic is soft when pierced with a knife; cool slightly.

2. Squeeze garlic into food processor. Add beans, reserved bean liquid, lemon juice and salt. Cover and process until uniform consistency.

3. Spoon dip into serving dish. Sprinkle with parsley. Serve with pita bread wedges.

16 servings (2 tablespoons each).

1 Serving: Calories 45 (Calories from Fat 10); Fat 1g (Saturated 0g); Cholesterol 0mg; Sodium 75mg; Carbohydrate 8g (Dietary Fiber 2g); Protein 3g
% Daily Value: Vitamin A 0%; Vitamin C 2%; Calcium 2%; Iron 6%
Diet Exchanges: 2 Vegetable

BETTY'S TIPS

❂ Time-Saver
Pick up a bulb of roasted garlic in the deli.

❂ Do-Ahead
Prepare this popular dip up to 1 day ahead of time. Cover and refrigerate until serving.

❂ Special Touch
Serve this mellow dip like they do in Turkey. Make a depression in the middle of the bowl of hummus, and spoon in 1 to 2 tablespoons of olive oil.

Roast an extra bulb of garlic to serve with the hummus.

Betty . . .
MAKES IT EASY

Brie in Puff Pastry with Cranberry Sauce

Prep: 30 min   Bake: 25 min   Cool: 30 min

Cranberry Sauce (below)
1   tablespoon butter or margarine
⅓   cup sliced almonds
½   package (17.3-ounce size) frozen puff pastry (1 sheet), thawed
1   round (14 to 15 ounces) Brie cheese
1   egg, beaten
Assorted crackers or sliced fresh fruit, if desired

1. Make Cranberry Sauce. Melt butter in 8-inch skillet over medium heat. Cook almonds in butter, stirring frequently, until golden brown.

2. Heat oven to 400°. Spray cookie sheet with cooking spray. Roll pastry into rectangle, 16 × 9 inches, on lightly floured surface; cut out one 8½-inch circle and one 7-inch circle.

3. Place cheese round on center of large circle. Spoon Cranberry Sauce and almonds over cheese. Bring pastry up and press around side of cheese. Brush top edge of pastry with egg. Place 7-inch circle on top, pressing around edge to seal. Brush top and side of pastry with egg. Cut decorations from remaining pastry and arrange on top; brush with egg. Place on cookie sheet.

4. Bake 20 to 25 minutes or until golden brown. Cool on cookie sheet on wire rack 30 minutes before serving. Serve with crackers.

12 servings.

Cranberry Sauce

1   cup fresh cranberries
6   tablespoons packed brown sugar
1   tablespoon orange juice
½   teaspoon grated orange peel

Mix cranberries, brown sugar and orange juice in 1-quart saucepan. Heat to boiling, stirring frequently; reduce heat. Simmer uncovered 15 to 20 minutes, stirring frequently, until mixture thickens and cranberries are tender. Stir in orange peel; remove from heat.

1 Serving: Calories 275 (Calories from Fat 170); Fat 19g (Saturated 9g); Cholesterol 70mg; Sodium 340mg; Carbohydrate 18g (Dietary Fiber 1g); Protein 9g
% Daily Value: Vitamin A 8%; Vitamin C 0%; Calcium 14%; Iron 6%
Diet Exchanges: 1 Starch, 1 High-Fat Meat, 2 Fat

Place cheese round on center of large puff pastry circle. Spoon Cranberry Sauce and almonds on top.

Place 7-inch circle on top, pressing around edge to seal.

Brie in Puff Pastry with Cranberry Sauce

Betty... ON BASICS

Olive Tapenade

Prep: 10 min

1½ cups pitted Kalamata or ripe olives
¼ cup chopped walnuts
3 tablespoons olive or vegetable oil
3 tablespoons capers, drained
1½ teaspoons fresh rosemary leaves
1 teaspoon Italian seasoning
2 cloves garlic
Chopped red bell pepper, if desired
Assorted crackers, if desired

Cover and process until mixture is slightly coarse.

1. Place all ingredients except bell pepper and crackers in food processor or blender. Cover and process, using quick on-and-off motions, until slightly coarse.

2. Spoon into serving bowl. Sprinkle with bell pepper. Serve with crackers.

14 servings (2 tablespoons each).

1 Serving: Calories 60 (Calories from Fat 55); Fat 6g (Saturated 1g); Cholesterol 0mg; Sodium 170mg; Carbohydrate 2g (Dietary Fiber 1g); Protein 1g
% Daily Value: Vitamin A 2%; Vitamin C 4%; Calcium 2%; Iron 2%
Diet Exchanges: 1 Fat

Quick & Low Fat

Olive Tapenade on Cucumber Stars

Prep: 15 min

2 large burpless cucumbers, cut into ⅜-inch slices (24 slices)

½ cup Olive Tapenade (opposite page) or purchased tapenade

Italian parsley sprigs, if desired

1. Cut cucumber slices into star or heart shapes, using cookie cutter, if desired.

2. Top each cucumber slice with 1 teaspoon Olive Tapenade. Garnish with parsley.

24 appetizers.

1 Appetizer: Calories 15 (Calories from Fat 10); Fat 1g (Saturated 0g); Cholesterol 0mg; Sodium 45mg; Carbohydrate 1g (Dietary Fiber 0g); Protein 0g
% Daily Value: Vitamin A 0%; Vitamin C 4%; Calcium 0%; Iron 0%
Diet Exchanges: Free Food

BETTY'S TIPS

⚙ **Variation**
Instead of using cucumbers, peel 1 pound of jicama, cut into ⅜-inch slices and cut slices into star or heart shapes.

⚙ **Do-Ahead**
Cut out the cucumber stars up to 3 hours before serving, and store in a plastic bag.

Olive Tapenade on Cucumber Stars

Holiday Bruschetta

Prep: 15 min

8 slices hard-crusted Italian bread, cut in half

2 cloves garlic

3 tablespoons olive or vegetable oil

1 jar (7 ounces) roasted red bell peppers, drained and cut into ½-inch strips

2 tablespoons chopped fresh parsley or 1 teaspoon parsley flakes

2 tablespoons shredded Parmesan cheese

1 tablespoon olive or vegetable oil

¼ teaspoon salt

¼ teaspoon pepper

1. Toast bread until golden brown on both sides.

2. Cut each garlic clove in half; rub cut sides over tops and sides of toast slices. Brush the 3 tablespoons oil over tops of toast slices.

3. Mix remaining ingredients. Spoon onto toast.

16 appetizers.

1 Appetizer: Calories 65 (Calories from Fat 35); Fat 4g (Saturated 1g); Cholesterol 0mg; Sodium 110mg; Carbohydrate 6g (Dietary Fiber 0g); Protein 1g
% Daily Value: Vitamin A 14%; Vitamin C 36%; Calcium 2%; Iron 2%
Diet Exchanges: 1 Vegetable, 1 Fat

BETTY'S TIPS

☺ **Substitution**
Sixteen baguette slices, ½ inch thick, can be used instead of the Italian bread. Toast slices in 400° oven about 4 to 5 minutes, turning once, until golden brown.

☺ **Do-Ahead**
You can toast the bread up to a day ahead of time if you like. You can also mix the bell pepper mixture, cover and store in the refrigerator up to 1 day.

Holiday Bruschetta

Herbed Seafood Bruschetta

Prep: 15 min   Chill: 1 hr   Broil: 6 min

1 can (6 ounces) crabmeat, drained, cartilage removed and flaked
1 can (4 to 4½ ounces) shrimp, rinsed and drained
2 medium roma (plum) tomatoes, seeded and chopped (½ cup)
⅓ cup chopped sweet onion
1 tablespoon chopped fresh chives
1 tablespoon chopped fresh basil leaves
1 tablespoon chopped fresh mint leaves
1 tablespoon olive or vegetable oil
1 tablespoon lemon juice
1 teaspoon finely chopped garlic
1 baguette (about 36 inches), cut into 36 slices
3 tablespoons olive or vegetable oil
  Freshly ground pepper to taste

1. Mix all ingredients except baguette, 3 tablespoons oil and the pepper. Cover and refrigerate at least 1 hour to blend flavors but no longer than 24 hours.

2. Place baguette slices on cookie sheet. Brush with some of the 3 tablespoons oil; sprinkle with pepper. Broil with tops 4 to 6 inches from heat 1 to 3 minutes or until light golden brown; turn. Brush with remaining oil; sprinkle with pepper. Broil 1 to 3 minutes longer or until light golden brown.

3. Place seafood mixture in bowl. Arrange bowl and toasted baguette slices on serving platter.

36 appetizers.

1 Appetizer: Calories 60 (Calories from Fat 20); Fat 2g (Saturated 0g); Cholesterol 10mg; Sodium 95mg; Carbohydrate 7g (Dietary Fiber 0g); Protein 3g
% Daily Value: Vitamin A 0%; Vitamin C 2%; Calcium 2%; Iron 2%
Diet Exchanges: ½ Starch, ½ Fat

BETTY'S TIPS

✪ **Variation**
Instead of letting guests assemble the bruschetta, you can spoon the seafood mixture onto the toasts and garnish each with a sprig of fresh mint.

✪ **Do-Ahead**
Toast slices for bruschetta up to 1 day ahead. Cool and store in an airtight container at room temperature.

✪ **Substitution**
You can substitute 3 tablespoons chopped fresh chives or basil rather than using 1 tablespoon each of chives, basil and mint.

Herbed Seafood Bruschetta

Salmon Crostini

Prep: 10 min   Bake: 5 min

- 18 slices pumpernickel cocktail bread
- 1/3 cup cream cheese, softened
- 3 tablespoons chopped red onion
- 2 tablespoons capers, drained
- 6 ounces salmon lox (18 slices)
- 1/4 cup chopped red bell pepper
   Chopped fresh dill weed

1. Heat oven to 400°. Place bread slices on cookie sheet. Bake 4 to 5 minutes or until crisp.

2. Spread each slice with cream cheese. Top with onion, capers, lox and bell pepper. Sprinkle with dill weed.

18 appetizers.

1 Appetizer: Calories 40 (Calories from Fat 20); Fat 2g (Saturated 1g); Cholesterol 5mg; Sodium 160mg; Carbohydrate 4g (Dietary Fiber 1g); Protein 3g
% Daily Value: Vitamin A 4%; Vitamin C 6%; Calcium 0%; Iron 2%
Diet Exchanges: 1/2 Starch

BETTY'S TIPS

☺ Substitution
One 4.75-ounce package of smoked salmon, chopped, can be used instead of the salmon lox. Use cream cheese flavored with smoked salmon or dill instead of regular cream cheese. Substitute a tomato, seeded and chopped, for the red bell pepper.

☺ Success Hint
Look for capers by the pickles in the supermarket.

☺ Variation
Use 18 slices of French bread, 1/4 inch thick, instead of the pumpernickel cocktail bread. Bake as directed.

Salmon Crostini

Barbecued Pork Crostini

Prep: 20 min   Marinate: 30 min   Bake: 30 min   Stand: 15 min

Marinade (right)

2   pork tenderloins (each about ¾ pound)

3   large red or yellow bell peppers, roasted and cut into strips

2   tablespoons olive or vegetable oil

1   tablespoon balsamic vinegar

Salt, to taste

2   cloves garlic, finely chopped

1   loaf (1 pound) French bread, cut into ½-inch slices

1. Make Marinade in resealable plastic food-storage bag. Add pork, turning to coat. Seal bag and refrigerate, turning pork occasionally, at least 30 minutes but no longer than 12 hours.

2. Mix bell peppers, oil, vinegar, salt and garlic. Set aside.

3. Heat oven to 425°. Remove pork from marinade; reserve marinade. Spray shallow roasting pan with cooking spray. Place pork in pan. Insert meat thermometer so tip is in thickest part of pork. Bake uncovered 25 to 30 minutes, brushing occasionally with marinade, until thermometer reads 155°. Discard any remaining marinade. Cover pork and let stand about 15 minutes or until thermometer reads 160° and pork is slightly pink in center. Cut pork into ¼-inch slices.

4. While pork is standing, place bread on ungreased cookie sheet. Bake 3 to 5 minutes or until toasted. Top bread with pork and bell peppers.

32 appetizers.

Marinade

½   cup barbecue sauce

2   tablespoons packed brown sugar

2   tablespoons olive or vegetable oil

2   tablespoons white wine vinegar

2   tablespoons soy sauce

1 to 2   teaspoons red pepper sauce

2   cloves garlic, finely chopped

Mix all ingredients.

1 Appetizer: Calories 335 (Calories from Fat 80); Fat 9g (Saturated 2g); Cholesterol 55mg; Sodium 750mg; Carbohydrate 40g (Dietary Fiber 2g); Protein 25g
% Daily Value: Vitamin A 48%; Vitamin C 66%; Calcium 6%; Iron 18%
Diet Exchanges: 2 Starch, 2 Lean Meat, 2 Vegetable

BETTY'S TIPS

✪ Success Hint
To roast the bell peppers, broil them with tops 5 inches from heat, turning occasionally, until skin is blistered and evenly browned but not burned. Place in plastic or paper bag, and close tightly. Let stand 10 minutes, then peel, seed and cut into strips.

✪ Do-Ahead
Make the bell pepper mixture and the marinade up to 2 days ahead of time. Cover and refrigerate.

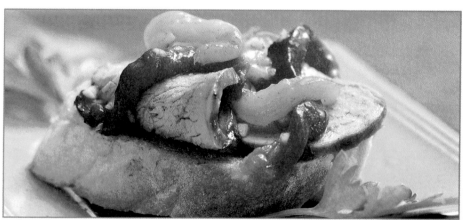

Barbecued Pork Crostini

Winter Fruit Kabobs with Peach Glaze

Denver Deviled Eggs

Winter Fruit Kabobs with Peach Glaze

Prep: 30 min   Broil: 4 min

6 cups bite-size pieces assorted fresh fruit (pineapple, pears, apples, kiwifruit, strawberries)
2 cups grapes
¾ cup peach or apricot preserves
2 tablespoons butter or margarine
2 tablespoons orange-flavored liqueur or orange juice
¼ teaspoon ground cinnamon

1. Thread 4 to 6 pieces of fruit on each of sixteen 8-inch skewers. Place skewers on large cookie sheet; set aside.

2. Heat preserves, butter, liqueur and cinnamon in 1-quart saucepan over medium-high heat, stirring frequently, until butter is melted. Brush about ¼ to ⅓ cup of preserves mixture over kabobs; reserve remaining preserves mixture.

3. Set oven control to broil. Broil kabobs with tops 4 to 6 inches from heat 2 minutes or until fruit is hot and glaze is bubbly. Serve warm or cold with remaining preserves mixture.

16 appetizers.

1 Appetizer: Calories 90 (Calories from Fat 20); Fat 2g (Saturated 1g); Cholesterol 5mg; Sodium 15mg; Carbohydrate 19g (Dietary Fiber 2g); Protein 1g
% Daily Value: Vitamin A 2%; Vitamin C 42%; Calcium 0%; Iron 2%
Diet Exchanges: 1½ Fruit

BETTY'S TIPS

☺ Success Hint
If using bamboo skewers, soak in water at least 30 minutes before using to prevent burning.

☺ Time-Saver
Speed the preparation of these yummy kabobs by purchasing fruit that's already cut up.

Denver Deviled Eggs

Prep: 15 min   Cook: 10 min   Stand: 18 min

12 eggs
½ cup mayonnaise or salad dressing
1 teaspoon ground mustard
¼ teaspoon salt
⅛ teaspoon pepper
2 tablespoons finely chopped red bell pepper
2 tablespoons finely chopped green bell pepper
2 tablespoons finely chopped fully cooked ham

1. Place eggs in 4-quart Dutch oven. Add enough cold water until it reaches 1 inch above eggs. Heat to boiling; remove from heat. Cover and let stand 18 minutes. Immediately cool eggs briefly in cold water to prevent further cooking.

2. Tap eggs to crack shells; roll eggs between hands to loosen shells, then peel. Cut eggs lengthwise in half. Carefully remove yolks and place in small bowl; reserve egg white halves. Mash yolks with fork. Stir in mayonnaise, mustard, salt and pepper until well blended. Stir in remaining ingredients.

3. Carefully spoon yolk mixture into egg white halves.

24 appetizers.

1 Appetizer: Calories 70 (Calories from Fat 55); Fat 6g (Saturated 1g); Cholesterol 110mg; Sodium 90mg; Carbohydrate 1g (Dietary Fiber 0g); Protein 3g
% Daily Value: Vitamin A 4%; Vitamin C 4%; Calcium 0%; Iron 2%
Diet Exchanges: ½ High-Fat Meat, ½ Fat

BETTY'S TIPS

☺ Success Hint
Very fresh eggs don't peel as easily as those that have aged a bit. Try to plan ahead and purchase eggs one week before making hard-cooked eggs.

Another trick for tough-to-peel eggs is to peel them under cold running water.

Cut a thin slice from the bottom of each egg white half before filling to keep the eggs from tipping on the serving plate.

☺ Do-Ahead
Prepare these zesty eggs up to 24 hours ahead of time. Cover and refrigerate until serving.

Antipasto Platter

Prep: 15 min

- 12 slices hard-crusted round Italian bread or 24 slices French bread, $\frac{1}{2}$ inch thick
- 2 cloves garlic
- 12 slices prosciutto or thinly sliced fully cooked ham (about 6 ounces), cut in half
- 12 slices provolone cheese (about $\frac{3}{4}$ pound), cut in half
- 24 thin slices Genoa salami (about $\frac{3}{4}$ pound)
- 24 marinated mushrooms
- 24 marinated artichoke hearts
- 24 Kalamata olives, pitted
- $\frac{1}{3}$ cup olive or vegetable oil
- $\frac{1}{2}$ medium lemon
- 1 tablespoon chopped fresh or $\frac{1}{2}$ teaspoon dried oregano leaves

1. If using Italian bread, cut each slice in half. Cut each garlic clove in half; rub cut sides over both sides of bread. Arrange bread and remaining ingredients except olive oil, lemon and oregano on serving platter.

2. To serve, top each bread slice with prosciutto, cheese, salami, mushroom, artichoke heart and olive. Drizzle with oil. Squeeze juice from lemon over top. Sprinkle with oregano.

24 appetizers.

1 Appetizer: Calories 210 (Calories from Fat 135); Fat 15g (Saturated 5g); Cholesterol 30mg; Sodium 780mg; Carbohydrate 10g (Dietary Fiber 2g); Protein 11g
% Daily Value: Vitamin A 4%; Vitamin C 6%; Calcium 12%; Iron 8%
Diet Exchanges: $\frac{1}{2}$ Starch, 1 Medium-Fat Meat, 2 Fat

BETTY'S TIPS

❂ **Success Hint**

For the very best flavor, use extra-virgin olive oil.

We also prefer imported Kalamata or Gaeta olives, but you can use large pitted ripe olives if you prefer.

❂ **Variation**

Add pepperoncini peppers (bottled Italian peppers) and cherry tomatoes to this easy Italian appetizer.

Antipasto Platter

Mini Pork Tacos

Prep: 10 min   Cook: 10 hr

2½   pounds pork boneless loin roast
1   medium onion, thinly sliced
2   cups barbecue sauce
¾   cup salsa
3   tablespoons chili powder
1   tablespoon Mexican seasoning
1   package (3.8 ounces) miniature taco shells (24 shells), heated
    Assorted toppings (shredded Cheddar cheese, chopped green onions, chopped fresh cilantro, cooked black beans, sour cream)

1. Remove excess fat from pork. Place pork in 3½- to 6-quart slow cooker; top with onion. Mix remaining ingredients except taco shells and toppings; pour over pork.

2. Cover and cook on low heat setting 8 to 10 hours or until pork is very tender.

3. Remove pork; place on large plate. Use 2 forks to pull pork into shreds. Stir pork back into slow cooker. Spoon pork mixture into taco shells. Serve with toppings.

24 appetizers.

1 Appetizer: Calories 150 (Calories from Fat 55); Fat 6g (Saturated 2g); Cholesterol 35mg; Sodium 320mg; Carbohydrate 13g (Dietary Fiber 1g); Protein 12g
% Daily Value: Vitamin A 10%; Vitamin C 2%; Calcium 4%; Iron 6%
Diet Exchanges: 1 Starch, 1 Lean Meat, ½ Fat

BETTY'S TIPS

☺ Serve-With
Serve the shredded pork in the slow cooker on low heat setting, and let your guests make their own mini tacos. Include a variety of your favorite Mexican toppings.

☺ Substitution
You can use 2 teaspoons of chili powder and 1 teaspoon ground cumin instead of the Mexican seasoning.

Quick

Corn and Crab Quesadillas

Prep: 10 min   Cook: 5 min

1   package (8 ounces) cream cheese, softened
1   can (11 ounces) whole kernel corn, drained
½   cup chopped fresh cilantro or parsley
5   medium green onions, chopped (⅓ cup)
1   jar (2 ounces) diced pimientos, drained
½   teaspoon black pepper
¼   teaspoon ground red pepper (cayenne)
1   pound chopped cooked crabmeat or imitation crabmeat (2 cups)
6   sun-dried tomato or spinach-cilantro flavored flour tortillas (8 to 10 inches in diameter)
1   tablespoon butter or margarine, melted

1. Mix cream cheese, corn, cilantro, onions, pimientos, black pepper and red pepper in medium bowl. Fold in crabmeat. Spread ⅔ cup of the crabmeat mixture over each tortilla; fold tortilla in half, pressing lightly. Brush butter over both sides of each tortilla.

2. Cook 3 tortillas at a time in 12-inch skillet over medium-high heat about 5 minutes, turning once, until light brown. Cut each quesadilla into 3 wedges.

18 servings.

1 Serving: Calories 140 (Calories from Fat 65); Fat 7g (Saturated 4g); Cholesterol 40mg; Sodium 220mg; Carbohydrate 12g (Dietary Fiber 1g); Protein 8g
% Daily Value: Vitamin A 8%; Vitamin C 4%; Calcium 6%; Iron 6%
Diet Exchanges: 1 Starch, 1 Lean Meat

BETTY'S TIPS

☺ Substitution
Roasted red bell peppers available in jars, drained and chopped, or chopped fresh red bell pepper can be used instead of the pimientos.

☺ Special Touch
Garnish with sour cream and fresh cilantro leaves.

Corn and Crab Quesadillas

Mini Pork Tacos

Maple Chicken Drummies

Maple Chicken Drummies

Prep: 15 min   Bake: 55 min

¼ cup real maple syrup or honey
¼ cup chili sauce
2 tablespoons chopped fresh chives
1 tablespoon soy sauce
½ teaspoon ground mustard
¼ teaspoon ground red pepper (cayenne), if desired
2 pounds chicken drummettes (about 20)

1. Heat oven to 375°. Mix all ingredients except chicken. Place chicken in ungreased jelly roll pan, 15½ × 10½ × 1 inch. Pour syrup mixture over chicken; turn chicken to coat.

2. Bake uncovered 45 to 55 minutes, turning once and brushing with sauce after 30 minutes, until juice of chicken is no longer pink when centers of thickest pieces are cut. Serve chicken with sauce.

20 appetizers.

1 Appetizer: Calories 60 (Calories from Fat 20); Fat 2g (Saturated 1g); Cholesterol 20mg; Sodium 100mg; Carbohydrate 4g (Dietary Fiber 0g); Protein 6g
% Daily Value: Vitamin A 0%; Vitamin C 0%; Calcium 0%; Iron 2%
Diet Exchanges: 1 Lean Meat

BETTY'S TIPS

✿ Variation
For extra flavor, marinate the drummettes in the maple syrup mixture in a zippered plastic bag in the refrigerator for up to 1 hour. Bake as directed.

✿ Special Touch
If desired, sprinkle with crumbled blue cheese and serve with blue cheese dressing.

Pesto Pepperoni Roll-Ups

Prep: 15 min

½ cup basil pesto
4 pesto-flavored flour tortillas (8 to 10 inches in diameter)
1 package (3¼ ounces) sliced pepperoni
2 roma (plum) tomatoes, seeded and chopped
¼ cup chopped yellow or orange bell pepper
¼ cup chopped ripe olives, drained
½ cup shredded mozzarella cheese (2 ounces)

1. Spread 2 tablespoons pesto evenly over each tortilla. Arrange 12 pepperoni slices on pesto. Sprinkle tomatoes, bell pepper, olives and cheese evenly over pepperoni to within ½ inch of edges of tortillas.

2. Roll up tortillas tightly. Cut each roll into 8 slices.

48 appetizers.

1 Appetizer: Calories 40 (Calories from Fat 25); Fat 3g (Saturated 1g); Cholesterol 5mg; Sodium 80mg; Carbohydrate 2g (Dietary Fiber 0g); Protein 1g
% Daily Value: Vitamin A 0%; Vitamin C 2%; Calcium 2%; Iron 0%
Diet Exchanges: 1 Fat

BETTY'S TIPS

✿ Do-Ahead
To make ahead, wrap each uncut roll tightly in plastic wrap and refrigerate up to 24 hours.

Pesto Pepperoni Roll-Ups

Betty... ON WHAT'S NEW

Set the Appetizer Table

Using a buffet-style setup for an appetizer party is the best way to cater to a large number of guests with a range of tastes and appetites. Because buffets are self-service, guests can help themselves to foods, leaving the host plenty of time to enjoy the guests.

Make as many foods ahead of time as possible, whether weeks ahead and freezing, or simply the morning of the party.

To create different levels of visual play, use pedestals, covered boxes and baskets, as well as trays and plates, to arrange and display foods. Candles, centerpieces and vases can provide visual interest, too.

Use different textures for your background. Instead of a tablecloth, consider pieces of velvet or a holiday tapestry as a runner for the table. Allow colors to contrast, and add gold or silver pieces that sparkle. Tie the corners of a tablecloth with brightly colored ribbon.

Clean pieces of granite, stone or tile or a marble chess or backgammon board work great as serving pieces. Arrange cheeses, crackers or fruits directly on the stone. Place a bowl under one or more stones to build different heights.

A mirror is a visually stunning way to display finger food. Leave space between individual pieces for the most dramatic effect.

Create a centerpiece with impact. You can use seasonal flowers, a miniature Christmas tree or a tree made of ornaments. Or try something from the kitchen such as an olive and cheese tree or a basket overflowing with different types of bread. You can also decorate the buffet with small potted seasonal flowers and then either give them as gifts or repot them.

Serving ware is handy when wrapped in napkins. Guests can handle all their serving utensils as one package. If you like, tie with a festive ribbon and place in a vase, clay pot or holiday-themed container.

Don't be afraid to be different by giving the buffet your own mix-and-match look! Try different containers: vases, boxes, baskets, pails. Mix different serving pieces: stone, wicker, clay, wood. Use a variety of shapes: square, round, oval, irregular.

After you've set up the buffet, there may be some open areas that could use a little filler. Try these ideas for items to weave around serving platters and bowls as space permits:

Branches: Real or artificial, depending on where you live and what's available.

Fruit: Bunches of grapes, whole strawberries, kiwifruit halves, pears and apples make for a beautiful, edible work of art.

Vegetables: Bell pepper strips, carrots, cucumbers, broccoli, purple kale or other greens add color and texture.

Spicy Sesame Chicken Strips

Prep: 20 min   Bake: 15 min

4 boneless, skinless chicken breast halves (about 1¼ pounds)
½ cup hoisin sauce
½ cup orange marmalade
2 tablespoons honey
1 teaspoon finely chopped gingerroot
¼ to ½ teaspoon ground red pepper (cayenne)
1 clove garlic, finely chopped
8 red pearl onions, peeled and halved, or 16 grape tomatoes
8 whole green onions
1 tablespoon sesame seed, toasted if desired

1. Heat oven to 425°. Line jelly roll pan, 15½ × 10½ × 1 inch, with aluminum foil.

2. Cut each chicken breast half lengthwise into 4 strips. Thread chicken strip on each of sixteen 8- to 10-inch skewers, leaving ½ inch space on pointed end. Place skewers in pan; set aside.

3. Mix remaining ingredients except pearl onions, green onions and sesame seed. Reserve ½ cup hoisin mixture. Spoon remaining hoisin mixture into small serving bowl; cover and refrigerate until serving. Brush chicken with ½ cup reserved hoisin mixture.

4. Bake 12 to 15 minutes, brushing chicken occasionally with pan drippings, until chicken is no longer pink in center. Thread 1 pearl onion half on end of each skewer. To serve, line serving platter with onions; arrange skewers on green onions. Sprinkle sesame seed over chicken. Serve with remaining hoisin mixture (heated if desired).

16 appetizers.

1 Appetizer: Calories 70 (Calories from Fat 10); Fat 1g (Saturated 0g); Cholesterol 20mg; Sodium 110mg; Carbohydrate 9g (Dietary Fiber 1g); Protein 7g
% Daily Value: Vitamin A 4%; Vitamin C 4%; Calcium 0%; Iron 2%
Diet Exchanges: ½ Starch, ½ Very Lean Meat

BETTY'S TIPS

⚙ **Success Hint**
To save time, purchase unbreaded chicken breast tenders, which can be skewered right from the package—no cutting needed.

If using bamboo skewers, soak in water at least 30 minutes before using to prevent burning.

To toast sesame seed, bake uncovered in ungreased shallow pan in 350° oven 8 to 10 minutes, stirring occasionally, until golden brown.

Spicy Sesame Chicken Strips

Baked Coconut Shrimp

Prep: 30 min   Bake: 8 min

Apricot Sauce (right)
¼ cup Gold Medal all-purpose flour
2 tablespoons packed brown sugar
¼ teaspoon salt
  Dash of ground red pepper (cayenne)
1 egg
1 tablespoon lime juice
1 cup shredded coconut
1 pound uncooked peeled deveined medium shrimp, thawed if frozen (about 40)
2 tablespoons butter or margarine, melted

1. Make Apricot Sauce. Move oven rack to lowest position. Heat oven to 425°. Spray rack in broiler pan with cooking spray.

2. Mix flour, brown sugar, salt and red pepper in shallow bowl. Beat egg and lime juice in another shallow bowl. Place coconut in third shallow bowl.

3. Coat each shrimp with flour mixture. Dip each side into egg mixture. Coat well with coconut. Place on rack in broiler pan. Drizzle with butter.

4. Bake 7 to 8 minutes or until shrimp are pink and firm and coating is beginning to brown. Serve with sauce.

About 40 appetizers.

Apricot Sauce

¾ cup apricot preserves
1 tablespoon lime juice
½ teaspoon ground mustard

Mix all ingredients in 1-quart saucepan. Cook over low heat, stirring occasionally, just until preserves are melted. Refrigerate while making shrimp.

1 Appetizer: Calories 40 (Calories from Fat 10); Fat 1g (Saturated 1g); Cholesterol 15mg; Sodium 35mg; Carbohydrate 6g (Dietary Fiber 0g); Protein 2g
% Daily Value: Vitamin A 0%; Vitamin C 0%; Calcium 0%; Iron 2%
Diet Exchanges: ½ Starch

BETTY'S TIPS

۞ Time-Saver
Serve these terrific low-fat appetizers with purchased cocktail sauce.

۞ Do-Ahead
Prepare the shrimp up to 2 hours ahead of time. Refrigerate covered, and bake just before serving.

Baked Coconut Shrimp

Caribbean Shrimp

Prep: 20 min   Marinate: 30 min   Bake: 8 min

1½ pounds uncooked peeled deveined medium shrimp (about 60)

2 medium green onions, chopped (2 tablespoons)

2 cloves garlic, finely chopped

2 teaspoons grated lime peel

¼ cup lime juice

1 tablespoon soy sauce

¼ teaspoon pepper

⅛ teaspoon crushed red pepper

2 teaspoons sesame oil

1. Mix all ingredients except oil in large glass or plastic bowl. Cover and refrigerate at least 30 minutes but no longer than 4 hours.

2. Heat oven to 400°. Spray rectangular pan, 13 × 9 × 2 inches, with cooking spray. Arrange shrimp in single layer in pan. Bake uncovered 7 to 8 minutes or until shrimp are pink and firm. Drizzle with oil. Serve hot.

12 servings (5 shrimp each).

1 Serving: Calories 50 (Calories from Fat 10); Fat 1g (Saturated 0g); Cholesterol 80mg; Sodium 120mg; Carbohydrate 0g (Dietary Fiber 0g); Protein 9g
% Daily Value: Vitamin A 2%; Vitamin C 2%; Calcium 2%; Iron 6%
Diet Exchanges: 1 Very Lean Meat

BETTY'S TIPS

☺ Success Hint

Choose raw, peeled shrimp that are firm, moist and translucent. If frozen, thaw before using. Leave the tails on the shrimp for more pizzazz.

☺ Health Twist

Your weight-conscious friends will love you for serving low-fat foods. This recipe is a terrific choice, with just 50 calories and 1 gram of fat for 5 shrimp.

Portabella and Brie Appetizer Pizza

Prep: 15 min   Bake: 10 min

1 package (6 ounces) fresh portabella mushrooms

1 tablespoon olive or vegetable oil

½ cup thinly sliced green bell pepper

½ cup thinly sliced red bell pepper

2 teaspoons chopped fresh or ½ teaspoon dried marjoram leaves

¼ teaspoon salt

1 package (10 ounces) ready-to-serve thin cheese pizza crust (12 inches in diameter)

½ cup sliced Brie cheese

1. Heat oven to 425°. Remove stems from mushrooms; thinly slice mushrooms.

2. Heat oil in 10-inch nonstick skillet over medium-high heat. Cook bell peppers in oil 2 minutes, stirring occasionally. Stir in mushrooms, marjoram and salt. Cook 1 to 2 minutes, stirring constantly, until mushrooms are just tender.

3. Place pizza crust on ungreased cookie sheet. Spread mushroom mixture over crust. Top with cheese.

4. Bake 8 to 10 minutes or until hot and cheese is melted. Cut into thin wedges to serve.

16 servings.

1 Serving: Calories 60 (Calories from Fat 20); Fat 2g (Saturated 1g); Cholesterol 3mg; Sodium 160mg; Carbohydrate 10g (Dietary Fiber 1g); Protein 2g
% Daily Value: Vitamin A 2%; Vitamin C 6%; Calcium 2%; Iron 4%
Diet Exchanges: ½ Starch, ½ Fat

BETTY'S TIPS

☺ Substitution

If portabella mushrooms are not available, you can use button or crimini mushrooms.

☺ Do-Ahead

Prepare the pizza up to 2 hours ahead of time. Refrigerate covered, and bake just before serving.

Portabella and Brie Appetizer Pizza

Caribbean Shrimp

Fresh Vegetable Appetizer Pizzas

Prep: 15 min
photo on page 41

1¼ cups finely chopped assorted raw vegetables (broccoli, carrots, red onion, yellow summer squash, red bell pepper, mushrooms)

¼ teaspoon salt

Dash of pepper

¼ teaspoon grated lemon peel

1 container (4 to 5 ounces) garlic-and-herb spreadable cheese

5 whole wheat flatbreads (6 inches in diameter)

⅓ cup finely shredded sharp Cheddar cheese

1. Place vegetables in small bowl. Sprinkle with salt, pepper and lemon peel.

2. Spread 2 tablespoons spreadable cheese over each flatbread. Top each with ¼ cup vegetable mixture. Sprinkle with Cheddar cheese. Cut each into 6 wedges.

30 servings.

1 Serving: Calories 25 (Calories from Fat 20); Fat 2g (Saturated 1g); Cholesterol 5mg; Sodium 45mg; Carbohydrate 1g (Dietary Fiber 0g); Protein 1g
% Daily Value: Vitamin A 4%; Vitamin C 2%; Calcium 0%; Iron 0%
Diet Exchanges: ½ Fat

BETTY'S TIPS

☻ Substitution
Crumbled feta cheese can be used in place of the Cheddar.

☻ Variation
If you like olives, toss ¼ cup halved pitted Kalamata or ripe olives with the vegetables.

Easy Pizzettes

Prep: 5 min   Bake: 10 min

1 cup pizza sauce

8 English muffins, split and toasted

2 cups shredded provolone cheese (8 ounces)

Assorted toppings (sliced mushrooms, sliced ripe olives, chopped bell pepper, chopped red onion)

1. Heat oven to 425°. Spread 1 tablespoon pizza sauce over each English muffin half. Sprinkle each with 1 tablespoon of the cheese.

2. Arrange toppings on pizzas. Sprinkle with remaining cheese. Place on ungreased cookie sheet. Bake 5 to 10 minutes or until cheese is melted.

16 appetizers.

1 Appetizer: Calories 125 (Calories from Fat 45); Fat 5g (Saturated 3g); Cholesterol 15mg; Sodium 360mg; Carbohydrate 15g (Dietary Fiber 1g); Protein 6g
% Daily Value: Vitamin A 8%; Vitamin C 6%; Calcium 16%; Iron 6%
Diet Exchanges: 1 Starch, ½ High-Fat Meat

BETTY'S TIPS

☻ Special Touch
Top with leftover grilled vegetables, such as mushrooms, zucchini, red onion, eggplant and bell peppers. Sprinkle toppings with chopped fresh basil, oregano or thyme

Easy Pizzettes

Stove-Top Sensations

Flavorful Soups, Stews, and Skillets

Rigatoni Pizza Stew (page 83)

Shrimp Bisque (page 75)

Tomato-Basil Soup with Garlic Croutons

Prep: 10 min   Cook: 8 min

1 can (14½ ounces) diced tomatoes with basil, garlic and oregano, undrained
1 can (10¾ ounces) condensed tomato soup
1½ cups whipping (heavy) cream
½ cup thinly sliced fresh basil leaves
4 slices French bread, each ½ inch thick
2 tablespoons olive or vegetable oil
1 clove garlic, finely chopped
1 tablespoon chopped fresh parsley

1. Cook tomatoes, soup and whipping cream in 2-quart saucepan over medium heat 5 to 8 minutes, stirring frequently, until hot (do not boil or soup may curdle). Stir in basil.

2. While soup is heating, set oven control to broil. Place bread slices on rack in broiler pan. Mix oil and garlic in small bowl. Brush oil mixture over tops of bread slices. Broil 4 to 6 inches from heat 1 to 2 minutes or until edges are golden brown.

3. Spoon soup into shallow soup bowls. Place bread on soup; sprinkle with parsley.

4 servings (about ¾ cup each).

1 Serving: Calories 470 (Calories from Fat 335); Fat 37g (Saturated 19g); Cholesterol 100mg; Sodium 780mg; Carbohydrate 31g (Dietary Fiber 3g); Protein 6g
% Daily Value: Vitamin A 42%; Vitamin C 22%; Calcium 12%; Iron 12%
Diet Exchanges: 1 Starch, 3 Vegetable, 7 Fat

BETTY'S TIPS

☺ Health Twist

To reduce the fat to 3 grams and the calories to 195 per serving, use fat-free half-and-half instead of the whipping cream; the soup will be a little bit thinner. Omit the olive oil; instead, spray the bread with cooking spray and sprinkle with the garlic.

☺ Serve-With

Serve this rich, flavorful soup with a simple tossed salad and a light-flavored dressing. A mango or raspberry sorbet would be an excellent dessert.

Tomato-Lentil Soup

Prep: 10 min   Cook: 40 min

1 tablespoon olive or vegetable oil
1 large onion, finely chopped (1 cup)
1 medium stalk celery, cut into ½-inch pieces
2 cloves garlic, finely chopped
2 medium carrots, cut into ½-inch pieces (1 cup)
1 cup dried lentils (8 ounces), sorted and rinsed
4 cups water
4 teaspoons chicken or vegetable bouillon granules
1 teaspoon dried thyme leaves
¼ teaspoon pepper
1 dried bay leaf
1 can (28 ounces) diced tomatoes, undrained

1. Heat oil in 3-quart saucepan over medium-high heat. Cook onion, celery and garlic in oil about 5 minutes, stirring occasionally, until softened.

2. Stir in remaining ingredients except tomatoes. Heat to boiling; reduce heat. Cover and simmer 15 to 20 minutes or until lentils and vegetables are tender.

3. Stir in tomatoes; reduce heat. Simmer uncovered about 15 minutes or until heated through. Remove bay leaf.

6 servings.

1 Serving: Calories 150 (Calories from Fat 25); Fat 3g (Saturated 0g); Cholesterol 0mg; Sodium 1060mg; Carbohydrate 30g (Dietary Fiber 9g); Protein 10g
% Daily Value: Vitamin A 84%; Vitamin C 20%; Calcium 8%; Iron 22%
Diet Exchanges: 1 Starch, 3 Vegetable

BETTY'S TIPS

☺ Did You Know?

Lentils are low in calories and a good source of fiber. They also don't have cholesterol and have very little fat. Lentils are available in a variety of colors: grayish brown (the most widely available), yellow and red. Use whatever color you like.

Tomato-Lentil Soup

Tomato-Basil Soup with Garlic Croutons

Betty ... ON BASICS

Homemade Broth and Chicken

Prep: 25 min   Cook: 1 hr

3 to 3½   pounds cut-up broiler-fryer chicken
     4½   cups cold water
      1   teaspoon salt
     ½   teaspoon pepper
      1   medium stalk celery with leaves, cut up
      1   carrot, cut up
      1   small onion, cut up
      1   sprig parsley

Using colander, strain broth; discard vegetables.

1. Place chicken, giblets (except liver) and neck in 4-quart Dutch oven. Add remaining ingredients; heat to boiling. Skim foam from broth; reduce heat. Cover and simmer about 45 minutes or until juice of chicken is no longer pink when centers of thickest pieces are cut.

2. Remove chicken from broth. Cool chicken about 10 minutes or just until cool enough to handle. Strain broth; discard vegetables.

3. Remove skin and bones from chicken. Cut chicken into ½-inch pieces. Skim fat from broth. Use immediately, or cover and refrigerate broth and chicken in separate containers up to 24 hours or freeze for future use.

About 4 cups broth and 2½ cups cooked chicken.

1 Serving: Calories 160 (Calories from Fat 55); Fat 6g (Saturated 2g); Cholesterol 80mg; Sodium 600mg; Carbohydrate 0g (Dietary Fiber 0g); Protein 32g
% Daily Value: Vitamin A 8%; Vitamin C 0%; Calcium 2%; Iron 8%
Diet Exchanges: 4½ Very Lean Meat

Mom's Homemade Chicken Soup

Prep: 15 min   Cook: 1 hr 25 min

Homemade Broth and Chicken (opposite page) or 1 can (49½ ounces) ready-to-serve chicken broth plus 2 cups cut-up cooked chicken

- 1 cup baby-cut carrots
- 2 medium stalks celery, sliced (1 cup)
- 1 medium onion, chopped (½ cup)
- 2 cloves garlic, chopped
- 2 tablespoons chicken bouillon granules
- 1 tablespoon chopped fresh parsley
- 1 tablespoon chopped fresh or 1 teaspoon dried thyme leaves
- 1 cup frozen egg noodles (from 12-ounce bag)

1. Make Homemade Broth and Chicken. Refrigerate cut-up chicken. Add enough water to broth to measure 6 cups.

2. Heat broth, carrots, celery, onion, garlic, bouillon granules, parsley and thyme to boiling in 4-quart Dutch oven. Add noodles; reduce heat. Simmer uncovered 20 to 25 minutes, adding chicken to Dutch oven for last 5 minutes, until vegetables and noodles are tender.

6 servings.

1 Serving: Calories 220 (Calories from Fat 55); Fat 6g (Saturated 1g); Cholesterol 50mg; Sodium 3290mg; Carbohydrate 21g (Dietary Fiber 2g); Protein 22g
% Daily Value: Vitamin A 80%; Vitamin C 8%; Calcium 6%; Iron 12%
Diet Exchanges: 1 Starch, 2 Very Lean Meat, 1 Vegetable, 1 Fat

BETTY'S TIPS

✪ Substitution

We love the old-fashioned taste of the egg noodles, but you can also use 1 cup uncooked bow-tie pasta or your favorite pasta. Reduce the cooking time to 15 to 20 minutes.

If using canned broth, omit the bouillon granules.

Mom's Homemade Chicken Soup

Asian Pork and Noodle Soup

Shrimp Bisque

Shrimp Bisque

Prep: 10 min   Cook: 8 min

1 cup dry white wine or chicken broth
2 tablespoons cocktail sauce
1 teaspoon salt
1 teaspoon white pepper
1 teaspoon celery seed
1 teaspoon paprika
1 teaspoon lemon juice
1 teaspoon Worcestershire sauce
1 teaspoon butter or margarine
1 bottle (8 ounces) clam juice (1 cup)
1 pound uncooked peeled deveined medium shrimp, thawed if frozen
3 cups half-and-half

1. Mix all ingredients except shrimp and half-and-half in 4-quart Dutch oven. Heat to boiling. Stir in shrimp; reduce heat. Simmer uncovered 2 to 3 minutes or until shrimp are pink and firm.

2. Gradually add half-and-half, stirring constantly, until half-and-half is just heated through.

4 servings.

1 Serving: Calories 355 (Calories from Fat 205); Fat 24g (Saturated 14g); Cholesterol 230mg; Sodium 1230mg; Carbohydrate 11g (Dietary Fiber 0g); Protein 24g
% Daily Value: Vitamin A 24%; Vitamin C 4%; Calcium 24%; Iron 18%
Diet Exchanges: 3 Very Lean Meat, 2 Vegetable, 4 Fat

BETTY'S TIPS

✪ **Variation**
Turn up the heat in this creamy soup by adding 4 dashes of red pepper sauce.

✪ **Extra Special**
Garnish with snipped fresh Italian parsley, chopped fresh chives or green onions.

Asian Pork and Noodle Soup

Prep: 10 min   Cook: 20 min

1 pound pork boneless sirloin or loin, cut into $\frac{1}{2}$-inch pieces
2 cloves garlic, finely chopped
2 teaspoons finely chopped gingerroot
2 cans (14$\frac{1}{2}$ ounces each) chicken broth
2 cups water
2 tablespoons soy sauce
2 cups uncooked fine egg noodles (4 ounces)
1 medium carrot, sliced ($\frac{1}{2}$ cup)
1 small red bell pepper, chopped ($\frac{1}{2}$ cup)
2 cups fresh spinach leaves

1. Spray 3-quart saucepan with cooking spray; heat over medium-high heat. Add pork, garlic and gingerroot; stir-fry 3 to 5 minutes or until pork is brown.

2. Stir in broth, water and soy sauce. Heat to boiling; reduce heat. Simmer uncovered 5 minutes. Stir in noodles, carrot and bell pepper. Simmer uncovered about 10 minutes or until noodles are tender.

3. Stir in spinach. Cook until heated through.

4 servings.

1 Serving: Calories 320 (Calories from Fat 100); Fat 11g (Saturated 4g); Cholesterol 95mg; Sodium 1450mg; Carbohydrate 24g (Dietary Fiber 2g); Protein 33g
% Daily Value: Vitamin A 100%; Vitamin C 34%; Calcium 4%; Iron 18%
Diet Exchanges: 1 Starch, 4 Very Lean Meat, 2 Vegetable, 1 Fat

BETTY'S TIPS

✪ **Success Hint**
To prepare gingerroot, use a small sharp knife to peel the tough skin. Cut gingerroot into slices, then finely chop.

✪ **Time-Saver**
Purchase already washed spinach in the produce section of the supermarket.

Ham Chowder with Sweet Potato Biscuits

Prep: 15 min   Bake/Cook: 20 min

Sweet Potato Biscuits (page 27) or Rolled Parmesan Biscuits (below)

2   cans (10¾ ounces each) condensed cream of potato soup

1   can (11 ounces) whole kernel corn, drained

3   small red potatoes, cut into ⅛-inch slices

1   medium stalk celery, sliced (½ cup)

1   cup diced fully cooked ham

1¾   cups milk

1. Make biscuits.

2. While biscuits are baking, cook remaining ingredients in 10-inch nonstick skillet over medium-high heat 15 to 20 minutes, stirring occasionally, until potatoes are tender.

3. Serve each serving of chowder with a biscuit.

8 servings.

Rolled Parmesan Biscuits

2¼   cups Original Bisquick

¼   cup grated Parmesan cheese

⅔   cup milk

Heat oven to 450°. Stir all ingredients until soft dough forms. Place dough on surface sprinkled with Bisquick.

Knead 10 times. Roll dough ½ inch thick. Cut with 2½-inch biscuit cutter. Place about 1 inch apart on ungreased cookie sheet. Brush with additional milk and sprinkle with additional Parmesan cheese if desired. Bake 8 to 10 minutes or until golden brown.

1 Serving: Calories 330 (Calories from Fat 90); Fat 10g (Saturated 4g); Cholesterol 20mg; Sodium 1470mg; Carbohydrate 50g (Dietary Fiber 3g); Protein 13g
% Daily Value: Vitamin A 4%; Vitamin C 8%; Calcium 22%; Iron 12%
Diet Exchanges: 2½ Starch, 1 Skim Milk, 1 Fat

BETTY'S TIPS

❂ **Substitution**
You can use two 10¾-ounce cans of ready-to-eat cream of potato soup instead of the condensed soup; decrease the milk to ½ cup.

❂ **Variation**
Clam chowder would taste great served over the special Parmesan biscuits. Use 2 cans of clam chowder instead of the potato soup and omit the ham.

❂ **Special Touch**
It's easy to make special Halloween biscuits. Use a cookie cutter with a pumpkin, ghost, bat, cat or half-moon shape.

Ham Chowder with Sweet Potato Biscuits

Beef 'n' Veggie Soup with Mozzarella (page 78)

Beef 'n' Veggie Soup with Mozzarella

Prep: 10 min   Cook: 20 min
Photo on page 77

1 pound ground beef
1 large onion, chopped (1 cup)
1 can (14½ ounces) diced tomatoes with green pepper, celery and onions, undrained
4 cups water
5 teaspoons beef bouillon granules
1½ teaspoons Italian seasoning
¼ teaspoon pepper
1 package (10 ounces) frozen mixed vegetables
1 cup shredded mozzarella cheese (4 ounces)

1. Cook beef and onion in 4-quart Dutch oven over medium-high heat, stirring occasionally, until beef is brown; drain.

2. Stir in remaining ingredients except cheese. Heat to boiling; reduce heat. Simmer uncovered 6 to 8 minutes, stirring occasionally, until vegetables are tender.

3. Sprinkle about 2 tablespoons cheese in each of 8 soup bowls; fill bowls with soup.

8 servings (about 1½ cups each).

1 Serving: Calories 185 (Calories from Fat 100); Fat 11g (Saturated 5g); Cholesterol 40mg; Sodium 1050mg; Carbohydrate 8g (Dietary Fiber 2g); Protein 16g
% Daily Value: Vitamin A 24%; Vitamin C 16%; Calcium 14%; Iron 8%
Diet Exchanges: 2 Medium-Fat Meat, 2 Vegetable

BETTY'S TIPS

☺ Substitution
Four cups of canned beef broth can be substituted for the water and bouillon granules.

If you don't have diced tomatoes with green pepper, celery and onions, use regular diced tomatoes and add chopped green bell pepper, celery and onions with the ground beef.

Easy Beans and Franks Soup

Prep: 10 min   Cook: 15 min

1 can (28 ounces) baked beans with bacon and brown sugar sauce, undrained
1 can (11½ ounces) eight-vegetable juice
6 franks, cut into 1-inch slices
3 medium carrots, chopped (1½ cups)
1 large onion, chopped (1 cup)
1 clove garlic, finely chopped
1 teaspoon Worcestershire sauce

1. Mix all ingredients in 2-quart saucepan.

2. Heat to boiling; reduce heat. Simmer uncovered 10 to 15 minutes or until carrots are tender.

6 servings.

1 Serving: Calories 420 (Calories from Fat 190); Fat 21g (Saturated 8g); Cholesterol 40mg; Sodium 970mg; Carbohydrate 49g (Dietary Fiber 5g); Protein 15g
% Daily Value: Vitamin A 100%; Vitamin C 18%; Calcium 10%; Iron 18%
Diet Exchanges: 3 Starch, ½ High-Fat Meat, 1 Vegetable, 2½ Fat

BETTY'S TIPS

☺ Substitution
The eight-vegetable juice adds a nice spicy flavor. For an all-family-appeal soup, however, you may want to use tomato juice instead of the eight-vegetable juice.

☺ Special Touch
Add a little fun by topping each serving with a slice of process American cheese.

Easy Beans and Franks Soup

Southwestern Stew with Corn Dumplings

Prep: 5 min   Cook: 10 min   Bake: 25 min

1 tablespoon vegetable oil

1 large onion, chopped (1 cup)

2 cups cubed peeled sweet potatoes or butternut squash

1 cup whole kernel corn

1 can (15 to 16 ounces) garbanzo beans, rinsed and drained

1 jar (16 ounces) salsa (2 cups)

1 cup water

1/4 teaspoon ground cinnamon

1 pouch (6.5 ounces) Betty Crocker golden corn muffin and bread mix

1/2 cup fat-free (skim) milk

1 tablespoon vegetable oil

1 tablespoon roasted sunflower nuts, if desired

1. Heat oven to 425°. Heat 1 tablespoon oil in ovenproof 4-quart Dutch oven over medium-high heat. Cook onion in oil about 5 minutes, stirring occasionally, until crisp-tender. Stir in sweet potatoes, corn, beans, salsa, water and cinnamon. Heat to boiling, stirring occasionally.

2. Mix corn muffin mix (dry), milk and 1 tablespoon oil. Stir in nuts. Drop dough by 8 spoonfuls onto vegetable mixture.

3. Bake uncovered 20 to 25 minutes or until toothpick inserted in center of dumplings comes out clean.

4 servings.

1 Serving: Calories 555 (Calories from Fat 110); Fat 12g (Saturated 1g); Cholesterol 0mg; Sodium 1140mg; Carbohydrate 107g (Dietary Fiber 14g); Protein 18g
% Daily Value: Vitamin A 100%; Vitamin C 38%; Calcium 16%; Iron 32%
Diet Exchanges: 6 Starch, 3 Vegetable

BETTY'S TIPS

❂ **Success Hint**
Sweet potatoes with darker-colored skins are generally more moist and flavorful than the lighter ones. Two medium sweet potatoes or half of a small butternut squash will give you 2 cups cubed.

❂ **Serve-With**
This stew is complete in itself, but a salad of melon slices and orange segments drizzled with honey adds a finishing touch.

Southwestern Stew with Corn Dumplings

Cheesy Chicken Pasta Stew

Prep: 5 min   Cook: 20 min

1 tablespoon butter or margarine

1 pound boneless, skinless chicken breasts, cut into 1-inch pieces

1 cup milk

1 package (3 ounces) cream cheese, softened

1 bag (1 pound) frozen pasta, broccoli and carrots in creamy Cheddar sauce

2 tablespoons chopped fresh chives

1. Melt butter in 12-inch nonstick skillet over medium-high heat. Cook chicken in butter 4 to 5 minutes, stirring occasionally, until brown.

2. Stir in milk and cream cheese. Cook, stirring frequently, until cheese is melted. Stir in pasta and vegetable mixture. Heat to boiling, stirring occasionally; reduce heat. Cover and simmer 3 to 7 minutes or until pasta and vegetables are tender. Sprinkle with chives.

4 servings.

1 Serving: Calories 410 (Calories from Fat 180); Fat 20g (Saturated 10g); Cholesterol 115mg; Sodium 570mg; Carbohydrate 26g (Dietary Fiber 2g); Protein 34g
% Daily Value: Vitamin A 50%; Vitamin C 14%; Calcium 20%; Iron 10%
Diet Exchanges: 2 Starch, 4 Lean Meat, 1 Fat

BETTY'S TIPS

⚙ **Substitution**
Chopped chives add a fresh taste and pretty color to this stew. If you don't have chives on hand, sprinkle the stew with chopped green onions or parsley instead.

⚙ **Serve-With**
Here's a hearty stew you can make in minutes that the whole family will enjoy. Serve with breadsticks and fresh fruit.

Cincinnati Chili

Prep: 10 min   Cook: 16 min

10 ounces uncooked spaghetti

1 tablespoon vegetable oil

1 pound ground turkey breast

1 medium onion, chopped (½ cup)

1 clove garlic, finely chopped

1 jar (26 to 28 ounces) chunky vegetable-style tomato pasta sauce

1 can (15 to 16 ounces) kidney beans, rinsed and drained

2 tablespoons chili powder

½ cup shredded Cheddar cheese (2 ounces), if desired

3 medium green onions, sliced, if desired

1. Cook and drain spaghetti as directed on package.

2. Heat oil in 10-inch skillet over medium heat. Cook turkey, chopped onion and garlic in oil 5 to 6 minutes, stirring occasionally, until turkey is no longer pink.

3. Stir in pasta sauce, beans and chili powder; reduce heat. Simmer uncovered 10 minutes, stirring occasionally. Serve sauce over spaghetti. Sprinkle with cheese and green onions.

6 servings.

1 Serving: Calories 495 (Calories from Fat 80); Fat 9g (Saturated 1g); Cholesterol 50mg; Sodium 840mg; Carbohydrate 80g (Dietary Fiber 9g); Protein 32g
% Daily Value: Vitamin A 34%; Vitamin C 18%; Calcium 8%; Iron 34%
Diet Exchanges: 5 Starch, 2 Lean Meat

BETTY'S TIPS

⚙ **Substitution**
You can use ground beef instead of the ground turkey.

⚙ **Time-Saver**
Make a double batch of this hearty chili and freeze for a quick meal another week.

Cheesy Chicken Pasta Stew

Cincinnati Chili

Home-Style Beef Stew

Prep: 5 min   Cook: 10 min   Bake: 25 min

1 pound ground beef

2 cups water

2 cans (14½ ounces each) diced tomatoes in olive oil, garlic and spices, undrained

1 can (6 ounces) tomato paste

1 bag (1 pound) frozen carrots, green beans and cauliflower (or other combination)

2¼ cups Original Bisquick

⅔ cup milk

1 tablespoon chopped fresh parsley

1. Heat oven to 425°. Cook beef in 4-quart ovenproof Dutch oven over medium heat, stirring occasionally, until brown; drain. Stir in water, tomatoes, tomato paste and vegetables. Heat to boiling, stirring occasionally; remove from heat.

2. Stir remaining ingredients until soft dough forms. Drop dough by 6 spoonfuls onto beef mixture.

3. Bake uncovered 20 to 25 minutes or until biscuits are golden brown and stew is bubbly.

6 servings.

1 Serving: Calories 420 (Calories from Fat 160); Fat 18g (Saturated 6g); Cholesterol 45mg; Sodium 1310mg; Carbohydrate 48g (Dietary Fiber 5g); Protein 22g
% Daily Value: Vitamin A 60%; Vitamin C 44%; Calcium 18%; Iron 22%
Diet Exchanges: 2 Starch, 1½ High-Fat Meat, 3 Vegetable, 1 Fat

BETTY'S TIPS

❂ **Substitution**
Is your family particular about the kinds of vegetables they'll eat? You can use any 1-pound bag of frozen vegetables that is popular with your family.

❂ **Health Twist**
For 305 calories and 5 grams of fat per serving, use Reduced Fat Bisquick in place of Original Bisquick and substitute ground turkey breast for the ground beef.

❂ **Serve-With**
Accompany this hearty homespun dinner with a crisp green salad topped with raisins and sunflower nuts, and for dessert, chocolate chip cookies.

Home-Style Beef Stew

Barley Burger Stew

Prep: 15 min   Cook: 25 min

- 1   pound ground beef
- 1   large onion, chopped (1 cup)
- ½   cup uncooked quick-cooking barley
- 4   cups tomato juice
- 1   cup water
- 2 to 3   teaspoons chili powder
- 1½   teaspoons salt
- ½   teaspoon pepper
- 1   medium stalk celery, chopped (½ cup)

1. Cook beef and onion in 4-quart Dutch oven over medium heat 8 to 10 minutes, stirring occasionally, until beef is brown; drain.

2. Stir in remaining ingredients. Heat to boiling; reduce heat. Cover and simmer about 15 minutes or until barley is tender and stew is desired consistency.

4 servings.

1 Serving: Calories 375 (Calories from Fat 155); Fat 17g (Saturated 7g); Cholesterol 65mg; Sodium 1840mg; Carbohydrate 36g (Dietary Fiber 6g); Protein 36g
% Daily Value: Vitamin A 46%; Vitamin C 40%; Calcium 6%; Iron 22%
Diet Exchanges: 2 Starch, 3 Lean Meat, 1 Vegetable, ½ Fat

BETTY'S TIPS

☺ **Time-Saver**
Double this recipe; leftovers make a great lunch.

☺ **Variation**
Add chopped carrots and/or green beans with the celery.

Barley Burger Stew

Rigatoni Pizza Stew

Prep: 15 min   Cook: 30 min
Photo on page 69

- 1   pound Italian sausage links, cut into ¼-inch slices
- 1   can (14½ ounces) Italian-style stewed tomatoes with basil, garlic and oregano, undrained
- 1   can (14½ ounces) beef broth
- 1   cup water
- ¼   cup Italian-style tomato paste
- 1   medium onion, coarsely chopped (½ cup)
- 2   medium carrots, cut into ½-inch slices (1 cup)
- 1½   cups uncooked rigatoni pasta (4½ ounces)
- 1   medium zucchini, cut lengthwise in half, then cut crosswise into ¼-inch slices (2 cups)
- ½   cup shredded mozzarella cheese (2 ounces)

1. Spray 4-quart Dutch oven with cooking spray. Cook sausage in Dutch oven over medium heat, stirring occasionally, until no longer pink; drain.

2. Stir tomatoes, broth, water, tomato paste, onion and carrots into sausage. Heat to boiling; reduce heat to medium-low. Cook about 10 minutes or until carrots are tender.

3. Stir in pasta and zucchini. Cook 10 to 12 minutes, stirring occasionally, until pasta is tender. Serve topped with cheese.

4 servings.

1 Serving: Calories 539 (Calories from Fat 225); Fat 25g (Saturated 9g); Cholesterol 70mg; Sodium 1700mg; Carbohydrate 52g (Dietary Fiber 5g); Protein 30g
% Daily Value: Vitamin A 100%; Vitamin C 24%; Calcium 18%; Iron 22%
Diet Exchanges: 2½ Starch, 3 Medium-Fat Meat, 2½ Vegetable, 1 Fat

BETTY'S TIPS

☺ **Substitution**
Turkey Italian sausage can be used in place of the regular sausage. Or for the pepperoni pizza lovers in your family, substitute sliced pepperoni, stirring it into the tomato mixture.

☺ **Success Hint**
Place the sausage in the freezer while you cut the vegetables. It will be much easier to slice when it is partially frozen.

Beef Taco Rice Skillet

Pizza Burgers

Beef Taco Rice Skillet

Prep: 5 min   Cook: 14 min   Stand: 10 min

- 1 pound ground beef
- 1 envelope (1¼ ounces) taco seasoning mix
- 1½ cups water
- 1 cup thick-and-chunky salsa
- 1 cup frozen whole kernel corn
- 1½ cups uncooked instant rice
- ¾ cup shredded taco-seasoned cheese (4 ounces)
- 1 cup shredded lettuce
- 1 medium tomato, chopped (¾ cup)
  Sour cream, if desired

1. Cook beef in 10-inch skillet over medium heat 8 to 10 minutes, stirring occasionally, until brown; drain.

2. Stir in seasoning mix, water, salsa and corn. Heat to boiling; stir in rice. Boil 1 minute; remove from heat. Cover and let stand 8 minutes.

3. Fluff rice mixture with fork; sprinkle with cheese. Cover and let stand 1 to 2 minutes or until cheese is melted. Sprinkle lettuce around edge of skillet; sprinkle tomato in circle next to lettuce. Serve with sour cream.

5 servings.

1 Serving: Calories 440 (Calories from Fat 170); Fat 19g (Saturated 9g); Cholesterol 70mg; Sodium 670mg; Carbohydrate 44g (Dietary Fiber 3g); Protein 26g
% Daily Value: Vitamin A 30%; Vitamin C 12%; Calcium 14%; Iron 20%
Diet Exchanges: 3 Starch, 2 High-Fat Meat

BETTY'S TIPS

☼ Variation
If you're lucky enough to have leftovers, wrap 'em up in a flour tortilla to serve for lunch the next day.

If you want a little more kick, use spicy salsa and add a few drops of red pepper sauce to the rice mixture.

Pizza Burgers

Prep: 5 min   Cook: 14 min

- 1 pound ground beef
- 1 medium onion, chopped (½ cup)
- 1 small green bell pepper, chopped (½ cup)
- 1 jar (14 ounces) pepperoni-flavored or regular pizza sauce
- ½ cup sliced ripe olives, if desired
- 6 sandwich buns, split
- 1 cup shredded pizza cheese blend (4 ounces)

1. Cook beef, onion and bell pepper in 10-inch skillet over medium heat 8 to 10 minutes, stirring occasionally, until beef is brown; drain.

2. Stir in pizza sauce and olives. Heat to boiling, stirring occasionally.

3. Spoon about ½ cup beef mixture on bottom half of each bun. Immediately sprinkle each with 2 tablespoons of the cheese; add tops of buns. Serve immediately or let stand about 2 minutes until cheese is melted.

6 sandwiches.

1 Sandwich: Calories 375 (Calories from Fat 190); Fat 21g (Saturated 8g); Cholesterol 60mg; Sodium 620mg; Carbohydrate 26g (Dietary Fiber 3g); Protein 23g
% Daily Value: Vitamin A 12%; Vitamin C 20%; Calcium 18%; Iron 16%
Diet Exchanges: 2 Starch, 2½ Medium-Fat Meat, 1 Fat

BETTY'S TIPS

☼ Substitution
Pizza cheese is a blend of shredded mozzarella and Cheddar cheeses. You can also use just mozzarella cheese.

☼ Do-Ahead
Cook large quantities of ground beef and onion ahead of time, and freeze in 1-pound packages. Defrost in the microwave oven, and add the bell pepper, pizza sauce and olives. Microwave until hot; continue as directed in step 3.

Beef and Salsa Skillet

Prep: 15 min   Cook: 20 min

1	pound ground beef
1	jar (16 ounces) thick-and-chunky salsa (2 cups)
1	can (15 to 16 ounces) kidney beans, undrained
1	can (8¾ ounces) whole kernel corn, undrained
1	can (8 ounces) tomato sauce
2	teaspoons chili powder
1½	cups Original Bisquick
½	cup water
½	cup shredded Colby-Monterey Jack cheese (2 ounces), if desired

1. Cook beef in 12-inch skillet over medium heat, stirring occasionally, until brown; drain. Stir in salsa, beans, corn, tomato sauce and 1 teaspoon of the chili powder. Heat to boiling; reduce heat to low.

2. Stir Bisquick, remaining 1 teaspoon chili powder and the water until soft dough forms. Drop by 6 spoonfuls onto simmering beef mixture.

3. Cook uncovered 10 minutes. Cover and cook 8 minutes longer. Sprinkle with cheese. Cover and cook about 2 minutes or until cheese is melted.

6 servings.

1 Serving: Calories 345 (Calories from Fat 145); Fat 16g (Saturated 5g); Cholesterol 45mg; Sodium 1120mg; Carbohydrate 34g (Dietary Fiber 3g); Protein 19g
% Daily Value: Vitamin A 18%; Vitamin C 16%; Calcium 8%; Iron 20%
Diet Exchanges: 2 Starch, 1½ Lean Meat, 1 Vegetable

BETTY'S TIPS

✪ Substitution
Make an equally delicious and quick meal by substituting ground turkey breast for the ground beef.

✪ Health Twist
For 9 grams of fat and 290 calories per serving, use ¾ pound extra-lean ground beef and 1½ cups Reduced Fat Bisquick.

✪ Serve-With
Complete this easy meal with a salad of sliced oranges, sliced avocado and red onion rings drizzled with your favorite vinaigrette dressing.

Beef and Salsa Skillet

Pasta Pronto

Nifty Noodles in 30 Minutes or Less

Turkey Pasta Primavera (page 88)

Timesaving Tortellini (page 102)

Turkey Pasta Primavera

Prep: 10 min   Cook: 8 min
Photo on page 87

1 package (9 ounces) refrigerated fettuccine or linguine
2 tablespoons Italian dressing
1 bag (1 pound) frozen broccoli, cauliflower and carrots, thawed and drained
2 cups cut-up cooked turkey or chicken
1 teaspoon salt
2 large tomatoes, seeded and chopped (2 cups)
¼ cup freshly grated Parmesan cheese
2 tablespoons chopped fresh parsley

1. Cook and drain fettuccine as directed on package.

2. While fettuccine is cooking, heat dressing in 10-inch skillet over medium-high heat. Cook vegetables in dressing, stirring occasionally, until crisp-tender.

3. Stir turkey, salt and tomatoes into vegetables. Cook about 3 minutes or just until turkey is hot. Spoon turkey mixture over fettuccine. Sprinkle with cheese and parsley.

4 servings.

1 Serving: Calories 435 (Calories from Fat 115); Fat 13g (Saturated 3g); Cholesterol 120mg; Sodium 880mg; Carbohydrate 52g (Dietary Fiber 6g); Protein 34g
% Daily Value: Vitamin A 82%; Vitamin C 46%; Calcium 16%; Iron 26%
Diet Exchanges: 3 Starch, 3 Lean Meat, 1 Vegetable

BETTY'S TIPS

⊙ **Success Hint**
To quickly thaw frozen vegetables, place them in a colander and run cool water over them.

⊙ **Serve-With**
Complete this meal with crusty breadsticks brushed with olive oil, a large leafy green salad and, for dessert, a bowl of fresh berries.

Southwest Fettuccine Bowl

Prep: 15 min   Cook: 6 min

8 ounces uncooked fettuccine
  Olive oil–flavored cooking spray
1 cup salsa
⅓ cup frozen whole kernel corn
¼ cup water
2 tablespoons chili sauce
½ teaspoon ground cumin
1 can (15 ounces) black beans, rinsed and drained
¼ cup chopped fresh cilantro

1. Cook and drain fettuccine as directed on package. Spray fettuccine 2 or 3 times with cooking spray, tossing after each spray. Remove from saucepan; cover to keep warm.

2. Mix remaining ingredients except cilantro in same saucepan used to cook fettuccine. Cook over medium heat 4 to 6 minutes, stirring occasionally, until corn is tender.

3. Divide fettuccine among 4 bowls. Top each with about ¾ cup sauce mixture. Sprinkle with cilantro.

4 servings.

1 Serving: Calories 350 (Calories from Fat 25); Fat 3g (Saturated 1g); Cholesterol 50mg; Sodium 800mg; Carbohydrate 73g (Dietary Fiber 10g); Protein 18g
% Daily Value: Vitamin A 16%; Vitamin C 10%; Calcium 12%; Iron 32%
Diet Exchanges: 4½ Starch

Southwest Fettuccine Bowl

Creamy Ham and Fettuccine

Prep: 10 min   Cook: 6 min

1 package (9 ounces) refrigerated fettuccine
1 tablespoon vegetable oil
1 clove garlic, finely chopped
2 medium green onions, sliced (2 tablespoons)
6 ounces thinly sliced fully cooked ham, cut into $\frac{1}{4}$-inch strips
1 cup frozen green peas
$\frac{1}{3}$ cup plain low-fat yogurt
$\frac{1}{4}$ cup ranch dressing
2 tablespoons milk

1. Cook and drain fettuccine as directed on package.

2. Heat oil in 12-inch skillet over medium-high heat. Add garlic and onions; stir-fry 1 minute. Add ham and peas; stir-fry 1 to 2 minutes or until hot. Reduce heat to low.

3. Stir in yogurt, dressing and milk. Add fettuccine. Cook 2 to 3 minutes, stirring constantly, until hot.

4 servings.

1 Serving: Calories 455 (Calories from Fat 145); Fat 16g (Saturated 3g); Cholesterol 30mg; Sodium 820mg; Carbohydrate 60g (Dietary Fiber 4g); Protein 22g
% Daily Value: Vitamin A 6%; Vitamin C 4%; Calcium 10%; Iron 20%
Diet Exchanges: 4 Starch, 1 High-Fat Meat, 1 Fat

BETTY'S TIPS

☼ Substitution
Refrigerated fresh pastas are convenient time-savers because they cook in just minutes. But you can also use 9 ounces of dried fettuccine. Cook as directed on the package.

You can substitute your favorite frozen vegetable for the peas.

☼ Success Hint
To serve pasta hot, pour hot water into the serving bowl a few minutes before pasta is done. Just before draining the pasta, pour out the water and wipe the bowl dry.

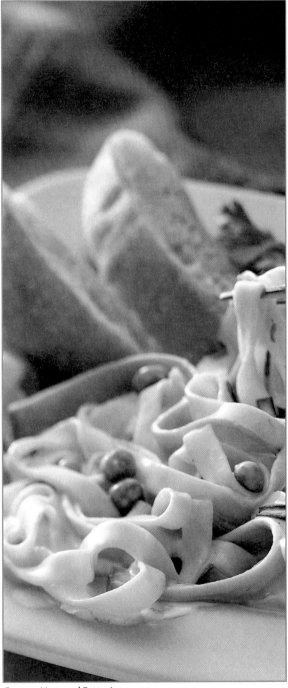

Creamy Ham and Fettucine

Italian Shrimp Stir-Fry

Prep: 15 min   Cook: 15 min

8 ounces uncooked linguine
¾ cup reduced-calorie Italian dressing
1½ teaspoons grated lemon peel
3 cloves garlic, finely chopped
¾ pound uncooked peeled and deveined medium shrimp, thawed if frozen
3 cups broccoli flowerets
1 medium yellow summer squash, cut lengthwise in half, then cut crosswise into slices (1½ cups)
2 tablespoons water
8 cherry tomatoes, cut in half
12 extra-large pitted ripe olives, cut in half
¼ cup chopped fresh basil leaves
   Grated Parmesan cheese, if desired

1. Cook and drain linguine as directed on package; keep warm. Mix dressing, lemon peel and garlic; set aside.

2. Spray 12-inch nonstick skillet with cooking spray; heat over medium-high heat. Add shrimp; stir-fry about 2 minutes or until shrimp are pink and firm. Remove shrimp from skillet.

3. Spray skillet with cooking spray; heat over medium-high heat. Add broccoli and squash; stir-fry 1 minute. Add water. Cover and simmer about 3 minutes, stirring occasionally, until vegetables are crisp-tender (add water if necessary to prevent sticking).

4. Stir in dressing mixture; cook 30 seconds. Stir in tomatoes, olives, basil, shrimp and linguine; stir-fry until hot. Sprinkle with cheese.

5 servings.

1 Serving: Calories 310 (Calories from Fat 70); Fat 8g (Saturated 1g); Cholesterol 100mg; Sodium 660mg; Carbohydrate 45g (Dietary Fiber 4g); Protein 19g
% Daily Value: Vitamin A 24%; Vitamin C 44%; Calcium 8%; Iron 24%
Diet Exchanges: 2 Starch, 1 Medium-Fat Meat, 3 Vegetable

BETTY'S TIPS

✪ Substitution
   This quick and easy stir-fry was a real winner in the Betty Crocker kitchens. If you prefer chicken to shrimp, use ¾ pound boneless, skinless chicken breasts, cut into 1-inch pieces. Stir-fry the chicken 3 to 4 minutes or until no longer pink in the center.

Italian Shrimp Stir-Fry

Quick & Low Fat

Beef Lo Mein

Prep: 15 min   Cook: 10 min

1 pound lean beef boneless sirloin steak, about ½ inch thick

½ pound snap pea pods (2 cups)

1 cup baby-cut carrots, cut lengthwise into ¼-inch sticks

1 package (9 ounces) refrigerated linguine, cut into 2-inch pieces

2 teaspoons cornstarch

1 teaspoon sugar

2 teaspoons cold water

⅓ cup chicken broth

1 tablespoon soy sauce

4 cloves garlic, finely chopped

2 teaspoons finely chopped gingerroot

½ cup thinly sliced red onion

1. Remove fat from beef. Cut beef into thin strips, about 1½ × ½ inch.

2. Heat 2 quarts water to boiling in 3-quart saucepan. Add pea pods, carrots and linguine; heat to boiling. Boil 2 to 3 minutes or just until linguine is tender; drain.

3. Mix cornstarch, sugar and cold water. Mix broth, soy sauce, garlic and gingerroot; stir in cornstarch mixture.

4. Spray 12-inch nonstick skillet with cooking spray; heat over medium-high heat. Add beef and onion; stir-fry about 4 minutes or until beef is no longer pink. Stir broth mixture; stir into beef mixture. Stir in linguine mixture. Cook 2 minutes, stirring occasionally.

4 servings.

1 Serving: Calories 405 (Calories from Fat 45); Fat 5g (Saturated 1g); Cholesterol 60mg; Sodium 370mg; Carbohydrate 61g (Dietary Fiber 5g); Protein 34g
% Daily Value: Vitamin A 100%; Vitamin C 24%; Calcium 6%; Iron 32%
Diet Exchanges: 3 Starch, 2½ Very Lean Meat, 3 Vegetable

BETTY'S TIPS

✪ Substitution
Improvise! If fresh pea pods are not available, use a 10-ounce package of frozen snap pea pods, thawed.

✪ Variation
Changing this recipe to suit your tastes is easy. If you prefer chicken, substitute it for the beef. If you are a veggie lover, add broccoli, water chestnuts and bell peppers, and forget the meat altogether.

✪ Special Touch
Sprinkle with toasted sesame seed if desired.

Beef Lo Mein

Bacon, Tomato and Red Onion Spaghetti

Hot and Spicy Chicken Pesto and Pasta

Bacon, Tomato and Red Onion Spaghetti

Prep: 5 min   Cook: 20 min

8   ounces uncooked spaghetti, broken in half
8   slices bacon, cut into ½-inch pieces
1   medium red onion, cut into thin strips
1   can (14½ ounces) diced tomatoes with basil, garlic and oregano, undrained
¼   teaspoon crushed red pepper
    Grated Parmesan cheese, if desired

1. Cook spaghetti in 3-quart saucepan as directed on package.

2. While spaghetti is cooking, cook bacon in 10-inch skillet over medium heat about 5 minutes, stirring occasionally, until partially crisp. Stir in onion. Cook, stirring occasionally, until bacon is crisp and onion is crisp-tender; drain.

3. Drain spaghetti; return to saucepan. Stir in tomatoes and red pepper. Cook over medium-high heat, stirring occasionally, until hot. Add bacon and onion; toss. Serve with cheese.

4 servings.

1 Serving: Calories 305 (Calories from Fat 65); Fat 7g (Saturated 2g); Cholesterol 10mg; Sodium 360mg; Carbohydrate 52g (Dietary Fiber 4g); Protein 13g
% Daily Value: Vitamin A 6%; Vitamin C 12%; Calcium 4%; Iron 16%
Diet Exchanges: 3 Starch, 1 Vegetable, 1 Fat

BETTY'S TIPS

⊕ **Substitution**
If you don't have seasoned tomatoes on hand, substitute a 14½-ounce can of diced tomatoes and add 1 teaspoon Italian seasoning.

Hot and Spicy Chicken Pesto and Pasta

Prep: 15 min   Cook: 8 min

2   packages (3 ounces each) chicken-flavored ramen noodle soup mix
1   cup water
½   cup basil pesto
2   teaspoons cornstarch
2   teaspoons chili puree with garlic
1   tablespoon vegetable oil
¾   pound boneless, skinless chicken breasts, cut into 1-inch pieces
1   large carrot, shredded (1 cup)
2   green onions, cut diagonally into 1-inch pieces

1. Reserve seasoning packets from noodles. Cook and drain noodles as directed on package.

2. Mix water, pesto, cornstarch, chili puree and contents of seasoning packets; set aside.

3. Heat oil in 12-inch skillet over medium-high heat. Add chicken; stir-fry 3 to 4 minutes or until no longer pink in center. Add carrot and onions; stir-fry 1 minute.

4. Stir in pesto mixture. Boil and stir 1 minute. Add noodles; toss to coat.

5 servings.

1 Serving: Calories 360 (Calories from Fat 205); Fat 23g (Saturated 5g); Cholesterol 45mg; Sodium 720mg; Carbohydrate 20g (Dietary Fiber 2g); Protein 20g
% Daily Value: Vitamin A 62%; Vitamin C 2%; Calcium 12%; Iron 12%
Diet Exchanges: 1 Starch, 2 Medium-Fat Meat, 1 Vegetable, 2½ Fat

BETTY'S TIPS

⊕ **Substitution**
For a peppery pork version, use ¾ pound pork tenderloin, cut into 1-inch pieces, and pork-flavored ramen noodles.

⊕ **Health Twist**
For 14 grams of fat and 280 calories per serving, use reduced-fat ramen noodles and decrease pesto to ⅓ cup. Stir in 1½ teaspoons dried basil leaves with the pesto if desired.

Kung Pao Noodles and Chicken

Prep: 5 min   Cook: 15 min

2   cups uncooked fine egg noodles (3 ounces)

1   tablespoon vegetable oil

1¼   pounds boneless, skinless chicken breasts, cut into 1-inch pieces

1   envelope (⅞ ounce) hot and spicy kung pao chicken Oriental seasoning mix

¾   cup water

1   tablespoon sugar

1   tablespoon soy sauce

6   medium green onions, cut into 1-inch pieces

½   cup dry-roasted peanuts

    Crushed red pepper, if desired

1. Cook and drain noodles as directed on package; keep warm.

2. Heat oil in 12-inch nonstick skillet over medium-high heat. Cook chicken in oil 4 to 5 minutes, stirring occasionally, until no longer pink in center.

3. Stir in seasoning mix (dry), water, sugar and soy sauce. Heat to boiling. Stir in onions. Boil 30 seconds to 1 minute, stirring constantly, until sauce is thickened. Stir in noodles; toss to coat.

4. Sprinkle with peanuts and red pepper.

4 servings.

1 Serving: Calories 405 (Calories from Fat 160); Fat 18g (Saturated 3g); Cholesterol 105mg; Sodium 750mg; Carbohydrate 23g (Dietary Fiber 3g); Protein 41g
% Daily Value: Vitamin A 4%; Vitamin C 2%; Calcium 4%; Iron 14%
Diet Exchanges: 1½ Starch, 5 Lean Meat

BETTY'S TIPS

✺ Substitution

Three-fourths cup Sichuan or any flavor stir-fry sauce can be substituted for the water, sugar and soy sauce. Because bottled stir-fry sauce will not thicken, you may want to choose a thicker variety of sauce.

Kung Pao Noodles and Chicken

Mediterranean Chicken with Rosemary Orzo

Prep: 10 min   Cook: 20 min

1 pound chicken breast tenders (not breaded)

2 cloves garlic, finely chopped

1⅓ cups uncooked rosamarina (orzo) pasta

1 can (14½ ounces) chicken broth

½ cup water

1 tablespoon chopped fresh or 1 teaspoon dried rosemary leaves

½ teaspoon salt

2 medium zucchini, cut lengthwise into fourths, then cut crosswise into slices (1½ cups)

3 roma (plum) tomatoes, cut into fourths and sliced (1½ cups)

1 medium bell pepper, chopped (1 cup)

1. Spray 10-inch skillet with cooking spray; heat over medium-high heat. Add chicken; stir-fry about 5 minutes or until brown.

2. Stir in garlic, pasta and broth. Heat to boiling; reduce heat. Cover and simmer about 8 minutes or until most of the liquid is absorbed.

3. Stir in remaining ingredients. Heat to boiling; reduce heat. Cover and simmer about 5 minutes, stirring once, until bell pepper is crisp-tender and pasta is tender.

4 servings.

1 Serving: Calories 335 (Calories from Fat 45); Fat 5g (Saturated 1g); Cholesterol 70mg; Sodium 820mg; Carbohydrate 41g (Dietary Fiber 4g); Protein 35g
% Daily Value: Vitamin A 22%; Vitamin C 34%; Calcium 4%; Iron 18%
Diet Exchanges: 2 Starch, 3 Very Lean Meat, 2 Vegetable

BETTY'S TIPS

⚙ **Substitution**
If chicken tenders are not available, substitute 1 pound boneless, skinless chicken breasts, cut lengthwise into 1-inch strips.

⚙ **Time-Saver**
Use 2 cups deli roast chicken instead of the chicken tenders. Cut the chicken into bite-size pieces, omit step 1 and add the deli chicken with the remaining ingredients in step 3.

Mediterranean Chicken with Rosemary Orzo

Spring Vegetable Fettuccine

Prep: 5 min   Cook: 12 min

1   package (9 ounces) refrigerated fettuccine
1   cup half-and-half
1   container (5 ounces) garlic-and-herb spreadable cheese
½   teaspoon garlic salt
1   bag (1 pound) frozen baby peas, carrots, pea pods and corn, thawed and drained
    Freshly ground pepper, if desired

1. Cook and drain fettuccine as directed on package.

2. While fettuccine is cooking, heat half-and-half to boiling in 12-inch nonstick skillet over medium heat. Stir in cheese and garlic salt. Cook, stirring constantly, until cheese is melted and mixture is smooth.

3. Stir in vegetables. Cook about 7 minutes, stirring occasionally, until vegetables are tender. Serve over fettuccine. Sprinkle with pepper.

4 servings.

1 Serving: Calories 460 (Calories from Fat 190); Fat 21g (Saturated 12g); Cholesterol 95mg; Sodium 370mg; Carbohydrate 58g (Dietary Fiber 5g); Protein 15g
% Daily Value: Vitamin A 100%; Vitamin C 14%; Calcium 14%; Iron 24%
Diet Exchanges: 3 Starch, 2 Vegetable, 4 Fat

BETTY'S TIPS

☺ Substitution
This recipe is ready in no time flat because it uses time-savers such as fresh pasta and flavored spreadable cheese.

You may want to try different vegetable mixtures for variety.

Look for the garlic-and-herb spreadable cheese in the dairy case near other cheese spreads.

☺ Variation
For **Shrimp Vegetable Fettuccine,** add ½ pound cooked peeled shrimp with the vegetables in step 3. Continue as directed.

Shrimp and Feta Radiatore

Prep: 10 min   Cook: 13 min

2   cups uncooked radiatore (nugget) pasta (6 ounces)
1   tablespoon butter or margarine
1   cup fat-free (skim) milk
2   tablespoons Gold Medal® all-purpose flour
¼   teaspoon salt
⅛   teaspoon pepper
¼   cup crumbled garlic-and-herb feta cheese
1   pound uncooked peeled deveined medium shrimp, thawed if frozen
3   cloves garlic, finely chopped
¼   cup thinly sliced fresh basil leaves (½ ounce)
12   Kalamata olives, pitted and chopped, if desired

1. Cook and drain pasta as directed on package.

2. While pasta is cooking, heat butter in 1½-quart saucepan over medium heat until melted and bubbly. Shake milk, flour, salt and pepper in tightly covered container. Gradually stir into butter. Heat to boiling, stirring constantly. Boil and stir 1 minute. Stir in cheese; keep warm.

3. Spray 10-inch nonstick skillet with cooking spray; heat over medium-high heat. Cook shrimp and garlic in skillet about 3 minutes, stirring frequently, just until shrimp are pink and firm. Toss pasta, sauce, shrimp and basil. Sprinkle with olives.

4 servings.

1 Serving: Calories 325 (Calories from Fat 65); Fat 7g (Saturated 4g); Cholesterol 180mg; Sodium 490mg; Carbohydrate 40g (Dietary Fiber 2g); Protein 27g
% Daily Value: Vitamin A 14%; Vitamin C 2%; Calcium 16%; Iron 26%
Diet Exchanges: 2½ Starch, 3 Very Lean Meat, ½ Fat

BETTY'S TIPS

☺ Serve-With
Serve with a Greek-style salad of thickly sliced cucumber, tomato and red onion drizzled with a vinaigrette dressing.

☺ Special Touch
A basil chiffonade adds a festive look to this dish, and it's easy to do! Simply roll up large basil leaves, slice them into long, thin strips and place on top of the pasta.

Spring Vegetable Fettuccine (shrimp variation)

Shrimp and Feta Radiatore

Bow-Ties with Salmon and Tarragon Mustard Sauce

Prep: 15 min   Cook: 15 min

1 package (16 ounces) farfalle (bow-tie) pasta
1 tablespoon olive or vegetable oil
1 medium onion, chopped (½ cup)
1 tablespoon chopped fresh tarragon leaves
1 tablespoon chopped fresh parsley
¼ cup dry white wine
1 cup whipping (heavy) cream or half-and-half
2 teaspoons stone-ground mustard
2 packages (3 to 4 ounces each) sliced salmon (smoked or cured), cut into ½-inch-wide strips
½ cup freshly grated or shredded Parmesan cheese

1. Cook and drain pasta as directed on package.

2. While pasta is cooking, heat oil in 10-inch skillet over medium heat. Cook onion, tarragon and parsley in oil about 5 minutes, stirring frequently, until onion is tender. Stir in wine. Cook uncovered about 4 minutes or until wine has evaporated. Stir in whipping cream and mustard. Heat to boiling; reduce heat. Simmer uncovered 5 to 10 minutes or until sauce is slightly thickened.

3. Add pasta, salmon and ¼ cup of the cheese to sauce in skillet; toss gently until pasta is evenly coated. Sprinkle with remaining ¼ cup cheese.

6 servings.

1 Serving: Calories 495 (Calories from Fat 180); Fat 20g (Saturated 10g); Cholesterol 60mg; Sodium 420mg; Carbohydrate 62g (Dietary Fiber 3g); Protein 20g
% Daily Value: Vitamin A 14%; Vitamin C 2%; Calcium 16%; Iron 18%
Diet Exchanges: 4 Starch, 1 Lean Meat, 3 Fat

BETTY'S TIPS

⊙ **Substitution**
Use chicken broth if you don't have any white wine on hand.

⊙ **Time-Saver**
You can cook the pasta up to 3 days ahead of time. Rinse with cold water, toss with a little olive oil and store in a resealable plastic bag in the refrigerator. Reheat in the microwave oven or plunge briefly into boiling water to reheat.

Bow-Ties with Salmon and Tarragon Mustard Sauce

Tuna Twist Casserole

Prep: 10 min   Bake: 20 min

½ cup reduced-fat Alfredo pasta sauce

2 eggs

1 clove garlic, finely chopped

4 cups cooked tricolor rotelle pasta

2 cups frozen broccoli, carrots and cauliflower (from 1-pound bag), thawed and drained

1 can (12 ounces) tuna in water, drained

1 cup seasoned croutons

1. Heat oven to 350°.

2. Mix Alfredo sauce, eggs and garlic in ungreased square baking dish, 8 × 8 × 2 inches. Stir in pasta, vegetables and tuna. Press lightly in baking dish.

3. Cover and bake about 20 minutes or until set. Sprinkle with croutons.

6 servings.

1 Serving: Calories 255 (Calories from Fat 45); Fat 5g (Saturated 2g); Cholesterol 25mg; Sodium 380mg; Carbohydrate 34g (Dietary Fiber 3g); Protein 22g
% Daily Value: Vitamin A 20%; Vitamin C 8%; Calcium 6%; Iron 14%
Diet Exchanges: 2 Starch, 2 Very Lean Meat, 1 Vegetable

BETTY'S TIPS

✪ Substitution

If you like, substitute frozen broccoli, thawed and drained, for the vegetable mixture.

✪ Health Twist

You can use regular Alfredo sauce and tuna in oil, but we've saved 8 grams of fat per serving by using the reduced-fat version of Alfredo sauce and tuna packed in water.

Tuna Twist Casserole

Lemon Basil Pasta with Ham

Prep: 10 min   Cook: 20 min

- 2 cups uncooked rotini pasta (6 ounces)
- 2 cups 1-inch pieces asparagus spears
- 1 cup diced fully cooked ham
- 1 tablespoon grated lemon peel
- 1 clove garlic, finely chopped
- ¼ cup olive or vegetable oil
- ½ cup sliced fresh basil leaves
- ½ cup shredded Swiss cheese (2 ounces)

1. Cook pasta as directed on package, adding asparagus during last 3 to 4 minutes of cooking; drain.

2. Return pasta mixture to saucepan. Stir in ham, lemon peel, garlic and oil. Cook over medium heat, stirring occasionally, until hot. Stir in basil. Sprinkle with cheese.

4 servings.

1 Serving: Calories 470 (Calories from Fat 200); Fat 22g (Saturated 5g); Cholesterol 30mg; Sodium 770mg; Carbohydrate 50g (Dietary Fiber 3g); Protein 21g
% Daily Value: Vitamin A 22%; Vitamin C 12%; Calcium 16%; Iron 18%
Diet Exchanges: 3 Starch, 1½ Medium-Fat Meat, 1 Vegetable, 2 Fat

BETTY'S TIPS

✪ Substitution

If you don't have fresh basil, use ½ cup chopped fresh parsley and add 1 teaspoon of dried basil leaves.

You can use ½ cup freshly shredded Parmesan cheese instead of the Swiss cheese.

Lemon Basil Pasta with Ham

Cheeseburger Pasta Toss

Prep: 5 min   Cook: 15 min

- 2 cups uncooked wagon wheel pasta (4 ounces)
- 1 pound ground beef
- 1 large onion, sliced or chopped (1 cup)
- 2 containers (8 ounces each) process sharp Cheddar cheese spread
- ½ cup milk
- ½ teaspoon garlic salt
- 1 large tomato, chopped (1 cup)
- ½ cup shredded Cheddar cheese (2 ounces)

1. Cook and drain pasta as directed on package.

2. While pasta is cooking, cook beef and onion in 10-inch skillet over medium-high heat, stirring occasionally, until beef is brown; drain.

3. Reduce heat to medium. Stir cheese spread, milk and garlic salt into beef; continue stirring until cheese is melted and mixture is well blended. Stir in pasta and tomato. Sprinkle with Cheddar cheese; cover 2 to 3 minutes or until cheese is melted.

5 servings.

1 Serving: Calories 705 (Calories from Fat 395); Fat 44g (Saturated 25g); Cholesterol 135mg; Sodium 1490mg; Carbohydrate 34g (Dietary Fiber 2g); Protein 45g
% Daily Value: Vitamin A 24%; Vitamin C 6%; Calcium 58%; Iron 18%
Diet Exchanges: 2 Starch, 5 High-Fat Meat, 1 Vegetable

BETTY'S TIPS

✪ Substitution

Try another all-time favorite burger combo—a bacon cheeseburger. For a smoky bacon flavor, use process sharp Cheddar cheese spread with bacon.

Tricolored rotini pasta can be substituted for the wagon wheel pasta.

✪ Serve-With

Serve this stick-to-your-ribs supper with a crisp, cold tossed salad and fresh fruit.

Cheeseburger Pasta Toss

Spicy Black Bean Sauce with Ravioli

Prep: 10 min   Cook: 15 min

1 tablespoon olive or vegetable oil
1 small green bell pepper, chopped (½ cup)
1 can (14½ ounces) stewed tomatoes, undrained
½ cup hot picante sauce
1 can (15 ounces) black beans with cumin and chili spices, undrained
1 package (9 ounces) refrigerated cheese-filled ravioli
   Chopped fresh cilantro, if desired

1. Heat oil in 2-quart saucepan over medium heat. Cook bell pepper in oil 2 to 3 minutes, stirring occasionally, until tender.

2. Stir in tomatoes, breaking up with spoon. Stir in picante sauce and beans. Heat to boiling; reduce heat. Simmer uncovered about 10 minutes or until slightly thickened.

3. Meanwhile, cook and drain ravioli as directed on package. Serve ravioli with sauce. Sprinkle with cilantro.

4 servings.

1 Serving: Calories 320 (Calories from Fat 90); Fat 10g (Saturated 3g); Cholesterol 65mg; Sodium 1370mg; Carbohydrate 49g (Dietary Fiber 9g); Protein 18g
% Daily Value: Vitamin A 14%; Vitamin C 28%; Calcium 22%; Iron 24%
Diet Exchanges: 3 Starch, 1 Lean Meat, 1 Vegetable

BETTY'S TIPS

⊙ **Substitution**
This sauce is quite spicy; you can use medium or mild picante sauce instead or substitute salsa for the picante sauce.

Fusilli, rotini and rotelle are perfect pastas to substitute for the ravioli. The twisted shape of these pastas will capture all the spicy bits and pieces of the sauce.

⊙ **Variation**
If you have any leftover sauce, simply add cut-up cooked chicken to it and spoon onto tortillas. Top with shredded lettuce, chopped tomatoes and sliced ripe olives, and fold them up.

Timesaving Tortellini

Prep: 10 min   Cook: 10 min

1 package (9 ounces) refrigerated cheese-filled tortellini
1 package (10 ounces) broccoli cuts (or other frozen vegetable)
2½ cups quartered cherry tomatoes
¼ cup chopped fresh basil leaves
1 tablespoon grated Parmesan or Romano cheese
1½ teaspoons olive or vegetable oil
4 medium green onions, sliced (¼ cup)
2 medium cloves garlic, finely chopped
   Salt and freshly ground pepper to taste, if desired

1. Cook tortellini as directed on package, adding broccoli for the last 2 to 3 minutes of cook time; drain thoroughly.

2. Add remaining ingredients except salt and pepper; toss. Sprinkle with salt and pepper.

4 servings.

1 Serving: Calories 210 (Calories from Fat 70); Fat 8g (Saturated 3g); Cholesterol 55mg; Sodium 85mg; Carbohydrate 31g (Dietary Fiber 4g); Protein 8g
% Daily Value: Vitamin A 30%; Vitamin C 22%; Calcium 8%; Iron 10%
Diet Exchanges: 2 Starch, ½ High-Fat Meat

BETTY'S TIPS

⊙ **Substitution**
If you don't have fresh basil, use chopped fresh parsley instead.

You can use your favorite tortellini. Spinach-, meat- or chicken-filled would be equally delicious.

Timesaving Tortellini

Spicy Black Bean Sauce with Ravioli

Penne with Spicy Sauce

Prep: 10 min   Cook: 20 min

1 package (16 ounces) penne rigate pasta

1 can (28 ounces) Italian-style (plum) tomatoes, undrained

2 tablespoons olive or vegetable oil

2 cloves garlic, finely chopped

½ to 1 teaspoon crushed red pepper

2 tablespoons chopped fresh parsley

1 tablespoon tomato paste

½ cup freshly grated or shredded Parmesan cheese

1. Cook and drain pasta as directed on package.

2. While pasta is cooking, place tomatoes with juice in food processor or blender. Cover and process until coarsely chopped; set aside.

3. Heat oil in 12-inch skillet over medium-high heat. Cook garlic, red pepper and parsley in oil about 5 minutes, stirring frequently, until garlic just begins to turn golden. Stir in chopped tomatoes and tomato paste. Heat to boiling; reduce heat. Cover and simmer about 10 minutes, stirring occasionally, until slightly thickened.

4. Add pasta and ¼ cup of the cheese to tomato mixture. Cook about 3 minutes, tossing gently, until pasta is evenly coated. Sprinkle with remaining ¼ cup cheese.

6 servings.

1 Serving: Calories 390 (Calories from Fat 80); Fat 9g (Saturated 2g); Cholesterol 5mg; Sodium 380mg; Carbohydrate 66g (Dietary Fiber 4g); Protein 15g
% Daily Value: Vitamin A 12%; Vitamin C 18%; Calcium 16%; Iron 22%
Diet Exchanges: 4 Starch, 1 Vegetable, 1 Fat

BETTY'S TIPS

✿ Success Hint

It is important to keep the cooking heat on the medium-high side to achieve the best release of potency from the hot pepper.

Serve the pasta at once while it is piping hot. Try rinsing your pasta bowl with hot water before adding the pasta to help keep it warm.

Penne with Spicy Sauce

Hot from the Oven

Hearty Home-Style Casseroles and Bakes

Dill Salmon and Couscous (page 112)

Crunchy Garlic Chicken (page 121)

South-of-the-Border Enchiladas

Prep: 25 min   Cook: 3 min   Bake: 25 min

1   can (14½ ounces) whole tomatoes, undrained
1   medium onion, chopped (½ cup)
1   clove garlic, finely chopped
¼   cup chopped fresh cilantro
2   teaspoons honey
⅛   teaspoon crushed red pepper
1   can (15 to 16 ounces) pinto beans, rinsed and drained
1   cup low-fat or regular ricotta cheese
1   small green bell pepper, chopped (½ cup)
1   teaspoon ground cumin
6   flour tortillas (8 inches in diameter)
¼   cup shredded Cheddar cheese (1 ounce)
¼   cup shredded Monterey Jack cheese (1 ounce)

1. Heat oven to 375°. Spray rectangular baking dish, 13 × 9 × 2 inches, with cooking spray.

2. Place tomatoes, onion and garlic in blender or food processor. Cover and blend until smooth. Cook blended mixture, 2 tablespoons of the cilantro, the honey and red pepper in 2-quart saucepan over medium heat 3 minutes, stirring occasionally.

3. Mix beans, ricotta cheese, bell pepper, cumin and remaining 2 tablespoons cilantro. Spread ½ cup tomato sauce in baking dish. Spoon ½ cup bean mixture down center of each tortilla. Roll up tortilla; place seam side down on tomato sauce in dish. Spoon remaining tomato sauce over filled tortillas. Sprinkle with cheeses.

4. Bake uncovered 20 to 25 minutes or until tomato sauce is bubbly and cheese is melted.

6 servings.

1 Serving: Calories 335 (Calories from Fat 90); Fat 10g (Saturated 5g); Cholesterol 20mg; Sodium 540mg; Carbohydrate 52g (Dietary Fiber 9g); Protein 18g
% Daily Value: Vitamin A 14%; Vitamin C 20%; Calcium 28%; Iron 22%
Diet Exchanges: 3 Starch, 1 Medium-Fat Meat, 1 Vegetable

BETTY'S TIPS

☺ Substitution
If you like enchiladas but would prefer beef or chicken, omit the beans and substitute 1½ cups cooked ground beef or chopped cooked chicken.

☺ Health Twist
The pinto beans in these enchiladas give a generous dose of fiber, and the cheeses provide over a fourth of your daily calcium needs.

South-of-the-Border Enchiladas

Quick

Gruyère Vegetable Bake

Prep: 10 min   Bake: 20 min

1 bag (1 pound) frozen broccoli, cauliflower and carrots
2 tablespoons butter or margarine
2 tablespoons Gold Medal all-purpose flour
¼ teaspoon salt
¼ teaspoon onion powder
¼ teaspoon caraway seed
1 cup milk
½ cup shredded Gruyère or Swiss cheese (2 ounces)
½ cup soft whole wheat or white bread crumbs
1 tablespoon butter or margarine, melted

1. Heat oven to 350°. Cook and drain vegetables as directed on package.

2. Melt 2 tablespoons butter in 1½-quart saucepan over medium heat. Stir in flour, salt, onion powder and caraway seed. Cook, stirring constantly, until mixture is smooth and bubbly; remove from heat. Stir in milk. Heat to boiling, stirring constantly. Boil and stir 1 minute. Stir in cheese until melted. Stir in vegetables.

3. Place vegetable mixture in ungreased 1½-quart casserole. Mix bread crumbs and 1 tablespoon butter; sprinkle around edge of casserole. Bake uncovered about 20 minutes or until crumbs are golden.

4 servings.

1 Serving: Calories 240 (Calories from Fat 125); Fat 14g (Saturated 9g); Cholesterol 40mg; Sodium 420mg; Carbohydrate 22g (Dietary Fiber 4g); Protein 11g
% Daily Value: Vitamin A 72%; Vitamin C 30%; Calcium 28%; Iron 8%
Diet Exchanges: 1 Starch, ½ High-Fat Meat, 2 Vegetable, 1½ Fat

BETTY'S TIPS

✪ Variation
This is a wonderful vegetarian casserole, but if you prefer to add meat, stir in 1 cup diced corned beef or fully cooked ham with the vegetables.

✪ Do-Ahead
Prepare the casserole as directed, but do not sprinkle on the bread crumbs. Cover casserole tightly and cover bread crumb mixture tightly, then refrigerate up to 48 hours. To bake, sprinkle bread crumb mixture around edge of casserole and bake uncovered at 350° about 40 minutes or until crumbs are golden and vegetables are hot.

Gruyère Vegetable Bake

Three-Cheese Rigatoni

Prep: 15 min   Bake: 30 min

3   cups uncooked rigatoni pasta (9 ounces)

2   medium stalks celery, sliced (1 cup)

1   small carrot, shredded (½ cup)

1   container (8 ounces) sour cream-and-chive dip

1   cup shredded Colby cheese (4 ounces)

1   cup shredded brick cheese (4 ounces)

¼   cup grated Parmesan cheese

¼   cup milk

1   tablespoon chopped fresh or 1 teaspoon dried basil leaves

¼   cup seasoned dry bread crumbs

1   tablespoon butter or margarine, melted

1. Heat oven to 375°. Cook and drain pasta as directed on package.

2. Mix pasta and remaining ingredients except bread crumbs and butter. Place pasta mixture in ungreased 2-quart casserole. Mix bread crumbs and butter; sprinkle around edge of casserole.

3. Bake uncovered 25 to 30 minutes or until hot and bubbly.

6 servings.

1 Serving: Calories 470 (Calories from Fat 205); Fat 23g (Saturated 14g); Cholesterol 60mg; Sodium 640mg; Carbohydrate 49g (Dietary Fiber 3g); Protein 20g
% Daily Value: Vitamin A 48%; Vitamin C 0%; Calcium 36%; Iron 14%
Diet Exchanges: 3 Starch, 1 High-Fat Meat, 1 Vegetable, 2½ Fat

BETTY'S TIPS

☺ Variation

If you'd like to serve a few more, you can add 1 to 1½ cups cooked shrimp, ham, chicken or beef to this triple-cheesy pasta bake.

☺ Do-Ahead

Prepare the casserole as directed, but do not sprinkle on the bread crumbs. Cover casserole tightly and cover bread crumb mixture tightly, then refrigerate up to 48 hours. To bake, sprinkle bread crumb mixture around edge of casserole and bake uncovered at 375° about 50 minutes or until hot and bubbly.

Three-Cheese Rigatoni

Roasted-Vegetable Lasagna

Prep: 25 min   Bake: 1 hr 15 min   Stand: 5 min

6 small red potatoes, cut into fourths

2 medium red, green or yellow bell peppers, each cut into 8 pieces

1 medium onion, cut into 8 wedges

1 large zucchini, cut into 2-inch pieces (2 cups)

1 package (8 ounces) whole mushrooms, cut in half

2 tablespoons olive or vegetable oil

½ teaspoon peppered seasoned salt

2 teaspoons chopped fresh or ½ teaspoon dried basil leaves

9 uncooked lasagna noodles (9 ounces)

1 container (15 ounces) ricotta cheese

½ cup basil pesto

1 egg, slightly beaten

2 cups shredded provolone cheese (8 ounces)

1 cup shredded mozzarella cheese (4 ounces)

1. Heat oven to 425°. Spray bottom and sides of jelly roll pan, 15½ × 10½ × 1 inch, with cooking spray. Place potatoes, bell peppers, onion, zucchini, mushrooms, oil, peppered seasoned salt and basil in large bowl; toss to coat. Spread vegetables in pan. Bake uncovered about 30 minutes or until crisp-tender. Cool slightly.

2. Reduce oven temperature to 350°. Spray bottom and sides of rectangular baking dish, 13 × 9 × 2 inches, with cooking spray. Cook and drain noodles as directed on package. Mix ricotta cheese, pesto and egg. Coarsely chop vegetables.

3. Place 3 noodles lengthwise in baking dish. Spread with half of the ricotta mixture. Top with 2 cups vegetables and 1 cup of the provolone cheese. Repeat layers, starting with noodles. Top with remaining 3 noodles and remaining vegetables. Sprinkle with mozzarella cheese.

4. Bake uncovered 40 to 45 minutes or until hot in center and top is golden brown. Let stand 5 minutes before cutting.

8 servings.

1 Serving: Calories 510 (Calories from Fat 250); Fat 28g (Saturated 12g); Cholesterol 80mg; Sodium 660mg; Carbohydrate 44g (Dietary Fiber 4g); Protein 26g
% Daily Value: Vitamin A 54%; Vitamin C 50%; Calcium 54%; Iron 18%
Diet Exchanges: 2 Starch, 2 High-Fat Meat, 3 Vegetable, 2 Fat

BETTY'S TIPS

☺ Do-Ahead
Roasting vegetables takes some time, but the richly flavored results are definitely worth it. If you want to get a jump start, roast vegetables up to 8 hours in advance and refrigerate.

☺ Special Touch
Topping off each serving of lasagna with a spoonful or two of warmed spaghetti sauce adds the finishing touch to this dish. Dress it up even more with a sprinkle of shredded Parmesan and fresh basil garnishing each plate.

Roasted-Vegetable Lasagna

Betty...
ON BASICS

— *Quick* —

White Sauce

Prep: 5 min   Cook: 5 min

Stir flour, salt and pepper into melted butter. Cook, stirring constantly, until mixture is smooth and bubbly.

  $\frac{1}{4}$ cup butter or margarine
  $\frac{1}{4}$ cup Gold Medal all-purpose flour
  $\frac{1}{2}$ teaspoon salt
  $\frac{1}{4}$ teaspoon pepper
  2 cups milk

1. Melt butter in 1½-quart saucepan over low heat. Stir in flour, salt and pepper. Cook over medium heat, stirring constantly, until mixture is smooth and bubbly; remove from heat.

2. Gradually stir in milk. Heat sauce to boiling, stirring constantly. Boil and stir 1 minute.

About 2 cups sauce.

1 Tablespoon: Calories 25 (Calories from Fat 20); Fat 2g (Saturated 1g); Cholesterol 5mg; Sodium 55mg; Carbohydrate 1g (Dietary Fiber 0g); Protein 1g
% Daily Value: Vitamin A 2%; Vitamin C 0%; Calcium 2%; Iron 0%
Diet Exchanges: 1 Serving is Free

Salmon Macaroni Casserole

Prep: 15 min   Bake: 30 min

1⅓ cups uncooked medium pasta shells or elbow macaroni (4 ounces)

White Sauce (opposite page)

1½ cups shredded sharp process American or Cheddar cheese (6 ounces)

1 tablespoon chopped fresh or 1 teaspoon dried marjoram leaves

2 cups cooked broccoli flowerets

1 can (6 ounces) skinless boneless pink salmon, drained and flaked

1. Heat oven to 350°. Cook and drain pasta as directed on package.

2. While pasta is cooking, make White Sauce. Stir 1 cup of the cheese and the marjoram into sauce until cheese is melted.

3. Mix pasta, broccoli, salmon and sauce in ungreased 2-quart casserole. Cover and bake 25 minutes.

4. Sprinkle with remaining ½ cup cheese. Bake uncovered about 5 minutes or until heated through.

4 servings.

1 Serving: Calories 590 (Calories from Fat 280); Fat 31g (Saturated 18g); Cholesterol 110mg; Sodium 950mg; Carbohydrate 50g (Dietary Fiber 4g); Protein 32g
% Daily Value: Vitamin A 50%; Vitamin C 26%; Calcium 50%; Iron 18%
Diet Exchanges: 3 Starch, 3 High-Fat Meat, 1 Vegetable, ½ Fat

BETTY'S TIPS

⊙ Substitution

With so many pasta shapes available, try a different shape next time you make this casserole. Be sure to use a pasta of similar size, though, such as wagon wheel, rotini, mini penne or farfalle.

Tuna can also be used in this casserole. Substitute a 6- or 9-ounce can of tuna, drained, for the salmon.

Salmon Macaroni Casserole

Dill Salmon and Couscous

Prep: 12 min Bake: 25 min

- 1 pound salmon fillets, about ¾ inch thick
- 1 package (5.6 ounces) toasted pine nut couscous mix
- 1½ cups hot water
- 1 tablespoon olive or vegetable oil
- 1 tablespoon lemon juice
- ½ teaspoon dried dill weed
- 1 small zucchini, coarsely chopped
- 1 small yellow summer squash, coarsely chopped
- ¼ teaspoon dried dill weed
- Toasted pine nuts, if desired

1. Heat oven to 350°. Spray square baking dish, 8 × 8 × 2 inches, with cooking spray. Cut fish into 4 serving pieces.

2. Stir couscous, seasoning packet from couscous mix, water, oil, lemon juice, ½ teaspoon dill weed, the zucchini and summer squash in baking dish. Place fish on couscous mixture. Sprinkle fish with ¼ teaspoon dill weed.

3. Cover and bake 20 to 25 minutes or until liquid is absorbed and fish flakes easily with fork. Sprinkle with pine nuts.

4 servings.

1 Serving: Calories 330 (Calories from Fat 90); Fat 10g (Saturated 2g); Cholesterol 75mg; Sodium 75mg; Carbohydrate 33g (Dietary Fiber 3g); Protein 30g
% Daily Value: Vitamin A 8%; Vitamin C 8%; Calcium 4%; Iron 8%
Diet Exchanges: 1½ Starch, 3 Lean Meat, 2 Vegetable

BETTY'S TIPS

☺ Substitution
Many kinds of fresh fish can be substituted for the salmon. We recommend sea bass, snapper, grouper or haddock.

☺ Health Twist
Packed with omega-3 fatty acids, salmon is low in fat and high in polyunsaturated oils.

Crispy Baked Fish with Salsa

Prep: 10 min Bake: 25 min

- 3 tablespoons butter or margarine
- ⅔ cup Original Bisquick
- ¼ cup yellow cornmeal
- 1 teaspoon chili powder
- 1¼ teaspoons salt
- 1 pound orange roughy fillets or other white fish fillets
- 1 egg, beaten
- 1½ cups thick-and-chunky salsa

1. Heat oven to 425°. Melt butter in rectangular pan, 13 × 9 × 2 inches, in oven.

2. Mix Bisquick, cornmeal, chili powder and salt. Dip fish into egg, then coat with Bisquick mixture. Place in pan.

3. Bake uncovered 10 minutes; turn fish. Bake about 15 minutes longer or until fish flakes easily with fork. Serve with salsa.

4 servings.

1 Serving: Calories 325 (Calories from Fat 135); Fat 15g (Saturated 7g); Cholesterol 140mg; Sodium 1610mg; Carbohydrate 25g (Dietary Fiber 2g); Protein 25g
% Daily Value: Vitamin A 22%; Vitamin C 10%; Calcium 8%; Iron 12%
Diet Exchanges: 1 Starch, 3 Lean Meat, 2 Vegetable, 1 Fat

BETTY'S TIPS

☺ Success Hint
Preheating the pan before adding the fish helps to create a crisp bottom crust.

☺ Serve-With
Serve with coleslaw and homemade oven potato fries. Cut potatoes into wedges; spray with cooking spray and sprinkle with seasoned salt. Bake on ungreased cookie sheet in 425° oven for about 25 minutes or until tender.

☺ Variation
A variety of bottled salsas would work well for this recipe. Try a fruit salsa such as peach, mango or pineapple or perhaps a green salsa for a change of pace. Or you may want to make your own fresh salsa.

Dill Salmon and Couscous

Crispy Baked Fish with Salsa

Shrimp and Pea Pod Casserole

Prep: 5 min   Cook: 15 min   Bake: 25 min

3 cups uncooked penne pasta (9 ounces)

½ cup butter or margarine

2 cups sliced fresh mushrooms (5 ounces)

2 cloves garlic, finely chopped

½ cup Gold Medal all-purpose flour

½ teaspoon salt

¼ teaspoon pepper

2 cups milk

2 tablespoons sherry or dry white wine, if desired

1 can (14½ ounces) chicken broth

¾ cup shredded Fontina or Swiss cheese (3 ounces)

1 pound cooked peeled deveined medium shrimp, thawed if frozen

2 cups frozen snap pea pods (from 1-pound bag), thawed and drained

⅓ cup finely shredded Parmesan cheese

¼ cup sliced almonds

1. Heat oven to 350°. Spray rectangular baking dish, 13 × 9 × 2 inches, with cooking spray. Cook and drain pasta as directed on package.

2. While pasta is cooking, melt butter in 3-quart saucepan over low heat. Cook mushrooms and garlic in butter, stirring occasionally, until mushrooms are tender. Stir in flour, salt and pepper. Cook over medium heat, stirring constantly, until mixture is smooth and bubbly. Gradually stir in milk, sherry and broth until smooth. Heat to boiling, stirring constantly. Stir in Fontina cheese until melted; remove from heat.

3. Stir pasta, shrimp and pea pods into mushroom mixture; pour into baking dish. Sprinkle with Parmesan cheese and almonds.

4. Bake uncovered 20 to 25 minutes or until cheese is golden brown.

6 servings.

1 Serving: Calories 505 (Calories from Fat 235); Fat 26g (Saturated 14g); Cholesterol 210mg; Sodium 940mg; Carbohydrate 38g (Dietary Fiber 3g); Protein 33g
% Daily Value: Vitamin A 24%; Vitamin C 20%; Calcium 36%; Iron 30%
Diet Exchanges: 2 Starch, 3 Lean Meat, 2 Vegetable, 3 Fat

BETTY'S TIPS

⊛ **Substitution**

You can use another pasta of similar size in place of the penne. Try cavatappi, farfalle, fusilli, gemelli or mostaccioli.

⊛ **Did You Know?**

Snap pea pods are a hybrid pea, a cross between an English pea and a flat snow pea. Because these peas are primarily available in the spring and fall, we've used the frozen peas. Using either fresh or frozen snap pea pods gives this upscale casserole a delicious twist.

Shrimp and Pea Pod Casserole

Chicken Alfredo Pot Pie

Prep: 15 min   Bake: 30 min

- 1   can (11 ounces) refrigerated soft breadsticks
- 1   jar (16 ounces) Alfredo pasta sauce
- ⅓   cup milk
- 1   bag (1 pound) frozen broccoli, cauliflower and carrots, thawed and drained
- 2   cups cut-up cooked chicken
- 2   tablespoons grated Parmesan cheese
- 1   teaspoon Italian seasoning

1. Heat oven to 375°. Unroll breadstick dough; separate at perforations to form 12 strips and set aside.

2. Mix pasta sauce, milk, vegetables and chicken in 3-quart saucepan. Heat to boiling, stirring occasionally. Spoon into ungreased rectangular pan, 13 × 9 × 2 inches.

3. Twist each dough strip; arrange crosswise over hot chicken mixture, gently stretching strips if necessary to fit. Sprinkle with cheese and Italian seasoning.

4. Bake uncovered 20 to 30 minutes or until breadsticks are deep golden brown.

6 servings.

1 Serving: Calories 525 (Calories from Fat 290); Fat 32g (Saturated 18g); Cholesterol 120mg; Sodium 750mg; Carbohydrate 36g (Dietary Fiber 4g); Protein 27g
% Daily Value: Vitamin A 60%; Vitamin C 20%; Calcium 32%; Iron 14%
Diet Exchanges: 2 Starch, 3 High-Fat Meat, 1 Vegetable, 1 Fat

BETTY'S TIPS

❂ **Substitution**
Use your favorite frozen vegetable combination.

❂ **Success Hint**
Here's a quick and easy pot pie your family will love. Make sure the pasta sauce mixture is hot before spooning it into the pan so the breadsticks will bake through.

Chicken Alfredo Pot Pie

Betty... MAKES IT EASY

Chicken Pot Pie

Prep: 10 min   Cook: 10 min   Bake: 35 min

1	package (10 ounces) frozen peas and carrots
⅓	cup butter or margarine
⅓	cup Gold Medal all-purpose flour
⅓	cup chopped onion
½	teaspoon salt
¼	teaspoon pepper
1¾	cups chicken broth
⅔	cup milk
2½ to 3	cups cut-up cooked chicken or turkey
1	package (15 ounces) refrigerated pie crusts

Carefully place top crust over filling. Fold and roll overhanging pastry under edge of bottom pastry pressing to seal.

1. Heat oven to 425°. Rinse frozen peas and carrots in cold water to separate; drain.

2. Melt butter in 2-quart saucepan over medium heat. Stir in flour, onion, salt and pepper. Cook, stirring constantly, until mixture is bubbly; remove from heat. Stir in broth and milk. Heat to boiling, stirring constantly. Boil and stir 1 minute. Stir in chicken and peas and carrots; remove from heat.

3. Roll one pastry to 12-inch circle. Ease into ungreased square pan, 9 × 9 × 2 inches. Pour chicken mixture into pastry-lined pan.

4. Place remaining circle over chicken mixture. Roll other pastry into 12-inch circle; place over chicken mixture. Turn edges of pastry under and flute. Bake about 35 minutes or until golden brown.

Place the index finger of one hand on outside of pastry rim and thumb and index finger of other hand on inside of pastry. Pinch pastry in V shape along edges.

6 servings.

1 Serving: Calories 635 (Calories from Fat 350); Fat 37 (Saturated 14g); Cholesterol 80mg; Sodium 1120mg; Carbohydrate 48g (Dietary Fiber 3g); Protein 26g
% Daily Value: Vitamin A 100%; Vitamin C 2%; Calcium 6%; Iron 20%
Diet Exchanges: 2 Starch, 2 Medium-Fat Meat, 3 Vegetable, 4 Fat

Chicken Pot Pie

Cowboy Chicken and Beans

Prep: 5 min   Bake: 40 min

- 2 cups Lloyd's® fully cooked shredded chicken in barbeque sauce
- 1 can (about 15 ounces) garbanzo beans, rinsed and drained
- 1 can (15 to 16 ounces) lima beans, rinsed and drained
- 1 can (15 to 16 ounces) kidney beans, rinsed and drained
- 1 cup shredded Cheddar cheese (4 ounces)

1. Heat oven to 350°. Spray 2-quart casserole with cooking spray. Mix chicken and beans in casserole.

2. Bake uncovered 30 to 35 minutes or until hot and bubbly. Sprinkle with cheese. Bake about 5 minutes longer or until cheese is melted.

6 servings.

1 Serving: Calories 400 (Calories from Fat 135); Fat 15g (Saturated 6g); Cholesterol 75mg; Sodium 910mg; Carbohydrate 43g (Dietary Fiber 11g); Protein 34g
% Daily Value: Vitamin A 6%; Vitamin C 4%; Calcium 16%; Iron 30%
Diet Exchanges: 2½ Starch, 3½ Lean Meat, 1 Vegetable

BETTY'S TIPS

✪ Substitution
You can also use shredded beef or pork in barbeque sauce in place of the chicken. If you can't find the barbeque chicken in the refrigerator case, you can mix 2 cups shredded cooked chicken and ½ cup of your favorite barbecue sauce.

Cowboy Chicken and Beans

Quick

Zesty Italian Chicken

Prep: 5 min   Bake: 20 min

- 4 boneless, skinless chicken breast halves (1¼ pounds)
- ¼ cup mayonnaise or salad dressing
- ¼ cup zesty Italian dressing
- 2 tablespoons chopped fresh basil leaves
- 1 tablespoon chopped fresh oregano leaves
- 1 teaspoon chopped fresh rosemary leaves

1. Heat oven to 375°. Place chicken in ungreased rectangular pan, 13 × 9 × 2 inches.

2. Mix remaining ingredients; brush half of mayonnaise mixture on chicken.

3. Cover and bake 10 minutes. Turn chicken; brush with remaining mayonnaise mixture. Bake uncovered about 10 minutes longer or until juice of chicken is no longer pink when centers of thickest pieces are cut. (If chicken browns too quickly, cover with aluminum foil.)

4 servings.

1 Serving: Calories 305 (Calories from Fat 190); Fat 21g (Saturated 3g); Cholesterol 85mg; Sodium 280mg; Carbohydrate 2g (Dietary Fiber 0g); Protein 27g
% Daily Value: Vitamin A 2%; Vitamin C 0%; Calcium 4%; Iron 6%
Diet Exchanges: 4 Lean Meat, 2 Fat

BETTY'S TIPS

✪ Variation
For **Zesty Italian Chicken with Sweet Potatoes,** peel 4 medium sweet potatoes and cut into 1½-inch pieces. Increase mayonnaise and zesty Italian dressing to ⅓ cup each. Arrange sweet potatoes around chicken. Brush mayonnaise mixture on chicken and sweet potatoes. Bake as directed or until potatoes are tender.

Zesty Italian Chicken

Cheesy Chicken Strips

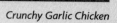

Crunchy Garlic Chicken

Crunchy Garlic Chicken

Prep: 30 min   Bake: 25 min

2 tablespoons butter or margarine, melted
2 tablespoons milk
1 tablespoon chopped fresh chives
½ teaspoon salt
½ teaspoon garlic powder
2 cups Country® Corn Flakes cereal, crushed (1 cup)
3 tablespoons chopped fresh parsley
½ teaspoon paprika
6 boneless, skinless chicken breast halves (1¾ pounds)
2 tablespoons butter or margarine, melted

1. Heat oven to 425°. Spray rectangular pan, 13 × 9 × 2 inches, with cooking spray.

2. Mix 2 tablespoons butter, the milk, chives, salt and garlic powder. Mix crushed cereal, parsley and paprika. Dip chicken into milk mixture, then coat lightly and evenly with cereal mixture. Place in pan. Drizzle with 2 tablespoons butter.

3. Bake uncovered 20 to 25 minutes or until chicken is no longer pink when centers of thickest pieces are cut.

6 servings.

1 Serving: Calories 245 (Calories from Fat 100); Fat 11g (Saturated 5g); Cholesterol 90mg; Sodium 410mg; Carbohydrate 8g (Dietary Fiber 0g); Protein 28g
% Daily Value: Vitamin A 14%; Vitamin C 6%; Calcium 2%; Iron 22%
Diet Exchanges: ½ Starch, 4 Lean Meat

BETTY'S TIPS

✪ **Substitution**
Chopped fresh parsley can be substituted for the chives.

✪ **Serve-With**
Add Betty Crocker® roasted garlic mashed potatoes and steamed broccoli spears or green beans to make your meal complete.

✪ **Do-Ahead**
Coat the chicken breasts with the crumbs the night before and then bake the next day when you get home from work.

Quick

Cheesy Chicken Strips

Prep: 10 min   Bake: 12 min

4 boneless, skinless chicken breast halves (1¼ pounds)
2 cups cheese-flavored crackers, crushed (1 cup)
½ cup finely shredded Cheddar cheese (2 ounces)
1 egg
   Barbecue sauce, ketchup or ranch dressing, if desired

1. Heat oven to 400°. Spray jelly roll pan, 15½ × 10½ × 1 inch, with cooking spray.

2. Cut chicken lengthwise into ½-inch strips. Mix crushed crackers and cheese in large resealable plastic bag. Beat egg in large bowl; add chicken strips to egg and toss to coat. Remove chicken from egg, allowing excess to drip off; place chicken in bag of cracker mixture. Seal bag and shake to coat evenly with cracker mixture. Place chicken strips in single layer in pan.

3. Bake uncovered 10 to 12 minutes or until no longer pink in center. Serve with barbecue sauce.

4 servings.

1 Serving: Calories 355 (Calories from Fat 155); Fat 17g (Saturated 7g); Cholesterol 130mg; Sodium 7mg; Carbohydrate 19g (Dietary Fiber 1g); Protein 34g
% Daily Value: Vitamin A 4%; Vitamin C 0%; Calcium 14%; Iron 14%
Diet Exchanges: 1 Starch, 5 Lean Meat

BETTY'S TIPS

✪ **Time-Saver**
Use chicken breast tenders instead of the chicken breasts; you won't have to cut the chicken into strips.

✪ **Serve-With**
Here's a perfect meal for kids to make! Serve with canned corn, Bisquick® biscuits and lots of fresh fruit.

Lemon Chicken with Broccoli

Prep: 5 min   Cook: 15 min   Bake: 40 min

2 cups uncooked farfalle (bow-tie) pasta (4 ounces)

¼ cup crushed butter-flavored crackers

1 teaspoon grated lemon peel

1 pound boneless, skinless chicken breasts, cut into ¼-inch strips

2 cloves garlic, finely chopped

2 cups frozen broccoli flowerets or broccoli cuts, thawed and drained

1 cup chicken broth

½ cup fat-free (skim) milk

2 tablespoons lemon juice

⅛ teaspoon pepper

1 can (10¾ ounces) condensed reduced-fat cream of chicken soup

1. Heat oven to 350°. Spray rectangular baking dish, 13 × 9 × 2 inches, with cooking spray. Cook and drain pasta as directed on package.

2. While pasta is cooking, mix crushed crackers and lemon peel in small bowl; set aside. Spray 10-inch nonstick skillet with cooking spray; heat over medium-high heat. Cook chicken and garlic in skillet 2 to 3 minutes, stirring frequently, until chicken is brown. Remove skillet from heat; stir in pasta and re-maining ingredients. Spoon chicken mixture into baking dish. Sprinkle with crumb mixture.

3. Cover and bake 25 minutes. Uncover and bake 10 to 15 minutes longer or until hot and bubbly.

6 servings.

1 Serving: Calories 275 (Calories from Fat 70); Fat 8g (Saturated 2g); Cholesterol 50mg; Sodium 740mg; Carbohydrate 29g (Dietary Fiber 3g); Protein 25g
% Daily Value: Vitamin A 24%; Vitamin C 22%; Calcium 8%; Iron 12%
Diet Exchanges: 1½ Starch, 3 Very Lean Meat, 1 Vegetable, ½ Fat

BETTY'S TIPS

✪ Substitution
If you don't have butter-flavored cracker crumbs, use regular cracker crumbs or seasoned bread crumbs.

✪ Health Twist
The broccoli in this casserole provides a good dose of vitamin C. In addition, using fat-free milk and reduced-fat soup gives it a lighter look.

✪ Serve-With
End your meal with an apple crisp or cobbler that you can bake after the casserole comes out of the oven. Serve with scoops of cinnamon or vanilla ice cream.

Lemon Chicken with Broccoli

Chicken Breasts Florentine

Prep: 10 min   Cook: 10 min   Bake: 45 min

- 2 cups uncooked egg noodles (4 ounces)
- 3 tablespoons butter or margarine
- 3 tablespoons Gold Medal all-purpose flour
- ¼ teaspoon pepper
- 1 cup milk
- 1 cup chicken broth
- 1 package (10 ounces) frozen chopped spinach, thawed and squeezed to drain
- ½ cup grated Parmesan cheese
- ¼ teaspoon ground nutmeg
- 4 boneless, skinless chicken breast halves (1¼ pounds)
- Additional ground nutmeg

1. Heat oven to 375°. Spray rectangular pan, 11 × 7 × 1½ inches, with cooking spray. Cook and drain noodles as directed on package.

2. While noodles are cooking, melt butter in 2-quart saucepan over medium heat. Stir in flour and pepper. Cook over medium heat, stirring constantly, until smooth and bubbly; remove from heat. Stir in milk and broth. Heat to boiling, stirring constantly. Boil and stir 1 minute; remove from heat.

3. Mix spinach, noodles, half of the sauce, ¼ cup of the cheese and ¼ teaspoon nutmeg. Spoon mixture into pan. Place chicken on spinach mixture. Pour remaining sauce over chicken. Sprinkle with remaining ¼ cup cheese and additional nutmeg.

4. Cover and bake 30 minutes. Uncover and bake about 15 minutes longer or until light brown on top and juice of chicken is no longer pink when centers of thickest pieces are cut.

4 servings.

1 Serving: Calories 445 (Calories from Fat 170); Fat 19g (Saturated 10g); Cholesterol 135mg; Sodium 690mg; Carbohydrate 29g (Dietary Fiber 2g); Protein 41g
% Daily Value: Vitamin A 92%; Vitamin C 4%; Calcium 34%; Iron 18%
Diet Exchanges: 1½ Starch, 5 Lean Meat, 1 Vegetable, ½ Fat

BETTY'S TIPS

✪ Serve-With
With the variety of breads available, be sure to experiment by serving an herb bread, a focaccia or sourdough rolls or bread with this casserole. Serve with a Caesar salad and a hearty cherry crisp for dessert.

✪ Did You Know?
Noodles come in a variety of forms and sizes, including fine, medium, wide, extra-wide, ribbons and dumplings. They can be fresh, frozen or dried and made with or without eggs. Almost any type of noodle can be used in this recipe, depending on your preference.

Chicken Breasts Florentine

Chicken Fettuccine Casserole

Prep: 20 min   Bake: 30 min

- 1 package (9 ounces) refrigerated fettuccine
- 3 tablespoons butter or margarine
- 3 tablespoons Gold Medal all-purpose flour
- 1 can (14½ ounces) chicken broth
- ½ cup half-and-half
- 1½ cups cubed cooked chicken
- ½ cup oil-packed sun-dried tomatoes, drained and cut into thin strips
- 2 slices bacon, crisply cooked and crumbled
- 3 tablespoons shredded Parmesan cheese

1. Heat oven to 350°. Spray square baking dish, 8 × 8 × 2 inches, with cooking spray. Cook and drain fettuccine as directed on package.

2. While fettuccine is cooking, melt butter in 2-quart saucepan over medium heat. Stir in flour. Gradually stir in broth. Heat to boiling, stirring constantly; remove from heat. Stir in half-and-half. Stir in chicken, tomatoes and bacon.

3. Add fettuccine to chicken mixture; toss gently to mix well. Spoon into baking dish. Sprinkle with cheese. Bake uncovered about 30 minutes or until hot in center.

4 servings.

1 Serving: Calories 530 (Calories from Fat 215); Fat 24g (Saturated 11g); Cholesterol 140mg; Sodium 760mg; Carbohydrate 51g (Dietary Fiber 3g); Protein 30g
% Daily Value: Vitamin A 16%; Vitamin C 12%; Calcium 14%; Iron 24%
Diet Exchanges: 3 Starch, 2½ High-Fat Meat, 1 Vegetable, ½ Fat

BETTY'S TIPS

☺ Success Hint
This casserole is sure to be a crowd-pleasing winner! You can easily double this recipe and bake it in a 13 × 9 × 2-inch baking dish.

☺ Do-Ahead
Make this dish up to 8 hours in advance. Cover the unbaked casserole tightly with aluminum foil and refrigerate no longer than 24 hours; uncover before baking. The casserole may need to bake an additional 5 to 10 minutes.

Cavatappi with Roasted Chicken and Vegetables

Prep: 25 min   Bake: 45 min

- 4 medium red potatoes, cut into ¾-inch cubes (2½ cups)
- 2 cups 1-inch cauliflowerets
- 1 large yellow or red bell pepper, cut into 1-inch pieces
- 4 medium roma (plum) tomatoes, cut into 1-inch pieces (1½ cups)
- 1 medium onion, coarsely chopped (½ cup)
- 2 tablespoons olive or vegetable oil
- 1 pound boneless, skinless chicken breast halves
- 1 tablespoon chicken seasoning
- 2 cups uncooked cavatappi or fusilli (corkscrew) pasta (6 ounces)
- ⅓ cup finely chopped fresh parsley
- 3 cloves garlic, finely chopped
- 2 tablespoons grated lemon peel

1. Heat oven to 425°. Mix potatoes, cauliflowerets, bell pepper, tomatoes, onion and oil in 6-quart roasting pan. Top with chicken. Sprinkle with chicken seasoning.

2. Bake uncovered about 45 minutes, stirring vegetables occasionally, until vegetables are very tender and juice of chicken is no longer pink when centers of thickest pieces are cut.

3. Cook and drain pasta as directed on package. Mix parsley, garlic and lemon peel; set aside.

4. Chop chicken. Toss chicken, vegetable mixture and pasta. Sprinkle with parsley mixture.

4 servings.

1 Serving: Calories 500 (Calories from Fat 90); Fat 10g (Saturated 2g); Cholesterol 70mg; Sodium 1120mg; Carbohydrate 74g (Dietary Fiber 7g); Protein 36g
% Daily Value: Vitamin A 21%; Vitamin C 100%; Calcium 6%; Iron 28%
Diet Exchanges: 4 Starch, 3 Very Lean Meat, 2 Vegetable, 1 Fat

BETTY'S TIPS

☺ Substitution
For a fun new flavor twist, substitute orange peel for the lemon peel.

Seasoned salt can be used instead of the chicken seasoning.

Cavatappi with Roasted Chicken and Vegetables

Chicken Fettuccine Casserole

Mexican Chicken Sour Cream Lasagna

Prep: 20 min   Bake: 1 hr   Stand: 15 min

12 uncooked lasagna noodles

2 cans (10¾ ounces each) condensed cream of chicken soup

1 container (8 ounces) sour cream

¼ cup milk

1¼ teaspoons ground cumin

½ teaspoon garlic powder

3 cups cubed cooked chicken

1 can (4 ounces) chopped green chilies, undrained

8 to 10 medium green onions, sliced (1 cup)

½ cup chopped fresh cilantro or parsley

3 cups finely shredded Mexican-style Cheddar-Monterey Jack cheese blend

1 large red bell pepper, chopped (1 cup)

1 can (2¼ ounces) sliced ripe olives, drained

1 cup crushed nacho cheese-flavored tortilla chips

Chopped or whole fresh cilantro leaves, if desired

1. Heat oven to 350°. Spray bottom and sides of rectangular baking dish, 13 × 9 × 2 inches, with cooking spray. Cook and drain noodles as directed on package. While noodles are cooking, mix soup, sour cream, milk, cumin, garlic powder, chicken and chilies in large bowl.

2. Spread about 1¼ cups of the chicken mixture in baking dish. Top with 4 noodles. Spread 1¼ cups chicken mixture over noodles; sprinkle with green onions and cilantro. Sprinkle with 1 cup of the cheese.

3. Top with 4 noodles. Spread 1¼ cups chicken mixture over noodles; sprinkle with bell pepper and olives. Sprinkle with 1 cup of the cheese. Top with 4 noodles; spread with remaining chicken mixture.

4. Bake uncovered 30 minutes; sprinkle with tortilla chips and remaining 1 cup cheese. Bake 15 to 30 minutes longer or until bubbly and hot in center. Sprinkle with cilantro. Let stand 15 minutes before cutting.

8 servings.

1 Serving: Calories 575 (Calories from Fat 290); Fat 32g (Saturated 15g); Cholesterol 110mg; Sodium 1060mg; Carbohydrate 42g (Dietary Fiber 3g); Protein 33g
% Daily Value: Vitamin A 52%; Vitamin C 38%; Calcium 34%; Iron 18%
Diet Exchanges: 3 Starch, 3 High-Fat Meat, 1 Fat

BETTY'S TIPS

☺ **Substitution**

We love the color and flavor of the nacho cheese tortilla chips, but you can also use regular tortilla chips for the topping.

Plain Cheddar or Monterey Jack cheese can be substituted for the Mexican cheese blend.

☺ **Special Touch**

Add a few drops red pepper sauce to the chicken mixture if you want a little more kick to your lasagna.

Mexican Chicken Sour Cream Lasagna

Chicken Enchiladas

Prep: 20 min   Bake: 25 min

- 1 cup mild green sauce (salsa verde) or salsa
- ¼ cup cilantro sprigs
- ¼ cup parsley sprigs
- 1 tablespoon lime juice
- 2 cloves garlic
- 2 cups chopped cooked chicken or turkey
- ¾ cup shredded mozzarella cheese (3 ounces)
- 6 flour tortillas (6 to 8 inches in diameter)
- 1 medium lime, cut into wedges

1. Heat oven to 350°. Spray rectangular baking dish, 11 × 7 × 1½ inches, with cooking spray. Place green sauce, cilantro, parsley, lime juice and garlic in blender or food processor. Cover and blend on high speed about 30 seconds or until smooth. Reserve half of mixture.

2. Mix remaining sauce mixture, the chicken and ¼ cup of the cheese. Spoon about ¼ cup chicken mixture onto each tortilla. Roll tortilla around filling; place seam side down in baking dish.

3. Pour reserved sauce mixture over enchiladas. Sprinkle with remaining ½ cup cheese. Bake uncov-ered 20 to 25 minutes or until hot. Serve with lime wedges.

6 servings.

1 Serving: Calories 205 (Calories from Fat 65); Fat 7g (Saturated 3g); Cholesterol 50mg; Sodium 420mg; Carbohydrate 17g (Dietary Fiber 2g); Protein 20g
% Daily Value: Vitamin A 14%; Vitamin C 8%; Calcium 16%; Iron 10%
Diet Exchanges: 1 Starch, 2½ Lean Meat

BETTY'S TIPS

⊙ **Success Hint**

Fresh cilantro and parsley will keep up to a week in the refrigerator. Place the herbs, stem end down, in a tall glass and fill with cold water until the ends are covered by 1 inch. Cover the herbs with a plastic bag. Just before using, wash the fresh herbs, and dry them with a paper towel.

⊙ **Serve-With**

Add Spanish rice to make this meal complete. Look for quick and easy Spanish rice mixes in the rice section of the supermarket.

Chicken Enchiladas

Baked Chicken and Rice with Autumn Vegetables

Home-Style Turkey and Potato Bake

Baked Chicken and Rice with Autumn Vegetables

Prep: 10 min   Cook: 5 min   Bake: 30 min

8	chicken drumsticks or thighs (1¼ pounds), skin removed
1	package (6 ounces) seasoned long-grain and wild rice
2	cups 1½-inch cubes butternut squash
1	medium zucchini, cut lengthwise in half, then cut crosswise into ¾-inch slices
1	medium red bell pepper, cut into 1-inch pieces (1 cup)
2	cups water
½	cup garlic-and-herb spreadable cheese

1. Heat oven to 425°. Spray 10-inch skillet with cooking spray; heat over medium-high heat. Cook chicken in skillet about 5 minutes, turning once, until brown. Remove chicken from skillet.

2. Mix rice, contents of seasoning packet, squash, zucchini and bell pepper in ungreased rectangular pan, 13 × 9 × 2 inches.

3. Add water to skillet; heat to boiling. Pour boiling water over rice mixture; stir to mix. Stir in cheese. Place chicken on rice mixture.

4. Cover and bake about 30 minutes or until liquid is absorbed and juice of chicken is no longer pink when centers of thickest pieces are cut.

4 servings.

1 Serving: Calories 285 (Calories from Fat 90); Fat 10g (Saturated 5g); Cholesterol 110mg; Sodium 170mg; Carbohydrate 22g (Dietary Fiber 3g); Protein 30g
% Daily Value: Vitamin A 100%; Vitamin C 60%; Calcium 8%; Iron 20%
Diet Exchanges: 1½ Starch, 3½ Very Lean Meat, 1 Fat

BETTY'S TIPS

✿ Substitution
Butternut squash is a tan-colored, elongated vegetable with a bulbous end and mildly sweet flavor. You can also use buttercup squash, which has a drier texture but is very sweet.

Boneless, skinless chicken breast halves can also be used in this recipe.

Home-Style Turkey and Potato Bake

Prep: 5 min   Cook: 10 min   Bake: 30 min

½	package (7.6-ounce size) Betty Crocker roasted garlic mashed potatoes (1 pouch)
1¼	cups hot water
½	cup milk
2	tablespoons butter or margarine
4	medium green onions, sliced (¼ cup)
2	cups chopped cooked turkey
1	bag (1 pound) frozen mixed vegetables, thawed and drained
1	jar (12 ounces) home-style turkey gravy
¼	teaspoon poultry seasoning

1. Heat oven to 350°. Spray 2-quart casserole with cooking spray. Make mashed potatoes as directed on package using water, milk and butter. Stir in onions.

2. Heat turkey, vegetables, gravy and poultry seasoning to boiling in 2-quart saucepan over medium-high heat. Pour turkey mixture into casserole. Spoon or pipe potatoes around edge of casserole.

3. Bake uncovered about 30 minutes or until heated through and potatoes are light brown.

6 servings.

1 Serving: Calories 300 (Calories from Fat 115); Fat 13g (Saturated 3g); Cholesterol 45mg; Sodium 720mg; Carbohydrate 22g (Dietary Fiber 6g); Protein 19g
% Daily Value: Vitamin A 54%; Vitamin C 22%; Calcium 6%; Iron 8%
Diet Exchanges: 2 Starch, 1½ Medium-Fat Meat, 1 Vegetable

BETTY'S TIPS

✿ Substitution
Poultry seasoning—a blend of thyme, sage, pepper, marjoram and other herbs and spices—marries well with the turkey in this recipe, but ground sage makes a good substitute.

✿ Special Touch
After spooning potatoes around edge of casserole, swirl the tops with the back of the spoon. For a fancier presentation, place potatoes in a pastry bag fitted with a large star tip and pipe onto the casserole; sprinkle with paprika.

Turkey and Ham Tetrazzini

Prep: 10 min   Bake: 35 min

1 package (9 ounces) refrigerated linguine
1 can (10¾ ounces) condensed cream of mushroom soup
1 can (10¾ ounces) condensed cream of chicken soup
¾ cup milk
2 tablespoons dry white wine or apple juice
2 cups cut-up cooked turkey or chicken
½ cup cut-up fully cooked smoked ham
1 small green bell pepper, chopped (½ cup)
¼ cup halved pitted ripe olives
½ cup grated Parmesan cheese
¼ cup slivered almonds, toasted

1. Heat oven to 375°. Cook and drain linguine as directed on package.

2. While linguine is cooking, mix soups, milk and wine in ungreased 2-quart casserole. Stir in linguine, turkey, ham, bell pepper and olives. Sprinkle with cheese.

3. Bake uncovered about 35 minutes or until hot and bubbly. Sprinkle with almonds.

6 servings.

1 Serving: Calories 450 (Calories from Fat 165); Fat 17g (Saturated 5g); Cholesterol 60mg; Sodium 1150mg; Carbohydrate 46g (Dietary Fiber 3g); Protein 29g
% Daily Value: Vitamin A 8%; Vitamin C 8%; Calcium 20%; Iron 18%
Diet Exchanges: 3 Starch, 3 Lean Meat, 1 Fat

BETTY'S TIPS

☼ Success Hint
To toast almonds, place in ungreased heavy skillet. Cook over medium heat 5 to 7 minutes, stirring frequently until almonds begin to brown, then stirring constantly until they are light brown.

☼ Health Twist
You can trim the fat in this classic creamy casserole. Use reduced-fat condensed soups and fat-free (skim) milk, and you'll save 3 grams of fat per serving.

☼ Do-Ahead
Assemble this family favorite, then cover and refrigerate it up to 24 hours before baking. It also can be easily doubled to serve a crowd.

Cheesy Italian Ravioli

Prep: 15 min   Bake: 25 min

½ pound ground beef
½ pound bulk Italian sausage
1 container (15 ounces) refrigerated marinara sauce
1 cup sliced mushrooms (3 ounces)
1 can (14½ ounces) diced tomatoes with Italian seasonings, undrained
1 package (9 ounces) refrigerated cheese ravioli
1 cup shredded mozzarella cheese or pizza cheese blend (4 ounces)

1. Heat oven to 375°. Cook beef and sausage in 10-inch skillet over medium heat 8 to 10 minutes, stirring occasionally, until brown; drain.

2. Stir marinara sauce, mushrooms and tomatoes into beef mixture. Pour half of sauce mixture into ungreased rectangular baking dish, 11 × 7 × 1½ inches. Arrange ravioli in sauce. Pour remaining sauce mixture over ravioli. Sprinkle with cheese.

3. Bake uncovered 20 to 25 minutes or until ravioli is tender and mixture is hot.

4 to 6 servings.

1 Serving: Calories 575 (Calories from Fat 295); Fat 33g (Saturated 13g); Cholesterol 135mg; Sodium 1330mg; Carbohydrate 39g (Dietary Fiber 3g); Protein 34g
% Daily Value: Vitamin A 30%; Vitamin C 28%; Calcium 32%; Iron 22%
Diet Exchanges: 2½ Starch, 4 Medium-Fat Meat, 2 Fat

BETTY'S TIPS

☼ Substitution
A can of plain diced tomatoes and ½ teaspoon dried Italian seasoning can be used instead of the diced tomatoes with Italian seasoning.

Meat- or cheese-filled tortellini can be substituted for the ravioli.

Turkey and Ham Tetrazzini

Cheesy Italian Ravioli

Hot from the Oven   131

Garlic Shepherd's Pie

Prep: 25 min   Bake: 30 min

1   pound ground beef
1   medium onion, chopped (½ cup)
2   cups frozen baby beans and carrots (from 1-pound bag)
1   cup sliced mushrooms (3 ounces)
1   can (14½ ounces) diced tomatoes, undrained
1   jar (12 ounces) beef gravy
2   tablespoons chili sauce
½   teaspoon dried basil leaves
⅛   teaspoon pepper
½   package (7.6-ounce size) Betty Crocker roasted garlic mashed potatoes (1 pouch)
1½ cups hot water
½   cup milk
2   teaspoons butter or margarine
2   teaspoons shredded Parmesan cheese

1. Heat oven to 350°. Cook beef and onion in 12-inch non-stick skillet over medium heat, stirring occasionally, until beef is brown; drain well. Stir in frozen vegetables, mushrooms, tomatoes, gravy, chili sauce, basil and pepper. Heat to boiling; reduce heat. Cover and simmer about 10 minutes or until vegetables are tender.

2. Cook potatoes as directed on package for 4 servings, using 1 pouch Potatoes and Seasoning, hot water, milk and butter. Let stand 5 minutes.

3. Spoon beef mixture into ungreased square baking dish, 8 × 8 × 2 inches, or 2-quart casserole. Spoon potatoes onto beef mixture around edge of dish. Sprinkle with cheese. Bake uncovered 25 to 30 minutes or until potatoes are firm and beef mixture is bubbly.

6 servings.

1 Serving: Calories 265 (Calories from Fat 135); Fat 15g (Saturated 6g); Cholesterol 50mg; Sodium 620mg; Carbohydrate 17g (Dietary Fiber 3g); Protein 19g
% Daily Value: Vitamin A 100%; Vitamin C 12%; Calcium 8%; Iron 14%
Diet Exchanges: 1 Starch, 2 Medium-Fat Meat, 1 Fat

BETTY'S TIPS
❂ Did You Know?
Shepherd's pie is a dish of cooked ground or diced meat mixed with gravy and vegetables and topped with mashed potatoes. It was originally created as an economical way to use leftover meat.

Garlic Shepherd's Pie

Manicotti

Prep: 15 min   Cook: 20 min   Bake: 1 hr 30 min

1   pound extra-lean ground beef

1   large onion, chopped (1 cup)

2   cloves garlic, finely chopped

1   can (28 ounces) whole tomatoes, undrained

1   package (8 ounces) sliced fresh mushrooms (3 cups)

¼   cup chopped fresh parsley

1   tablespoon chopped fresh or 1 teaspoon dried basil leaves

1   teaspoon fennel seed

¼   teaspoon salt

2   cups fat-free cottage cheese

⅓   cup grated Parmesan cheese

¼   teaspoon ground nutmeg, if desired

¼   teaspoon pepper

2   packages (10 ounces each) frozen chopped spinach, thawed and squeezed to drain

14   uncooked manicotti shells

2   tablespoons shredded Parmesan cheese

1. Heat oven to 350°. Cook beef, onion and garlic in 10-inch nonstick skillet over medium heat 8 to 10 minutes, stirring occasionally, until beef is brown; drain. Stir in tomatoes, mushrooms, parsley, basil, fennel seed and salt, breaking up tomatoes. Heat to boiling; reduce heat. Cover and simmer 10 minutes.

2. Spread about one-third of the beef mixture in ungreased rectangular baking dish, 13 × 9 × 2 inches.

3. Mix cottage cheese, ⅓ cup Parmesan cheese, the nutmeg, pepper and spinach. Fill uncooked manicotti shells with spinach mixture; place shells on beef mixture in baking dish. Pour remaining beef mixture evenly over shells, covering shells completely. Sprinkle with 2 tablespoons Parmesan cheese.

4. Cover and bake about 1 hour 30 minutes or until manicotti shells are tender.

7 servings.

1 Serving: Calories 345 (Calories from Fat 90); Fat 10g (Saturated 5g); Cholesterol 45mg; Sodium 650mg; Carbohydrate 39g (Dietary Fiber 5g); Protein 30g
% Daily Value: Vitamin A 52%; Vitamin C 24%; Calcium 24%; Iron 26%
Diet Exchanges: 2 Starch, 2½ Lean Meat, 2 Vegetable

BETTY'S TIPS

✿ Substitution
For a meatless version, you can omit the beef and use frozen (thawed) vegetarian crumbles.

✿ Success Hint
Filling uncooked manicotti shells makes this recipe very convenient and easy. The liquid from the beef mixture will rehydrate the pasta shells, and they will cook completely as they bake.

✿ Health Twist
This too-good-to-be-true manicotti is a good source of fiber. A serving also provides almost a fourth of your daily requirements for vitamin C, calcium and iron and over half of the requirement for vitamin A.

Manicotti

Italian Fettucine Pie

Italian Fettuccine Pie

Prep: 15 min　Cook: 15 min　Bake: 30 min　Stand: 10 min

½ pound ground beef

1 small onion, finely chopped (¼ cup)

1 can (8 ounces) stewed tomatoes, undrained

1 can (8 ounces) tomato sauce

½ teaspoon Italian seasoning

6 ounces uncooked fettuccine

2 eggs

1 tablespoon butter or margarine, melted

1 cup shredded mozzarella cheese (4 ounces)

1 cup small curd creamed cottage cheese

1 cup chopped fresh broccoli or frozen (thawed) chopped broccoli

¼ cup grated Parmesan cheese

1. Heat oven to 350°. Cook beef and onion in 10-inch skillet over medium heat, stirring occasionally, until beef is brown; drain. Stir in tomatoes, tomato sauce and Italian seasoning. Heat to boiling; reduce heat. Cover and simmer 10 minutes, stirring occasionally.

2. Meanwhile, cook and drain fettuccine as directed on package. Beat one of the eggs and the butter in medium bowl. Stir in fettuccine and mozzarella cheese. Spoon mixture into ungreased quiche dish or pie plate, 9 × 1½ inches; press evenly on bottom and up side of plate.

3. Mix cottage cheese and remaining egg; spread over fettuccine mixture on bottom of pie plate. Sprinkle with broccoli. Spoon beef mixture evenly over top. Sprinkle with Parmesan cheese.

4. Bake uncovered about 30 minutes or until hot in center. Let stand 10 minutes before cutting.

6 servings.

1 Serving: Calories 350 (Calories from Fat 145); Fat 16g (Saturated 8g); Cholesterol 140mg; Sodium 730mg; Carbohydrate 28g (Dietary Fiber 2g); Protein 25g
% Daily Value: Vitamin A 20%; Vitamin C 20%; Calcium 26%; Iron 14%
Diet Exchanges: 1½ Starch, 3 Lean Meat, 1 Vegetable, 1 Fat

BETTY'S TIPS

☺ Success Hint
An easy way to form the pasta shell is to spoon the fettuccine mixture into the pie plate and then press firmly with another pie plate.

☺ Do-Ahead
Wrap unbaked pie tightly and label. Freeze no longer than 1 month. About 2¼ hours before serving, heat oven to 400°. Unwrap and re-cover with aluminum foil. Bake about 2 hours or until hot in center. Let stand 10 minutes before cutting.

Pastitsio

Prep: 15 min   Bake: 40 min

1	cup uncooked elbow macaroni (3½ ounces)
1	egg white
¼	cup grated Parmesan cheese
2	tablespoons milk
¾	pound ground lamb
1½	cups cubed peeled eggplant
1	can (14½ ounces) whole tomatoes, drained
1	medium onion, chopped (½ cup)
½	teaspoon salt
¼	teaspoon ground cinnamon
¼	teaspoon ground nutmeg
1	clove garlic, finely chopped
1	cup milk
1	tablespoon cornstarch
2	tablespoons grated Parmesan cheese
1	egg, beaten

1. Heat oven to 350°. Cook and drain macaroni as directed on package. Stir in egg white, ¼ cup cheese and 2 tablespoons milk.

2. Meanwhile, cook lamb in 10-inch skillet over medium heat about 10 minutes, stirring occasionally, until no longer pink; drain. Stir in eggplant, tomatoes, onion, salt, cinnamon, nutmeg and garlic, breaking up tomatoes.

3. Cook 1 cup milk and the cornstarch in 1-quart saucepan over medium heat, stirring constantly, until mixture thickens and boils. Stir in 2 tablespoons cheese and the egg.

4. Place half of the macaroni mixture in ungreased 1½-quart casserole. Top with lamb mixture, remaining macaroni mixture and the sauce. Bake uncovered about 40 minutes or until set in center.

6 servings.

1 Serving: Calories 265 (Calories from Fat 110); Fat 12g (Saturated 5g); Cholesterol 80mg; Sodium 480mg; Carbohydrate 23g (Dietary Fiber 2g); Protein 18g
% Daily Value: Vitamin A 8%; Vitamin C 8%; Calcium 18%; Iron 12%
Diet Exchanges: 1 Starch, 1½ Medium-Fat Meat, 2 Vegetable, ½ Fat

BETTY'S TIPS

✿ Did You Know?

Pastitsio is a popular Greek casserole made up of layers of pasta, lamb, cheeses and a creamy white sauce. The delicate seasoning blend of cinnamon and nutmeg gives it its unique flavor.

✿ Substitution

Ground beef can be used instead of the ground lamb.

Pastitsio

Ham and Asparagus with Cashews

Prep: 10 min   Bake: 35 min

1   can (10¾ ounces) condensed reduced-fat cream of chicken soup
½   cup fat-free (skim) milk
½   cup reduced-fat sour cream
½   teaspoon ground mustard
2   cups chopped fully cooked lean ham
1   package (10 ounces) frozen asparagus cuts, thawed and drained
3   cups cooked brown or white rice
¼   cup cashew pieces

1. Heat oven to 350°. Spray 2-quart casserole with cooking spray.

2. Mix soup, milk, sour cream and mustard in casserole. Stir in remaining ingredients except cashews. Sprinkle with cashews.

3. Bake uncovered 30 to 35 minutes or until asparagus is tender.

6 servings.

1 Serving: Calories 305 (Calories from Fat 100); Fat 11g (Saturated 3g); Cholesterol 35mg; Sodium 1140mg; Carbohydrate 33g (Dietary Fiber 3g); Protein 18g
% Daily Value: Vitamin A 14%; Vitamin C 8%; Calcium 8%; Iron 10%
Diet Exchanges: 2 Starch, 1½ Lean Meat, 1 Vegetable, 1 Fat

BETTY'S TIPS

☺ Health Twist
By using reduced-fat cream of chicken soup, fat-free milk, reduced-fat sour cream and lean ham, this casserole has saved 4 grams of fat per serving.

Using the brown rice makes this a good source of fiber, too.

☺ Serve-With
The casserole is an all-in-one meal, so serve with slices of whole-grain or marble rye bread and a tossed salad.

☺ Variation
Change a few ingredients to make **Chicken and Broccoli with Cashews.** Use cooked chicken and frozen broccoli cuts instead of the ham and asparagus.

Low Fat

Pork Tenderloin with Roasted Vegetables

Prep: 10 min   Bake: 40 min   Stand: 5 min

2   pork tenderloins (each about ¾ pound)
1   pound baby-cut carrots
2   pounds new potatoes (16 to 20), cut in half
1   medium onion, cut into wedges
6   whole cloves garlic
1   tablespoon olive or vegetable oil
2   teaspoons dried rosemary leaves, crumbled
1   teaspoon dried sage leaves, crumbled
¼   teaspoon salt
¼   teaspoon pepper

1. Heat oven to 450°. Spray shallow roasting pan with cooking spray. Place pork in pan. Insert meat thermometer so tip is in thickest part of pork. Place carrots, potatoes, onion and garlic around pork. Drizzle with oil; sprinkle with rosemary, sage, salt and pepper.

2. Bake uncovered 25 to 30 minutes or until thermometer reads 155°. Remove pork from pan. Stir vegetables and continue baking 5 to 10 minutes or until tender. Cover pork and let stand 10 to 15 minutes or until thermometer reads 160° and pork is slightly pink in center. Serve pork with vegetables and garlic.

6 servings.

1 Serving: Calories 305 (Calories from Fat 55); Fat 6g (Saturated 2g); Cholesterol 70mg; Sodium 190mg; Carbohydrate 39g (Dietary Fiber 5g); Protein 29g
% Daily Value: Vitamin A 100%; Vitamin C 20%; Calcium 4%; Iron 18%
Diet Exchanges: 2 Starch, 3 Very Lean Meat, 2 Vegetable

BETTY'S TIPS

☺ Substitution
Use dried thyme leaves instead of the sage leaves.

☺ Success Hint
If the baby carrots are rather large, cut them in half before baking.

☺ Serve-With
This easy one-dish meal is perfect for casual entertaining. Serve with a crisp tossed salad.

Pork Tenderloin with Roasted Vegetables

Ham and Asparagus with Cashews

Curried Fruit Pork Chops

Spiced Pork Chop Bake

Curried Fruit Pork Chops

Prep: 10 min   Cook: 10 min   Bake: 30 min

- 6 pork loin or rib chops, about ¾ inch thick (about 2¼ pounds)
- ¼ teaspoon salt
- ¼ teaspoon pepper
- 1 cup uncooked instant brown rice
- 1 cup diced dried fruit and raisin mixture
- ¼ cup sliced almonds
- 1¼ cups hot water
- 1 cup apple juice
- 1 tablespoon butter or margarine
- ¾ teaspoon curry powder
- ½ teaspoon salt
- ¼ teaspoon pepper

1. Heat oven to 350°. Spray rectangular baking dish, 13 × 9 × 2 inches, with cooking spray.

2. Remove fat from pork. Sprinkle both sides of pork with ¼ teaspoon salt and ¼ teaspoon pepper. Spray 12-inch nonstick skillet with cooking spray; heat over medium-high heat. Cook pork in skillet about 6 minutes, turning once, until brown.

3. Meanwhile, mix remaining ingredients in baking dish. Place pork on rice mixture. Cover and bake about 30 minutes or until pork is slightly pink when cut near bone and rice is tender.

6 servings.

1 Serving: Calories 385 (Calories from Fat 115); Fat 13g (Saturated 4g); Cholesterol 70mg; Sodium 360mg; Carbohydrate 44g (Dietary Fiber 4g); Protein 27g
% Daily Value: Vitamin A 8%; Vitamin C 0%; Calcium 4%; Iron 12%
Diet Exchanges: 2 Starch, 3 Lean Meat, 1 Fruit

BETTY'S TIPS

☺ Health Twist
Brown rice and dried fruit give this casserole a good dose of fiber while adding a nutty, sweet flavor.

☺ Did You Know?
Curry powder is a blend of many spices, herbs and seeds, not a single spice. Indian cooks grind their curry powder daily. Commonly used fresh ingredients are chilies, turmeric, cinnamon, cardamom, cloves, pepper, cumin, nutmeg, fennel seed, sesame seed and saffron. Curry powder varies with the cook and the region and can range from mild to hot.

Spiced Pork Chop Bake

Prep: 15 min   Cook: 6 min   Bake: 55 min

- 6 pork loin or rib chops, about ½ inch thick
- ¼ teaspoon salt
- ⅛ teaspoon pepper
- 2 medium onions, sliced and separated into rings
- 2 medium acorn squash, cut into 1-inch rings and seeded
- 3 medium apples, cored and cut into 1-inch rings
- ¼ cup butter or margarine, melted
- 2 tablespoons honey
- 2 tablespoons water
- 1 teaspoon pumpkin pie spice

1. Heat oven to 350°. Cook pork in 12-inch nonstick skillet over medium heat about 6 minutes, turning once, until brown.

2. Place pork in ungreased rectangular baking dish, 13 × 9 × 2 inches; sprinkle with salt and pepper. Arrange onions, squash and apples on pork. Mix remaining ingredients; pour over apples.

3. Cover and bake 45 to 55 minutes or until pork is slightly pink when cut near bone and squash is tender. Serve pan drippings with pork.

6 servings.

1 Serving: Calories 375 (Calories from Fat 135); Fat 15g (Saturated 7g); Cholesterol 80mg; Sodium 190mg; Carbohydrate 40g (Dietary Fiber 5g); Protein 25g
% Daily Value: Vitamin A 16%; Vitamin C 18%; Calcium 8%; Iron 12%
Diet Exchanges: 2 Starch, 2 Medium-Fat Meat, 2 Vegetable

BETTY'S TIPS

☺ Health Twist
This sweet-spicy pork chop casserole is a good source of protein, thiamin and vitamin A.

☺ Did You Know?
Apples are in such an abundance in the fall, and the varieties are endless. Good choices for this casserole are slightly tangy apples such as Jonathon, Northern Spy, Winesap and York Imperial. Or try your personal favorite!

Spicy Orange Pork Chops

Prep: 10 min   Cook: 8 min   Bake: 45 min

⅔ cup orange marmalade

2 tablespoons butter or margarine, melted

½ teaspoon ground cinnamon

½ teaspoon ground ginger

2 tablespoons dried cranberries

2 medium sweet potatoes, peeled and cut into ½-inch slices

¾ cup Original Bisquick

¼ teaspoon ground red pepper (cayenne)

4 pork boneless loin chops, ½ inch thick (1 pound)

2 tablespoons soy sauce or water

1. Heat oven to 350°. Mix marmalade, butter, cinnamon and ginger in medium bowl. Stir in cranberries and sweet potatoes; set aside.

2. Mix Bisquick and red pepper. Dip pork into soy sauce, then coat with Bisquick mixture. Spray 10-inch skillet with cooking spray; heat over medium-high heat. Cook pork in skillet 6 to 8 minutes, turning once, until coating is brown.

3. Place pork in ungreased rectangular baking dish, 13 × 9 × 2 inches. Arrange sweet potato mixture around pork. Bake uncovered 40 to 45 minutes or until sweet potatoes are tender and pork is slightly pink in center.

4 servings.

1 Serving: Calories 510 (Calories from Fat 155); Fat 17g (Saturated 7g); Cholesterol 80mg; Sodium 880mg; Carbohydrate 66g (Dietary Fiber 3g); Protein 26g
% Daily Value: Vitamin A 100%; Vitamin C 16%; Calcium 8%; Iron 12%
Diet Exchanges: 3 Starch, 2 Medium-Fat Meat, 1½ Fruit, 1 Fat

BETTY'S TIPS

✪ **Substitution**
Use dried cherries or raisins instead of the cranberries for a colorful addition to this dinner.

✪ **Success Hint**
Follow cook times for pork carefully. Today's pork is lean and requires shorter cooking times. Overcooking pork will make it tough.

✪ **Time-Saver**
Looking for a shortcut? Use an 18-ounce can of vacuum-packed sweet potatoes, cut crosswise in half, for the fresh sweet potatoes.

Spicy Orange Pork Chops

Great Grilling

Great Grilling

Outdoor Cooking Made Easy

Mediterranean Grilled Tuna Sandwich (page 155)

Italian Beef Roast (page 162)

Easy Italian Grilled Veggies

Prep: 15 min   Grill: 20 min

- ¼ cup butter or margarine, softened
- 2 tablespoons lemon pepper
- 1 large potato, cut lengthwise into fourths
- 1 medium zucchini, cut lengthwise in half
- 1 medium yellow summer squash, cut lengthwise in half
- 2 large bell peppers, cut lengthwise into fourths and seeded
- 1 medium onion, cut into ½-inch slices
- ¼ cup Italian dressing

1. Heat coals or gas grill for direct heat. Mix butter and lemon pepper. Brush on potato, zucchini, squash, bell peppers and onion.

2. Cover and grill vegetables 4 inches from medium heat 10 to 20 minutes, turning frequently, until tender.

3. As vegetables become done, remove from grill to platter. Sprinkle with dressing. Serve warm.

4 servings.

1 Serving: Calories 260 (Calories from Fat 160); Fat 18g (Saturated 7g); Cholesterol 35mg; Sodium 730mg; Carbohydrate 26g (Dietary Fiber 5g); Protein 4g
% Daily Value: Vitamin A 24%; Vitamin C 70%; Calcium 6%; Iron 10%
Diet Exchanges: ½ Starch, 3 Vegetable, 3 Fat

BETTY'S TIPS

☺ Time-Saver
For a delicious do-ahead marinated salad, sprinkle the dressing over the vegetables and chill in the refrigerator for at least 2 hours before serving.

☺ Health Twist
For 0 grams of fat and 105 calories per serving, omit the butter, spray vegetables with butter-flavored cooking spray before grilling and use fat-free Italian dressing.

Quick

Grilled Spring Vegetables

Prep: 5 min   Grill: 8 min

- Herb Butter (below)
- 1 pound asparagus
- 1 pound green beans
- ½ pound mushrooms, cut in half
- ¼ cup chopped walnuts

1. Heat coals or gas grill for direct heat.

2. Make Herb Butter in large bowl. Add remaining ingredients except walnuts; toss to coat with butter.

3. Place vegetables in grill basket. Cover and grill vegetables 5 inches from medium heat 6 to 8 minutes, turning vegetables once or twice, until tender. Sprinkle with walnuts.

8 servings.

Herb Butter

- ¼ cup butter or margarine, melted
- 2 tablespoons chopped fresh thyme or 2 teaspoons dried thyme leaves
- 1 tablespoon chopped fresh chives
- ¼ teaspoon salt

Mix all ingredients.

1 Serving: Calories 90 (Calories from Fat 65); Fat 7g (Saturated 3g); Cholesterol 10mg; Sodium 110mg; Carbohydrate 6g (Dietary Fiber 2g); Protein 3g
% Daily Value: Vitamin A 14%; Vitamin C 8%; Calcium 4%; Iron 6%
Diet Exchanges: 1 Vegetable, 1½ Fat

BETTY'S TIPS

☺ Substitution
If you don't have a grill basket, use a sheet of heavy-duty aluminum foil and poke a few holes in the foil with a fork.

Olive oil can be substituted for the butter. Or omit the butter and spray the vegetables with cooking spray, then sprinkle with the seasonings.

☺ Success Hint
When grilling a variety of vegetables at once, be prepared to take each off the grill at a different time.

For maximum flavor, season the vegetables with salt and pepper both before and after grilling.

Easy Italian Grilled Veggies

Grilled Spring Vegetables

Portabella Mushrooms with Herbs

Portabella Mushrooms with Herbs

Prep: 10 min   Marinate: 1 hr   Grill: 10 min

2   tablespoons olive or vegetable oil
1   tablespoon balsamic vinegar
1   teaspoon chopped fresh or ¼ teaspoon dried oregano leaves
1   teaspoon chopped fresh or ¼ teaspoon dried thyme leaves
⅛   teaspoon salt
1   clove garlic, finely chopped
4   fresh portabella mushroom caps (about 4 inches in diameter)
¼   cup crumbled feta cheese with herbs

1. Mix oil, vinegar, oregano, thyme, salt and garlic in large glass or plastic bowl or resealable plastic food-storage bag. Add mushrooms; turn to coat with marinade. Cover dish or seal bag and refrigerate 1 hour.

2. Heat coals or gas grill for direct heat. Remove mushrooms from marinade (mushrooms will absorb most of the marinade). Cover and grill mushrooms 4 inches from medium heat 8 to 10 minutes or until tender. Sprinkle with cheese.

4 servings.

1 Serving: Calories 100 (Calories from Fat 80); Fat 9g (Saturated 2g); Cholesterol 10mg; Sodium 180mg; Carbohydrate 3g (Dietary Fiber 1g); Protein 3g
% Daily Value: Vitamin A 0%; Vitamin C 0%; Calcium 4%; Iron 4%
Diet Exchanges: ½ Vegetable, 2 Fat

BETTY'S TIPS

✪ Serve-With
This makes a perfect appetizer or side dish. It's a terrific accompaniment to Italian Beef Roast (page 162).

✪ Did You Know?
Portabella mushrooms are usually about 4 to 6 inches in diameter and have a dense, meaty texture that makes them perfect for grilling.

Smoky Cheddar Potatoes

Prep: 10 min   Grill: 1 hr

4   medium potatoes, cut into 1-inch chunks
½   teaspoon salt
2   tablespoons butter or margarine
1   cup shredded Cheddar cheese (4 ounces)
2   tablespoons Betty Crocker Bac-Os® bacon flavor chips
2   medium green onions, sliced (2 tablespoons)

1. Heat coals or gas grill for direct heat. Place potatoes on 30 × 18-inch piece of heavy-duty aluminum foil. Sprinkle with salt. Dot with butter. Sprinkle with cheese and bacon chips.

2. Wrap foil securely around potatoes; pierce top of foil once or twice with fork to vent steam. Cover and grill foil packet, seam side up, 4 to 6 inches from medium heat 45 to 60 minutes or until potatoes are tender. Sprinkle with onions.

4 servings.

1 Serving: Calories 310 (Calories from Fat 145); Fat 16g (Saturated 10g); Cholesterol 45mg; Sodium 580mg; Carbohydrate 33g (Dietary Fiber 3g); Protein 12g
% Daily Value: Vitamin A 10%; Vitamin C 16%; Calcium 18%; Iron 12%
Diet Exchanges: 2 Starch, ½ High-Fat Meat, 2 Fat

BETTY'S TIPS

✪ Substitution
Use Swiss cheese instead of the Cheddar cheese. Instead of the bacon chips, you can use chopped red bell pepper.

Smoky Cheddar Potatoes

Betty ... MAKES IT EASY

Tangy Onion Flowers

Prep: 20 min   Grill: 1 hr

Cut ½-inch slice from top of each onion.

4	medium onions (each 4 to 5 ounces)
	Vegetable oil
¼	cup balsamic or cider vinegar
1	tablespoon chopped fresh or 1 teaspoon dried oregano leaves
1	tablespoon packed brown sugar
¼	teaspoon salt
¼	teaspoon pepper
⅓	cup seasoned croutons, crushed

1. Heat coals or gas grill for direct heat. Peel onions; cut ½-inch slice from top of each onion and leave root end. Cut each onion from top into 8 wedges to within ½ inch of root end. Gently pull wedges apart.

2. Brush four 18 × 12-inch pieces of heavy-duty aluminum foil with vegetable oil. Place 1 onion on each square; loosely shape foil around onion. Sprinkle onions with vinegar, oregano, brown sugar, salt and pepper. Wrap foil securely around onions.

3. Cover and grill onions 4 inches from medium heat 50 to 60 minutes or until very tender. To serve, sprinkle onions with croutons.

4 servings.

1 Serving: Calories 70 (Calories from Fat 20); Fat 2g (Saturated 0g); Cholesterol 0mg; Sodium 190mg; Carbohydrate 16g (Dietary Fiber 2g); Protein 2g
% Daily Value: Vitamin A 2%; Vitamin C 6%; Calcium 2%; Iron 2%
Diet Exchanges: 1 Starch

Cut each onion into 8 wedges.

Place onion on foil square, and sprinkle with topping.

Wrap foil securely around onion.

Tangy Onion Flowers

Baked Potatoes on the Grill

Prep: 5 min   Grill: 1 hr 15 min

4   medium baking potatoes
    Rock or kosher salt

1. Heat coals or gas grill for direct heat. Gently scrub potatoes. Pierce potatoes several times with fork to allow steam to escape while potatoes bake.

2. Pour 1-inch layer of salt in bottom of 2 disposable aluminum loaf pans, 8½ × 4½ × 2½ inches. Place 2 potatoes in salt in each pan; pour salt over potatoes until completely covered.

3. Cover and grill potatoes over medium heat 1 hour to 1 hour 15 minutes or until potatoes feel tender when pierced in center with fork. Carefully remove potatoes from salt.

4 servings.

1 Serving: Calories 125 (Calories from Fat 0); Fat 0g (Saturated 0g); Cholesterol 0mg; Sodium 305mg; Carbohydrate 31g (Dietary Fiber 3g); Protein 3g
% Daily Value: Vitamin A 0%; Vitamin C 12%; Calcium 0%; Iron 8%
Diet Exchanges: 1 Starch, 1 Fruit

Baked Potatoes on the Grill

Veggie Burger Pitas

Prep: 10 min   Grill: 10 min

1   medium bell pepper, cut into thin strips
1   medium onion, cut into thin slices
1   cup sliced mushrooms (3 ounces)
1   package (about 12.8 ounces) frozen vegetable burgers (4 burgers)
    Cooking spray
¼   teaspoon seasoned salt
    Dill Cucumber Topping (right)
2   pita breads (6 inches in diameter), cut in half to form pockets
4   leaves red leaf lettuce

1. Heat coals or gas grill for direct heat. Place bell pepper, onion and mushrooms in grill basket. Spray vegetables and burgers with cooking spray; sprinkle with seasoned salt.

2. Cover and grill vegetables and burgers 8 to 10 minutes or until vegetables are tender and burgers are hot.

3. Spread Dill Cucumber Topping on insides of pita bread pockets. Fill each pita bread half with lettuce, burger and vegetables.

4 sandwiches.

Dill Cucumber Topping

2   tablespoons mayonnaise or salad dressing
2   tablespoons sour cream
1   tablespoon chopped cucumber
1   tablespoon chopped fresh dill weed

Mix all ingredients.

1 Sandwich: Calories 255 (Calories from Fat 100); Fat 11g (Saturated 2g); Cholesterol 10mg; Sodium 690mg; Carbohydrate 24g (Dietary Fiber 3g); Protein 18g
% Daily Value: Vitamin A 4%; Vitamin C 24%; Calcium 6%; Iron 22%
Diet Exchanges: 1 Starch, 2 Lean Meat, 2 Vegetable, ½ Fat

BETTY'S TIPS

✪ Substitution
Use 4 whole wheat buns or pita bread folds instead of the pita breads. Plain yogurt can be used instead of the sour cream in the Dill Cucumber Topping.

✪ Time-Saver
The Dill Cucumber Topping can be made up to a day ahead of time and stored in the refrigerator.

Veggie Burger Pitas

Lemon Shrimp with Squash

Prep: 10 min   Marinate: 15 min   Grill: 14 min

Lemon Rosemary Marinade (below)
1 pound uncooked fresh or frozen large shrimp in shells
2 medium zucchini, cut into 1-inch slices
2 medium yellow summer squash, cut into 1-inch slices
1 small bell pepper, cut into 1-inch wedges
1 small lemon, cut into wedges

1. Make Lemon Rosemary Marinade. Add shrimp, zucchini, yellow squash and bell pepper to marinade; stir to coat. Cover dish or seal bag and refrigerate 15 to 30 minutes, stirring occasionally. Heat coals or gas grill for direct heat.

2. Remove shrimp and vegetables from marinade; discard marinade. Place shrimp and vegetables in grill basket.

3. Cover and grill shrimp and vegetables 4 to 5 inches from medium heat 12 to 14 minutes or until shrimp are pink and firm and vegetables are tender. To serve, peel shrimp. Serve with lemon wedges.

4 servings.

Lemon Rosemary Marinade
2 tablespoons honey
1 teaspoon grated lemon peel
¼ cup lemon juice
1 teaspoon chopped fresh or ½ teaspoon dried rosemary leaves, crumbled

Mix all ingredients in shallow glass or plastic dish or resealable plastic food-storage bag.

1 Serving: Calories 110 (Calories from Fat 10); Fat 1g (Saturated 0g); Cholesterol 105mg; Sodium 130mg; Carbohydrate 14g (Dietary Fiber 3g); Protein 14g
% Daily Value: Vitamin A 22%; Vitamin C 34%; Calcium 6%; Iron 14%
Diet Exchanges: 1½ Very Lean Meat, 3 Vegetable

BETTY'S TIPS

☺ **Success Hint**
If you use medium shrimp, add the shrimp for the last 5 to 7 minutes of grilling and cook until the shrimp are pink and firm.

Lemon Garlic Halibut Steaks

Prep: 5 min   Marinate: 10 min   Grill: 15 min

¼ cup lemon juice
1 tablespoon vegetable oil
¼ teaspoon salt
¼ teaspoon pepper
2 cloves garlic, finely chopped
4 halibut or tuna steaks, about 1 inch thick (about 2 pounds)
¼ cup chopped fresh parsley
1 tablespoon grated lemon peel

1. Brush grill rack with vegetable oil. Heat coals or gas grill for direct heat. Mix lemon juice, oil, salt, pepper and garlic in shallow glass or plastic dish or resealable plastic food-storage bag. Add fish; turn several times to coat with marinade. Cover dish or seal bag and refrigerate 10 minutes.

2. Remove fish from marinade; reserve marinade. Cover and grill fish 4 to 6 inches from medium heat 10 to 15 minutes, turning once and brushing with marinade, until fish flakes easily with fork. Discard any remaining marinade.

3. Sprinkle fish with parsley and lemon peel.

4 servings.

1 Serving: Calories 220 (Calories from Fat 45); Fat 5g (Saturated 1g); Cholesterol 120mg; Sodium 290mg; Carbohydrate 1g (Dietary Fiber 0g); Protein 43g
% Daily Value: Vitamin A 6%; Vitamin C 4%; Calcium 4%; Iron 4%
Diet Exchanges: 6½ Very Lean Meat

BETTY'S TIPS

☺ **Success Hint**
You will need 1 large lemon for 1 tablespoon grated lemon peel and ¼ cup of juice.

☺ **Serve-With**
Fish on the grill makes a quick and easy weeknight meal. Serve with grilled lemon halves. Cover and grill lemons, cut sides down, 2 to 3 minutes. Heating helps release the juices.

Lemon Shrimp with Squash

Lemon Garlic Halibut Steaks

Salmon with Tropical Fruit Salsa

Prep: 15 min   Chill: 1 hr

2   kiwifruit, peeled and chopped

1   mango, cut lengthwise in half, pitted and chopped

1   papaya, peeled, seeded and chopped

1   jalapeño chili, seeded and finely chopped

1   cup pineapple chunks

1   tablespoon finely chopped red onion

1   tablespoon chopped fresh cilantro

2   tablespoons lime juice

8   salmon fillets (5 ounces each)

1. Mix all ingredients in glass or plastic bowl.

2. Cover and refrigerate 1 to 2 hours to blend flavors.

3. Heat coals or gas grill for direct heat. Spray grill grid with cooking spray. Place fish on grill grid. Cover and grill fish 5 to 6 inches from medium heat for 8 minutes, turning once, or until fish flakes easily. Serve with the salsa.

8 servings.

Per Serving: Calories 320 (Calories from Fat 140); Fat 16g (Saturated 3g); Cholesterol 85mg; Sodium 85mg; Carbohydrate 17g (Dietary Fiber 2g); Protein 29g
% Daily Value: Vitamin A 25%; Vitamin C 100%; Calcium 4%; Iron 4%
Diet Exchanges: 4 Lean Meat, 1 Fruit, 1 Fat

BETTY'S TIPS

⊛ **Substitution**
If mango and papaya are not available, try substituting a combination of peaches, nectarines, plums and apricots.

⊛ **Success Hint**
We find this salsa has the fullest flavor when served at room temperature, so let it stand a few minutes after it has been refrigerated.

Salmon with Tropical Fruit Salsa

Mediterranean Grilled Tuna Sandwich

Prep: 10 min   Marinate: 30 min   Grill: 15 min   Chill: 30 min
Photo on page 143

¼ cup olive or vegetable oil

1 tablespoon chopped fresh or 1 teaspoon dried thyme leaves

1 tablespoon red wine vinegar

¼ teaspoon salt

Dash of pepper

1 clove garlic, finely chopped

½ pound tuna, or marlin fillets, ¾ to 1 inch thick

1 medium tomato, seeded and coarsely chopped (¾ cup)

¼ medium red onion, thinly sliced

2 tablespoons chopped pitted Kalamata or ripe olives

2 tablespoons chopped fresh Italian or regular parsley

2 teaspoons capers

1 loaf (½ pound) unsliced crusty Italian, French or sourdough bread

2 leaves romaine, shredded

1. Mix oil, thyme, vinegar, salt, pepper and garlic. Pour half of oil mixture over fish fillets in shallow glass or plastic dish or resealable plastic food-storage bag; turn fish to coat with marinade. Cover dish or seal bag and refrigerate at least 30 minutes but no longer than 1 hour. Mix remaining oil mixture, the tomato, onion, olives, parsley and capers; cover and refrigerate.

2. Heat coals or gas grill for direct heat. Remove fish from marinade; reserve marinade. Cover and grill fish 5 to 6 inches from medium heat 10 to 15 minutes, brushing 2 or 3 times with marinade and turning once, until fish flakes easily with fork. Break fish into chunks.

3. Cut off top one-third of bread loaf. Hollow out both parts, leaving ½-inch-thick crust. Arrange romaine on bottom half of bread. Top with fish. Spoon tomato mixture evenly over fish. Replace top piece of bread. Wrap loaf in plastic wrap or aluminum foil and refrigerate 30 to 60 minutes. Unwrap and cut into 4 pieces.

4 servings.

1 Serving: Calories 325 (Calories from Fat 145); Fat 16g (Saturated 3g); Cholesterol 35mg; Sodium 660mg; Carbohydrate 31g (Dietary Fiber 2g); Protein 16g
% Daily Value: Vitamin A 12%; Vitamin C 8%; Calcium 6%; Iron 14%
Diet Exchanges: 2 Starch, 2 Lean Meat, 1 Fat

BETTY'S TIPS

❂ **Serve-With**
Enjoy these sandwiches with a colorful assortment of fresh fruit.

❂ **Do-Ahead**
This wonderful grilled sandwich is perfect for picnics. It can be made up to an hour before serving and transported to the picnic in a cooler.

Barbecued Chicken Tortilla Pizzas

Prep: 5 min   Grill: 8 min

2   flour tortillas (10 inches in diameter)
1½ cups Lloyd's barbeque shredded chicken (from 32-ounce tub)
⅔   cup chopped tomato
2   cups shredded Monterey Jack cheese with jalapeño peppers (8 ounces)
    Salsa, if desired

1. Heat coals or gas grill for direct heat. Top each tortilla with ¾ cup of the chicken, ⅓ cup of the tomatoes and 1 cup of the cheese.

2. Place tortillas on grill. Cover and grill 5 inches from medium heat 6 to 8 minutes or until chicken is hot and cheese is melted. Cut each tortilla into 8 wedges. Serve with salsa.

16 appetizers.

1 Appetizer: Calories 110 (Calories from Fat 55); Fat 6g (Saturated 3g); Cholesterol 20mg; Sodium 280mg; Carbohydrate 8g (Dietary Fiber 0g); Protein 6g
% Daily Value: Vitamin A 4%; Vitamin C 2%; Calcium 12%; Iron 4%
Diet Exchanges: ½ Starch, ½ Lean Meat, 1 Fat

BETTY'S TIPS

☺ Substitution
If you prefer a little less spice, use plain Monterey Jack cheese. Chopped red bell pepper can be used instead of the tomato.

Barbecued Chicken Tortilla Pizzas

Spicy Southwest Chicken Kabobs

Prep: 10 min   Grill: 20 min

1   tablespoon garlic pepper
2   tablespoons olive or vegetable oil
4   small ears fresh corn, husks removed
1½ pounds boneless, skinless chicken breasts, cut into 1-inch cubes
2   medium yellow or red bell peppers, cut into 1½-inch pieces
¾   cup ranch dressing
1   canned chipotle chili in adobo sauce, chopped

1. Heat coals or gas grill for direct heat. Mix garlic pepper and oil. Cut each ear of corn into 3 pieces. Thread chicken, corn and bell peppers alternately on each of six 10- to 12-inch metal skewers, leaving space between each piece. Brush kabobs with oil mixture.

2. Cover and grill kabobs 4 to 5 inches from medium heat 15 to 20 minutes, turning 2 or 3 times, until chicken is no longer pink in center.

3. Mix dressing and chili. Serve with kabobs.

6 servings.

1 Serving: Calories 390 (Calories from Fat 205); Fat 23g (Saturated 3g); Cholesterol 80mg; Sodium 400mg; Carbohydrate 20g (Dietary Fiber 2g); Protein 28g
% Daily Value: Vitamin A 6%; Vitamin C 64%; Calcium 6%; Iron 10%
Diet Exchanges: 1 Starch, 3 Lean Meat, 1 Vegetable, 2½ Fat

BETTY'S TIPS

☺ Variation
The ranch dressing mixture makes a great-tasting dip for vegetables.

☺ Do-Ahead
For quick and easy grilling, cut the chicken and vegetables the night before. Store in resealable plastic food-storage bags in the refrigerator.

Spicy Southwest Chicken Kabobs

Italian Chicken Packets

Prep: 10 min   Grill: 22 min

4 boneless, skinless chicken breast halves (about 1¼ pounds)

1 medium yellow bell pepper, cut into 4 wedges

4 roma (plum) tomatoes, cut in half

1 small red onion, cut into 8 wedges

½ cup Italian vinaigrette dressing

1. Heat coals or gas grill for direct heat. Place 1 chicken breast half, 1 bell pepper wedge, 2 tomato halves and 2 onion wedges on one side of four 18 × 12-inch sheets of heavy-duty aluminum foil. Pour 2 table-spoons dressing over chicken and vegetable mixture on each packet.

2. Fold foil over chicken and vegetables so edges meet. Seal edges, making tight ½-inch fold, fold again. Allow space on sides for circulation and expansion.

3. Grill packets 4 to 5 inches from medium heat 18 to 22 minutes or until juice of chicken is no longer pink when centers are cut. Place packets on plates. Cut large X across tops of packets; fold back foil.

4 servings.

1 Serving: Calories 290 (Calories from Fat 145); Fat 16g (Saturated 2g); Cholesterol 75mg; Sodium 340mg; Carbohydrate 9g (Dietary Fiber 1g); Protein 28g
% Daily Value: Vitamin A 10%; Vitamin C 54%; Calcium 6%; Iron 8%
Diet Exchanges: 3½ Lean Meat, 2 Vegetable, 1 Fat

BETTY'S TIPS

⚙ **Success Hint**
If you have time, marinate the chicken in Italian dressing for 1 to 2 hours before grilling.

⚙ **Serve-With**
These colorful packets are a meal in themselves. Serve with French bread to sop up the flavorful juices.

Italian Chicken Packets

Orange-Marinated Chicken with Peppers and Potatoes

Prep: 20 min   Marinate: 1 hr   Grill: 20 min

4   medium red potatoes, cut into fourths
Orange Marinade (below)

4   boneless, skinless chicken breast halves
(1¼ pounds)

2   medium bell peppers, each cut lengthwise
into eighths
Sliced green onions, if desired

1. Place potatoes in microwavable dish. Cover tightly and microwave on High 2 minutes.

2. Make Orange Marinade. Add potatoes, chicken and bell peppers to marinade; turn to coat. Cover dish or seal bag and refrigerate at least 1 hour but no longer than 24 hours.

3. Heat coals or gas grill for direct heat. Remove potatoes, chicken and peppers from marinade; discard marinade. Place potatoes and bell peppers in grill basket or on grill; add chicken to grill. Grill chicken, potatoes and bell peppers uncovered 4 to 6 inches from medium heat 15 to 20 minutes, turning once, until vegetables are tender and juice of chicken is no longer pink when centers of thickest pieces are cut. Garnish with onions.

4 servings.

Orange Marinade

¼   cup frozen (thawed) orange juice concentrate

¼   cup olive or vegetable oil

1   tablespoon chopped fresh or 1 teaspoon dried thyme leaves

2   tablespoons white vinegar

2   tablespoons honey

2   teaspoons grated orange peel

¼   teaspoon salt

Mix all ingredients in shallow glass or plastic dish or re-sealable plastic food-storage bag.

1 Serving: Calories 405 (Calories from Fat 115); Fat 13g (Saturated 2g); Cholesterol 75mg; Sodium 180mg; Carbohydrate 46g (Dietary Fiber 4g); Protein 30g
% Daily Value: Vitamin A 4%; Vitamin C 70%; Calcium 2%; Iron 16%
Diet Exchanges: 2 Starch, 3 Lean Meat, 3 Vegetable

BETTY'S TIPS

⊙ Do-Ahead
Get a start on this one-dish meal in the morning by marinating the potatoes, chicken and peppers during the day. By dinnertime, the food will be flavorful and ready to cook.

Orange-Marinated Chicken with Peppers and Potatoes

Grilled Rib Eye Sandwiches

Turkey Breast with Lemon and Basil

Turkey Breast
with Lemon and Basil

Prep: 15 min   Grill: 1 hr 5 min   Stand: 10 min

2   pound boneless turkey breast half with untorn skin
1   small lemon, thinly sliced
10   fresh basil leaves
     Olive or vegetable oil
½   teaspoon lemon pepper

1. If using charcoal grill, place drip pan directly under grilling area, and arrange coals around edge of firebox. Heat coals or gas grill for indirect heat. Loosen skin on turkey in 4 or 5 places. Carefully place lemon slices and basil leaves under skin. Rub turkey skin with oil; sprinkle with lemon pepper. Insert barbeque meat thermometer so tip is in thickest part of turkey.

2. Cover and grill turkey, skin side down, over drip pan or over unheated side of gas grill and 4 to 6 inches from medium heat 20 minutes; turn. Cover and grill 35 to 45 minutes longer or until thermometer reads 170° and juice of turkey is no longer pink when center is cut.

3. Remove turkey from grill; cover with aluminum foil tent and let stand 10 minutes. Slice turkey.

6 servings.

1 Serving: Calories 225 (Calories from Fat 100); Fat 11g (Saturated 3g); Cholesterol 85mg; Sodium 70mg; Carbohydrate 0g (Dietary Fiber 0g); Protein 31g
% Daily Value: Vitamin A 2%; Vitamin C 0%; Calcium 2%; Iron 6%
Diet Exchanges: 3½ Lean Meat

BETTY'S TIPS

✲ Success Hint
Don't slice the turkey the minute you take it off the grill because this will cause the juices to run out. Instead, cover the turkey with foil and let it rest for a few minutes.

✲ Serve-With
Fresh lemon and basil combine to give this turkey breast a moist texture and subtle Italian flavor. Enjoy with Grilled Spring Vegetables (page 144) and a tossed salad.

Grilled Rib Eye
Sandwiches

Prep: 10 min   Bake: 16 min   Grill: 12 min

¼   cup steak sauce
4   beef boneless rib eye steaks (about 5 ounces each)
4   slices French bread, 1 inch thick, toasted
1   package (8 ounces) frozen onion rings, baked

1. Heat coals or gas grill for direct heat. Brush steak sauce on both sides of beef.

2. Cover and grill beef 4 to 5 inches from medium heat 7 to 12 minutes, turning once, until desired doneness.

3. Serve beef on bread slices and top with onion rings. Serve with additional steak sauce if desired.

4 sandwiches.

1 Sandwich: Calories 540 (Calories from Fat 235); Fat 26g (Saturated 9g); Cholesterol 80mg; Sodium 720mg; Carbohydrate 41g (Dietary Fiber 2g); Protein 37g
% Daily Value: Vitamin A 4%; Vitamin C 2%; Calcium 6%; Iron 26%
Diet Exchanges: 3 Starch, 4 Medium-Fat Meat

BETTY'S TIPS

✲ Substitution
Serve with grilled sliced onions instead of the onion rings. Cut 2 red onions into ¼-inch slices and place on heavy-duty aluminum foil. Wrap the foil around the onions, and pierce the foil with a fork. Grill 5 to 10 minutes or until tender.

✲ Serve-With
Enjoy this sizzling summer sandwich with Smoky Cheddar Potatoes (page 147) and fresh fruit.

Garlic and Mustard Burgers

Prep: 15 min   Grill: 15 min

1	pound ground beef
3	tablespoons country-style Dijon mustard
5	cloves garlic, finely chopped
4	hamburger buns, split
4	slices (1 ounce each) Monterey Jack cheese
	Lettuce leaves
1	jar (7 ounces) roasted red bell peppers, drained

1. Heat coals or gas grill for direct heat. Mix beef, mustard and garlic. Shape mixture into 4 patties, about ¾ inch thick.

2. Cover and grill patties 4 to 5 inches from medium heat 13 to 15 minutes, turning once, until no longer pink in center and juice is clear. Add buns, cut sides down, for last 4 minutes of grilling or until toasted. Top burgers with cheese.

3. Serve burgers on buns with lettuce and bell peppers.

4 servings.

1 Serving: Calories 475 (Calories from Fat 245); Fat 27g (Saturated 12g); Cholesterol 90mg; Sodium 750mg; Carbohydrate 28g (Dietary Fiber 2g); Protein 32g
% Daily Value: Vitamin A 64%; Vitamin C 72%; Calcium 28%; Iron 20%
Diet Exchanges: 2 Starch, 4 Medium-Fat Meat

Garlic and Mustard Burgers

Italian Beef Roast

Prep: 5 min   Grill: 2 hr   Stand: 15 min

3- to 4	pound beef boneless sirloin tip roast
1 to 2	tablespoons olive or vegetable oil
1	envelope (0.7 ounce) Italian dressing mix

1. If using charcoal grill, place drip pan directly under grilling area, and arrange coals around edge of firebox. Heat coals or gas grill for indirect heat.

2. Brush beef with oil; sprinkle evenly with dressing mix (dry). Insert barbecue meat thermometer so tip is in thickest part of beef.

3. Cover and grill beef over drip pan or over unheated side of gas grill and 4 to 5 inches from medium heat 1 hour 30 minutes to 2 hours or until thermometer reads 140°. Cover beef with aluminum foil and let stand about 15 minutes or until thermometer reads 145°. (Temperature will continue to rise about 5°, and beef will be easier to carve.)

12 to 14 servings.

1 Serving: Calories 135 (Calories from Fat 45); Fat 5g (Saturated 1g); Cholesterol 60mg; Sodium 45mg; Carbohydrate 0g (Dietary Fiber 0g); Protein 23g
% Daily Value: Vitamin A 0%; Vitamin C 0%; Calcium 0%; Iron 12%
Diet Exchanges: 3 Very Lean Meat, 1 Fat

BETTY'S TIPS

☼ Do-Ahead

Grill the roast on the weekend, and use the leftovers for salads and sandwiches during the week.

Or you can freeze any leftovers for later use. Seal in a freezer container and freeze up to 4 months. Thaw frozen beef by placing the container in the refrigerator about 8 hours.

Italian Beef Roast

Cuban Pork Chops

Prep: 5 min   Grill: 10 min

4   pork boneless loin or rib chops, about 1 inch
     thick (about 2 pounds)
     Cuban Rub (below)
     Mango slices, if desired

1. Heat coals or gas grill for direct heat. Remove excess
   fat from pork. Make Cuban Rub; rub evenly on both
   sides of pork.

2. Cover and grill pork 4 to 6 inches from medium heat
   8 to 10 minutes, turning frequently, until slightly pink
   in center. Garnish with mango slices.

4 servings.

Cuban Rub

2   tablespoons grated lime peel
1   tablespoon cracked black pepper
1   tablespoon cumin seed
2   tablespoons olive or vegetable oil
½   teaspoon salt
1   clove garlic, finely chopped

Mix all ingredients.

1 Serving: Calories 410 (Calories from Fat 215); Fat 24g (Saturated 7g);
Cholesterol 140mg; Sodium 380mg; Carbohydrate 1g (Dietary Fiber
0g); Protein 48g
% Daily Value: Vitamin A 0%; Vitamin C 2%; Calcium 0%; Iron 10%
Diet Exchanges: 7 Lean Meat, 1 Fat

BETTY'S TIPS

⚙ **Substitution**
If you don't have cumin seed on hand, use 1 teaspoon
ground cumin.

⚙ **Serve-With**
Round out these flavor-packed pork chops with corn on
the cob and cooked rice tossed with black beans.

⚙ **Variation**
The Cuban Rub is also delicious on chicken breasts.

Cuban Pork Chops

Pork Tenderloin with Grilled Plums

Prep: 15 min   Marinate: 1 hr   Grill: 25 min

   Port Wine Marinade (right)
2 pork tenderloins (about ¾ pound each)
6 plums, pitted and cut in half
¼ cup plum jam

1. Make Port Wine Marinade. Place pork in shallow glass or plastic dish. Using meat injector, fill injector container to 1-ounce line. Inject marinade into pork every 1 to 2 inches, pushing plunger down slowly. Refill container and continue to inject marinade until marinade is used. Cover and refrigerate 1 hour.

2. Heat coals or gas grill for direct heat. Cover and grill pork 4 to 5 inches from medium heat 20 to 25 minutes, brushing with jam during last minute of grilling, until pork is slightly pink in center. Add plums to grill for last 4 to 6 minutes, brushing with jam during last minute of grilling, until hot.

3. Cut pork into slices; serve with plums.

6 servings.

Port Wine Marinade

¼ cup port wine
¼ cup orange juice
1 tablespoon cider vinegar
½ teaspoon garlic salt

Mix all ingredients.

1 Serving: Calories 220 (Calories from Fat 45); Fat 5g (Saturated 2g); Cholesterol 70mg; Sodium 110mg; Carbohydrate 19g (Dietary Fiber 1g); Protein 26g
% Daily Value: Vitamin A 2%; Vitamin C 8%; Calcium 0%; Iron 8%
Diet Exchanges: 4 Very Lean Meat, 1 Fruit, ½ Fat

BETTY'S TIPS

✪ **Substitution**
You can use apple juice instead of the port wine.

✪ **Variation**
If you do not have an injector, pour the marinade over the pork in a shallow glass dish, and cover and refrigerate 1 hour.

Pork Tenderloin with Grilled Plums

Betty . . .
ON WHAT'S COOKING

Grill Master's Guide

KEEPING SAFE

These tips will ensure your grilled meal is safe to eat.

▦ Trim visible fat from meats to avoid flare-ups.

▦ Always marinate foods in the refrigerator, not on the counter.

▦ Always serve grilled meat on a clean plate. Never serve cooked meat from the same unwashed plate you used to carry raw meat to the grill.

▦ If you want to reuse a marinade (that has had raw meat in it) as a sauce, heat the marinade to boiling, then boil one minute before serving.

▦ Perishable food should be eaten within two hours; one hour if the temperature is 90° or above.

If you're grilling. . .	use this grilling method. . .	and grill over this heat. . .	for this long. . .	or until . . .
Hamburgers (¾ inch thick)	Direct	Medium	13 to 15 minutes	no longer pink in the center and juice is clear
Hot dogs or cooked bratwurst	Direct	Medium	10 to 15 minutes	hot
Fish fillets (¾ to 1 inch thick)	Direct	Medium	10 to 15 minutes	fish flakes easily with fork
Fish steaks (¾ to 1 inch thick)	Direct	Medium	15 to 20 minutes	fish flakes easily with fork
Whole fish (1½ pounds)	Direct	Medium	20 to 25 minutes	fish flakes easily with fork
Shrimp (1 pound large)	Direct	Medium	3 to 5 minutes	pink and firm
Chicken breast halves (bone-in) (1 pound)	Direct	Medium	20 to 25 minutes	juice of chicken is no longer pink
Cut-up broiler-fryer chicken (3 to 3½ pounds)	Direct	Medium	35 to 55 minutes	juice of chicken is no longer pink
Chicken legs (2 pounds)	Direct	Medium	20 to 25 minutes	juice of chicken is no longer pink
Chicken thighs (2½ to 3 pounds)	Direct	Medium	20 to 25 minutes	juice of chicken is no longer pink
Chicken wings (2 to 2½ pounds)	Direct	Medium	12 to 18 minutes	juice of chicken is no longer pink
Chicken breasts and thighs (boneless) (1¼ pounds)	Direct	Medium	15 to 20 minutes	juice of chicken is no longer pink

If you're grilling...	use this grilling method...	and grill over this heat...	for this long...	or until . . .
Whole broiler-fryer chicken (3 to 3½ pounds)	Indirect	Medium	1½ to 2¼ hours	meat thermometer reads 180° and juice of chicken is no longer pink
Turkey breast tenderloins (1 to 1½ pounds)	Direct	Medium	20 to 30 minutes	juice of turkey is no longer pink
Whole turkey breast (3½ to 4 pounds)	Indirect	Medium	1¼ to 1½ hours	meat thermometer reads 170° and juice of turkey is no longer pink
Whole turkey (8 to 10 pounds)	Indirect	Medium	2¾ to 3 hours	meat thermometer reads 180° and juice of turkey is no longer pink
Pork chops (1 inch thick)	Direct	Medium	8 to 12 minutes	slightly pink when cut near bone
Pork ribs (3 to 4 pounds)	Indirect	Medium	50 to 70 minutes	no longer pink when cut near bone
Pork loin roast (3 pounds)	Indirect	Medium-Low	1 hour	meat thermometer reads 160°
Pork tenderloin (1 pound)	Direct	Medium	15 to 20 minutes	meat thermometer reads 160°
Beef T-bone steaks (1 inch thick)	Direct	Medium	14 to 16 minutes	desired doneness
Beef flank steak (1½ pounds)	Direct	Medium	12 to 15 minutes	desired doneness
Beef rib eye steaks (¾ inch thick)	Direct	Medium	6 to 8 minutes	desired doneness
Beef sirloin steak (¾ inch thick)	Direct	Medium	13 to 16 minutes	desired doneness
Corn on the cob	Direct	Medium	20 to 30 minutes	tender
Zucchini slices, whole green beans, bell pepper strips	Direct	Medium	10 to 15 minutes	crisp-tender
Whole mushrooms, small whole onions, onion slices, asparagus spears	Direct	Medium	5 to 10 minutes	tender

Zesty Lemon Spareribs

Prep: 15 min   Cook: 1 hr 30 min
Marinate: 4 hr   Grill: 30 min

6   pounds pork spareribs, cut into serving pieces
1   can (6 ounces) frozen lemonade concentrate, thawed
¾   cup purchased barbecue sauce

1. Place pork in 4-quart Dutch oven. Add enough water to cover pork. Heat to boiling; reduce heat to low. Cover and simmer about 1 hour 30 minutes or until tender.

2. Remove pork to rectangular baking dish, 13 × 9 × 2 inches, or resealable plastic food-storage bag. Mix lemonade concentrate and barbecue sauce. Reserve some marinade for basting. Pour over pork; turn pork to coat with marinade. Cover dish or seal bag and refrigerate, turning pork occasionally, at least 4 hours but no longer than 24 hours.

3. Heat coals or gas grill for direct heat. Remove pork from marinade; discard the reserved marinade. Grill pork, meaty sides up, uncovered and 4 inches from medium heat about 30 minutes, turning and brushing frequently with marinade, until glazed and heated through. Discard any remaining marinade.

8 servings.

1 Serving: Calories 630 (Calories from Fat 390); Fat 43g (Saturated 15g); Cholesterol 160mg; Sodium 160mg; Carbohydrate 14g (Dietary Fiber 0g); Protein 40g
% Daily Value: Vitamin A 6%; Vitamin C 4%; Calcium 6%; Iron 16%
Diet Exchanges: 1 Starch, 5½ High-Fat Meat

BETTY'S TIPS

✪ Serve-With
Serve these sweet, lemony ribs with a platter of farmers' market vegetables hot off the grill. Most vegetables can be grilled in 10 to 15 minutes (see page 165).

✪ Did You Know?
Zippered plastic food-storage bags are great for mess-free marinating. Place meat and marinade in bag and squeeze out all the air, allowing marinade to completely coat the food. When it's time to grill, take the bag outside and transfer the marinated meat to the grill.

Focaccia with Grilled Garlic

Prep: 5 min   Grill: 35 min

2   large bulbs garlic
1   tablespoon olive or vegetable oil
1   teaspoon chopped fresh or ¼ teaspoon dried thyme leaves
1   round focaccia bread, 12 inches in diameter (16 ounces)

1. Heat coals or gas grill for direct heat. Peel loose paperlike layers from garlic bulbs, but do not separate cloves. Place each garlic bulb on 18-inch square of heavy-duty aluminum foil. Brush with oil; sprinkle with thyme. Wrap bulbs securely in foil.

2. Cover and grill garlic 4 to 6 inches from medium heat 25 to 35 minutes or until garlic cloves are very soft. Add focaccia to side of grill for last 8 to 10 minutes of grilling, turning once, until golden brown. To serve, squeeze garlic out of individual cloves onto slices of focaccia.

6 servings.

1 Slice: Calories 240 (Calories from Fat 80); Fat 9g (Saturated 1g); Cholesterol 0mg; Sodium 0mg; Carbohydrate 36g (Dietary Fiber 1g); Protein 5g
% Daily Value: Vitamin A 0%; Vitamin C 0%; Calcium 0%; Iron 12%
Diet Exchanges: 2 Starch, 1 Vegetable, 1½ Fat

BETTY'S TIPS

✪ Substitution
Two 8-inch focaccias or 6-inch Italian pizza crusts can be used instead of the 12-inch focaccia.

✪ Success Hint
If focaccia browns too quickly, place a piece of aluminum foil between the focaccia and the grill.

Zesty Lemon Spareribs

Focaccia with Grilled Garlic

Stuffed French Bread

Prep: 15 min   Grill: 10 min

1   loaf (8 ounces) or ½ loaf (1-pound size) unsliced French bread

⅓   cup sun-dried tomato pesto or basil pesto

1   cup shredded mozzarella cheese (4 ounces)

1. Heat coals or gas grill for direct heat. Spray 18-inch piece of heavy-duty aluminum foil with cooking spray.

2. Cut bread loaf diagonally into 12 slices to within ½ inch of bottom of loaf. Spread pesto on both sides of slices. Sprinkle slices with cheese. Securely wrap loaf in aluminum foil.

3. Grill bread uncovered 5 to 6 inches from medium heat about 10 minutes, turning once, until hot.

6 servings.

1 Serving: Calories 225 (Calories from Fat 105); Fat 12g (Saturated 4g); Cholesterol 10mg; Sodium 440mg; Carbohydrate 20g (Dietary Fiber 1g); Protein 10g
% Daily Value: Vitamin A 4%; Vitamin C 0%; Calcium 22%; Iron 8%
Diet Exchanges: 1½ Starch, 1 High-Fat Meat

BETTY'S TIPS

⊙ **Success Hint**
If you don't have heavy-duty aluminum foil, use two sheets of regular foil.

⊙ **Do-Ahead**
You can assemble the bread and wrap it in foil up to 8 hours ahead of time. Keep it in the refrigerator until you're ready to grill.

Stuffed French Bread

On the Side

Family-Favorite Vegetables and Salads

Cranberry Streusel Sweet Potatoes (page 183)

Caribbean Crunch Squash (page 178)

Glazed Carrots

Prep: 5 min   Cook: 20 min

1½ pounds baby-cut carrots

⅓ cup packed brown sugar

2 tablespoons butter or margarine

½ teaspoon salt

½ teaspoon grated orange peel

1. Heat 1 inch water to boiling in 2-quart saucepan. Add carrots. Heat to boiling; reduce heat. Simmer uncovered 6 to 9 minutes or until crisp-tender; drain and set aside.

2. Cook remaining ingredients in 12-inch skillet over medium heat, stirring constantly, until bubbly.

3. Stir in carrots. Cook over low heat about 5 minutes, stirring occasionally, until carrots are glazed and hot.

6 servings.

1 Serving: Calories 120 (Calories from Fat 35); Fat 4g (Saturated 2g); Cholesterol 10mg; Sodium 260mg; Carbohydrate 23g (Dietary Fiber 3g); Protein 1g
% Daily Value: Vitamin A 100%; Vitamin C 8%; Calcium 4%; Iron 4%
Diet Exchanges: 2 Vegetable, 1 Fruit

BETTY'S TIPS

✪ Substitution
Instead of the baby-cut carrots, you can use 1½ bags (1-pound size) frozen sliced carrots, cooked as directed on package, or 1½ pounds regular carrots, cut into julienne strips, cooked as directed in step 1.

✪ Success Hint
If some of the baby-cut carrots are large, cut them lengthwise in half so all of the carrots cook in the same amount of time.

Carrots and Zucchini with Herbs

Prep: 10 min   Cook: 15 min

2 medium carrots, sliced (1 cup)

4 medium zucchini, cut into julienne strips (3 cups)

2 tablespoons butter or margarine

1 tablespoon chopped fresh or 1 teaspoon dried sage leaves

1 teaspoon chopped fresh or ¼ teaspoon dried dill weed

2 teaspoons lemon juice

¼ teaspoon salt

¼ teaspoon pepper

1. Place steamer basket in ½ inch water in saucepan (water should not touch bottom of basket). Place carrots in basket. Cover tightly and heat to boiling; reduce heat. Steam carrots 3 minutes. Add zucchini. Steam 4 to 6 minutes longer or until carrots and zucchini are crisp-tender.

2. Melt butter in 12-inch skillet over medium heat. Stir in carrots, zucchini and remaining ingredients. Cook uncovered 2 to 3 minutes, stirring gently, until hot.

4 servings.

1 Serving: Calories 90 (Calories from Fat 55); Fat 6g (Saturated 1g); Cholesterol 15mg; Sodium 200mg; Carbohydrate 9g (Dietary Fiber 3g); Protein 3g
% Daily Value: Vitamin A 100%; Vitamin C 16%; Calcium 4%; Iron 6%
Diet Exchanges: 2 Vegetable, 1 Fat

BETTY'S TIPS

✪ Health Twist
Zucchini is a summer squash variety that offers a mere 9 calories per half-cup. A colorful addition to many cooked dishes, zucchini can also be enjoyed raw. For a low-calorie snack, dip zucchini sticks into salsa or a fat-free sour cream dip.

Carrots and Zucchini with Herbs

Glazed Carrots

Betty ... MAKES IT EASY

Festive Pepper Bundles

Prep: 30 min   Cook: 2 min

Place 6 pepper strips on center of chive.

> 12 fresh chives (at least 6 inches long) or green part of green onion, cut into thin strips
> 2 medium red bell peppers
> 2 medium green bell peppers
>   Lemon Pepper Butter (below)
> ⅓ cup water

1. Place chives in shallow dish. Pour enough boiling water over chives just to cover; let stand 10 seconds so chives become pliable. Drain well; set aside.

2. Cut each pepper into eighteen 3 × ¼-inch strips (there may be extra strips; reserve for another use). To form each bundle, place 3 pepper strips side by side on center of chive. Top with 3 more pepper strips (alternate colors if desired). Tie chive around bundle. Repeat with remaining pepper strips and chives.

3. Make Lemon Pepper Butter; set aside.

4. Carefully transfer bundles to 10-inch nonstick skillet; add water. Heat to boiling; boil about 1 minute or until crisp-tender. Remove bundles to small serving plate, using slotted spoon or pancake turner; drizzle with Lemon Pepper Butter. Serve immediately.

Tie chive around bundle.

6 servings.

Lemon Pepper Butter
> ¼ cup butter or margarine
> 2 teaspoons finely shredded lemon peel
> ½ teaspoon lemon pepper

Heat all ingredients until butter is melted, stirring occasionally.

1 Serving: Calories 90 (Calories from Fat 70); Fat 8g (Saturated 5g); Cholesterol 20mg; Sodium 55mg; Carbohydrate 5g (Dietary Fiber 2g); Protein 1g
% Daily Value: Vitamin A 56%; Vitamin C 89%; Calcium 0%; Iron 2%
Diet Exchanges: 1 Vegetable, 1½ Fat

Festive Pepper Bundles

Lemon Pepper Crunch Vegetables

Prep: 5 min   Cook: 8 min

1   bag (1 pound) frozen cauliflower nuggets, carrots and pea pods

1¼ cups Country Corn Flakes cereal, coarsely crushed (½ cup)

1   tablespoon butter or margarine, melted

½   teaspoon lemon pepper

1. Cook vegetables as directed on package; drain well.

2. Just before serving, mix crushed cereal, butter and lemon pepper; sprinkle over vegetables and stir to coat. Serve immediately.

4 servings.

1 Serving: Calories 80 (Calories from Fat 25); Fat 3g (Saturated 2g); Cholesterol 10mg; Sodium 140mg; Carbohydrate 15g (Dietary Fiber 3g); Protein 3g
% Daily Value: Vitamin A 100%; Vitamin C 26%; Calcium 4%; Iron 20%
Diet Exchanges: ½ Starch, 1½ Vegetable

Nut- and Fruit-Filled Squash

Prep: 15 min   Bake: 50 min

1   buttercup squash (2 to 2½ pounds)

3   tablespoons butter or margarine, melted

¼   teaspoon salt

1   cup Basic 4® cereal, coarsely crushed (½ cup)

1   teaspoon grated orange peel

1. Heat oven to 350°. Cut squash into fourths; remove seeds and fibers. Place squash, cut sides up, in ungreased rectangular baking dish, 13 × 9 × 2 inches.

2. Brush cut sides of squash with 2 tablespoons of the butter; sprinkle with salt. Pour water into baking dish until ¼ inch deep. Cover and bake 40 to 50 minutes or until tender.

3. Mix remaining 1 tablespoon butter (melt again if necessary), cereal and orange peel; spoon into squash indentations.

4 servings.

1 Serving: Calories 180 (Calories from Fat 90); Fat 10g (Saturated 6g); Cholesterol 25mg; Sodium 290mg; Carbohydrate 26g (Dietary Fiber 6g); Protein 3g
% Daily Value: Vitamin A 100%; Vitamin C 16%; Calcium 10%; Iron 10%
Diet Exchanges: 1 Starch, 1 Fruit, 1 Fat

BETTY'S TIPS

✪ Substitution

Two acorn squash (1 to 1½ pounds each) can be substituted for the buttercup squash. This squash is also delicious with Honey Nut Clusters® or Harmony™ cereal sprinkled on top instead of the Basic 4 cereal.

Lemon Pepper Crunch Vegetables

Nut- and Fruit-Filled Squash

Caribbean Crunch Squash

Prep: 15 min   Bake: 1 hr

1 buttercup squash (2 to 2½ pounds)
2 tablespoons butter or margarine, melted
2 tablespoons peach or apricot preserves
2 tablespoons graham cracker crumbs
2 tablespoons shredded coconut
¼ teaspoon ground ginger
⅛ teaspoon ground allspice
⅛ teaspoon pepper

1. Heat oven to 350°. Cut squash into fourths; remove seeds and fibers. Place squash, cut sides up, in ungreased rectangular pan, 13 × 9 × 2 inches.

2. Mix butter and preserves. Brush about half of preserves mixture over cut sides of squash pieces. Mix remaining ingredients; sprinkle over squash. Drizzle with remaining preserves mixture.

3. Bake uncovered 45 to 60 minutes or until tender.

4 servings.

1 Serving: Calories 160 (Calories from Fat 70); Fat 8g (Saturated 5g); Cholesterol 15mg; Sodium 65mg; Carbohydrate 25g (Dietary Fiber 5g); Protein 2g
% Daily Value: Vitamin A 100%; Vitamin C 14%; Calcium 2%; Iron 4%
Diet Exchanges: ½ Starch, 1 Fruit, 1½ Fat

BETTY'S TIPS

☺ **Substitution**
Two acorn squash (1 to 1½ pounds each) can be substituted for the buttercup squash.

☺ **Serve-With**
Grilled pork chops, pork roast and pork tenderloin are excellent choices to serve with this sweetly spiced squash.

Caribbean Crunch Squash

Pan-Roasted Potatoes

Prep: 10 min   Bake: 50 min

6   medium baking potatoes (2 pounds)

1   medium red onion, coarsely chopped

2   tablespoons chopped fresh rosemary leaves

4   cloves garlic, finely chopped

½   teaspoon salt

½   teaspoon pepper

¼   cup olive or vegetable oil

¼   cup freshly grated or shredded Parmesan cheese

1. Heat oven to 375°. Peel potatoes if desired; cut into 1½-inch pieces. Toss potatoes, onion, rosemary, garlic, salt and pepper in rectangular pan, 15 × 10 × 2 inches. Drizzle with oil.

2. Bake uncovered 40 minutes, stirring occasionally. Sprinkle with cheese; toss until potatoes are evenly coated. Bake about 10 minutes longer or until potatoes are tender and golden brown.

4 servings.

1 Serving: Calories 310 (Calories from Fat 110); Fat 12g (Saturated 3g); Cholesterol 5mg; Sodium 430mg; Carbohydrate 47g (Dietary Fiber 5g); Protein 8g
% Daily Value: Vitamin A 4%; Vitamin C 24%; Calcium 12%; Iron 6%
Diet Exchanges: 3 Starch, 1½ Fat

BETTY'S TIPS

✪ Substitution

Two teaspoons of dried rosemary leaves can be substituted for the fresh rosemary.

We like the color of the red onion, but yellow onions can also be used.

Pan-Roasted Potatoes

Potatoes Stuffed with Pesto and Sun-Dried Tomatoes

Rosemary Parmesan Mashers

Potatoes Stuffed with Pesto and Sun-Dried Tomatoes

Prep: 20 min   Bake: 1 hr 35 min

         3   large baking potatoes (8 to 10 ounces each)
¼ to ½   cup milk
         ½   cup basil pesto
         ⅓   cup julienne sun-dried tomatoes packed in oil and herbs, drained
         ¼   cup sliced ripe olives, well drained
         ½   cup finely shredded Parmesan cheese
             Chopped fresh basil or parsley, if desired
             Additional shredded Parmesan cheese, if desired

1. Heat oven to 375°. Gently scrub potatoes, but do not peel. Pierce potatoes several times with fork. Bake 1 hour to 1 hour 15 minutes or until potatoes are tender when pierced in center with fork. Let stand until cool enough to handle.

2. Cut each potato lengthwise in half; scoop out inside, leaving a thin shell. Mash potatoes and milk in medium bowl with potato masher or electric mixer until no lumps remain (amount of milk needed will vary depending on type of potato used). Stir in pesto, tomatoes, olives and ½ cup cheese. Fill potato shells with mashed potato mixture. Place on ungreased cookie sheet.

3. Bake about 20 minutes or until hot. Sprinkle with basil and additional cheese.

6 servings.

1 Serving: Calories 235 (Calories from Fat 135); Fat 15g (Saturated 4g); Cholesterol 10mg; Sodium 410mg; Carbohydrate 19g (Dietary Fiber 2g); Protein 8g
% Daily Value: Vitamin A 6%; Vitamin C 12%; Calcium 22%; Iron 6%
Diet Exchanges: 1 Starch, 1 Vegetable, 3 Fat

BETTY'S TIPS

❂ **Do-Ahead**
Refrigerate filled potatoes tightly covered up to 48 hours. To reheat in oven, bake uncovered on ungreased cookie sheet at 375° about 30 minutes or until hot.

To reheat in microwave, arrange potatoes in circle on 10-inch microwavable plate. Cover loosely with plastic wrap and microwave on High 12 to 15 minutes, rotating plate one-half turn after 5 minutes, until hot.

Rosemary Parmesan Mashers

Prep: 10 min   Cook: 30 min   Stand: 5 min

         6   medium Yukon gold potatoes (2 pounds)
⅓ to ½   cup chicken broth
         ¼   cup olive or vegetable oil
         1   teaspoon chopped fresh or ¼ teaspoon dried rosemary leaves, crumbled
         ½   teaspoon salt
         1   cup shredded Parmesan cheese

1. Place potatoes in 2-quart saucepan; add enough water just to cover potatoes. Heat to boiling; reduce heat. Cover and simmer 20 to 30 minutes or until potatoes are tender; drain. Shake pan with potatoes over low heat to dry (this will help mashed potatoes be fluffier).

2. Mash potatoes in pan until no lumps remain. Add broth in small amounts, mashing after each addition (amount of broth needed to make potatoes smooth and fluffy will vary).

3. Add oil, rosemary, salt and cheese. Mash vigorously until potatoes are light and fluffy. Cover and let stand 5 minutes. Sprinkle with additional rosemary and Parmesan cheese if desired.

6 servings (about ½ cup each).

1 Serving: Calories 270 (Calories from Fat 125); Fat 14g (Saturated 4g); Cholesterol 15mg; Sodium 570mg; Carbohydrate 29g (Dietary Fiber 3g); Protein 10g
% Daily Value: Vitamin A 2%; Vitamin C 12%; Calcium 24%; Iron 10%
Diet Exchanges: 2 Starch, ½ Lean Meat, 2 Fat

BETTY'S TIPS

❂ **Substitution**
We love the buttery, rich taste of Yukon gold potatoes, but round red or round white potatoes can also be used.

❂ **Success Hint**
Mash potatoes only until they're light; overmixing will cause them to turn sticky and starchy.

❂ **Did You Know?**
Leaving the skin on adds lots of flavor and extra nutrition to mashed potatoes.

Mashed Potato Torta

Prep: 15 min   Bake: 30 min

1 teaspoon butter or margarine

16 medium green onions, sliced (1 cup)

1 teaspoon butter or margarine

1 medium red bell pepper, chopped (1 cup)

3 cups hot water

1 cup half-and-half

¼ cup butter or margarine

1 package Betty Crocker roasted garlic mashed potatoes (2 packets)

1½ cups shredded Cheddar cheese (6 ounces)

1. Heat oven to 350°. Lightly grease bottom and side of 1-quart casserole with shortening.

2. Melt 1 teaspoon butter in 8-inch nonstick skillet over medium-high heat. Cook onions in butter 1 minute, stirring occasionally. Remove from skillet; set aside. Melt 1 teaspoon butter in same skillet over medium-high heat. Cook bell pepper in butter 2 minutes, stirring occasionally. Remove from heat; set aside.

3. Heat water, half-and-half and ¼ cup butter to boiling in 2-quart saucepan; remove from heat. Stir in both packets of potatoes (and seasoning) just until moistened. Let stand about 1 minute or until liquid is absorbed. Beat with fork until smooth.

4. Spoon 1⅓ cups of the potatoes into casserole; sprinkle with peppers and ¾ cup of the cheese. Spoon another 1⅓ cups potatoes over cheese; carefully spread to cover. Sprinkle evenly with onions. Top with remaining potatoes; carefully spread to cover. Sprinkle with remaining ¾ cup cheese.

5. Bake uncovered about 30 minutes or until heated through.

8 servings.

1 Serving: Calories 290 (Calories from Fat 170); Fat 19g (Saturated 11g); Cholesterol 50mg; Sodium 530mg; Carbohydrate 23g (Dietary Fiber 2g); Protein 9g
% Daily Value: Vitamin A 34%; Vitamin C 28%; Calcium 16%; Iron 4%
Diet Exchanges: 1½ Starch, ½ High-Fat Meat, 3 Fat

BETTY'S TIPS

⚙ **Substitution**
Half-and-half is what makes these potatoes so rich and creamy. If you don't have it on hand, though, you can substitute milk.

⚙ **Do-Ahead**
You can make this yummy side dish up to 24 hours ahead of time. Follow directions through step 4. Cover and refrigerate up to 24 hours. Bake about 45 minutes or until heated through.

⚙ **Extra Special**
Get creative when topping this dish. After baking, garnish with tomato wedges, chopped bell pepper or sliced green onions.

Mashed Potato Torta

Cranberry Streusel Sweet Potatoes

Prep: 15 min   Cook: 30 min   Bake: 30 min

6 medium sweet potatoes, peeled
2 tablespoons butter or margarine
½ teaspoon salt
½ cup soft bread crumbs (about 1 slice bread)
¼ cup dried cranberries
¼ cup coarsely chopped pecans
2 tablespoons butter or margarine, melted

1. Place sweet potatoes in 3-quart saucepan; add enough water to cover. Cover and heat to boiling; reduce heat. Simmer 20 to 25 minutes or until tender; drain. Shake potatoes in saucepan over low heat to dry.

2. Heat oven to 350°. Mash potatoes with 2 tablespoons butter and the salt until no lumps remain. Spoon into ungreased 1-quart casserole. Mix remaining ingredients. Sprinkle over potatoes.

3. Bake uncovered about 30 minutes or until heated through and streusel mixture is golden brown.

6 servings.

1 Serving: Calories 265 (Calories from Fat 100); Fat 11g (Saturated 5g); Cholesterol 20mg; Sodium 290mg; Carbohydrate 44g (Dietary Fiber 5g); Protein 3g
% Daily Value: Vitamin A 100%; Vitamin C 30%; Calcium 4%; Iron 4%
Diet Exchanges: 1 Starch, 2 Fruit, 1½ Fat

BETTY'S TIPS

☺ Simplify
Substitute a 23-ounce can of sweet potatoes, drained, for the cooked fresh sweet potatoes. Mash as directed in step 2.

☺ Do-Ahead
To make this a day ahead of time, follow directions through step 2. Cover and refrigerate up to 24 hours. Bake uncovered 45 to 60 minutes or until heated through and streusel mixture is golden brown.

Cranberry Streusel Sweet Potatoes

Caramelized-Onion and Sweet Potato Skillet

Prep: 10 min   Cook: 20 min

1 teaspoon vegetable oil

¼ large sweet onion (Bermuda, Maui, Spanish or Vidalia), sliced

3 medium sweet potatoes, peeled and sliced (3½ cups)

2 tablespoons packed brown sugar

½ teaspoon jerk seasoning (dry)

1 tablespoon chopped fresh parsley

1. Heat oil in 10-inch nonstick skillet over medium heat. Cook onion and sweet potatoes in oil about 5 minutes, stirring occasionally, until light brown; reduce heat to low. Cover and cook 10 to 12 minutes, stirring occasionally, until potatoes are tender.

2. Stir in brown sugar and jerk seasoning. Cook uncovered about 3 minutes, stirring occasionally, until glazed. Sprinkle with parsley.

4 servings.

1 Serving: Calories 115 (Calories from Fat 10); Fat 1g (Saturated 0g); Cholesterol 0mg; Sodium 125mg; Carbohydrate 28g (Dietary Fiber 3g); Protein 2g
% Daily Value: Vitamin A 100%; Vitamin C 18%; Calcium 2%; Iron 2%
Diet Exchanges: ½ Starch, 1 Vegetable, 1 Fruit

Caramelized-Onion and Sweet Potato Skillet

Garden Medley Salad

Prep: 15 min

Caraway Vinaigrette (below)

1 medium cucumber

8 cups bite-size pieces salad greens

1 medium tomato, cut into wedges

4 medium green onions, sliced (¼ cup)

1. Make Caraway Vinaigrette.

2. Cut cucumber lengthwise in half; scrape out seeds. Cut halves diagonally into ½-inch slices.

3. Toss salad greens, tomato, cucumber, onions and vinaigrette.

8 servings.

Caraway Vinaigrette

¼ cup olive or vegetable oil

1 tablespoon chopped fresh parsley

2 tablespoons red wine vinegar

½ teaspoon caraway seed

½ teaspoon salt

1 clove garlic, finely chopped

Shake all ingredients in tightly covered container. Shake again before using.

1 Serving: Calories 80 (Calories from Fat 65); Fat 7g (Saturated 1g); Cholesterol 0mg; Sodium 160mg; Carbohydrate 4g (Dietary Fiber 2g); Protein 1g
% Daily Value: Vitamin A 28%; Vitamin C 20%; Calcium 2%; Iron 4%
Diet Exchanges: 1 Vegetable, 1 Fat

BETTY'S TIPS

✪ Substitution
You can substitute 1 teaspoon parsley flakes for the fresh parsley.

✪ Do-Ahead
The dressing can be made up to a couple of days ahead of time. Store it covered in the refrigerator, and shake well before using.

Garden Medley Salad

Sherried Greens with Fruit and Blue Cheese

Prep: 15 min

Sherry Vinaigrette (below)
8 cups bite-size pieces mixed salad greens
1 medium pear, thinly sliced
1 cup sliced strawberries
1 small red onion, thinly sliced
¼ cup finely crumbled blue cheese (1 ounce)

1. Make Sherry Vinaigrette.

2. Arrange salad greens, pear, strawberries and onion on 8 salad plates. Pour vinaigrette over salads. Sprinkle with cheese.

8 servings.

Sherry Vinaigrette
¼ cup dry sherry or apple juice
2 tablespoons raspberry, balsamic or red wine vinegar
1 tablespoon sugar
1 teaspoon toasted sesame oil

Shake all ingredients in tightly covered container until sugar is dissolved.

1 Serving: Calories 80 (Calories from Fat 20); Fat 2g (Saturated 1g); Cholesterol 5mg; Sodium 75mg; Carbohydrate 10g (Dietary Fiber 2g); Protein 7g
% Daily Value: Vitamin A 34%; Vitamin C 38%; Calcium 6%; Iron 4%
Diet Exchanges: ½ Lean Meat, 2 Vegetable

BETTY'S TIPS

⊙ **Substitution**
If you can't find toasted sesame oil, you can substitute vegetable oil and sprinkle the salad with toasted sesame seed.

⊙ **Simplify**
Feeling rushed? Skip the scratch vinaigrette, and dress the salad with your favorite bottled vinaigrette such as balsamic, raspberry or champagne.

Sherried Greens with Fruit and Blue Cheese

Beet and Arugula Salad

Prep: 15 min   Cook: 55 min   Cool: 1 hr   Chill: 2 hr   Stand: 30 min

6 medium beets (4 to 6 ounces each)
¼ cup olive or vegetable oil
2 tablespoons red wine vinegar or cider vinegar
1 tablespoon Dijon mustard
1 teaspoon sugar
2 cups arugula leaves, watercress or bite-size pieces salad greens
½ cup crumbled chévre (goat) cheese (2 ounces)
1 tablespoon chopped walnuts, toasted, if desired

1. Remove greens from beets, leaving about ½ inch of stem. Do not trim or cut root. Wash beets well. Place beets in 2-quart saucepan; add enough water to cover. Cover and heat to boiling; reduce heat. Simmer 40 to 50 minutes or until tender; drain.

2. Cool beets 1 hour. Remove skins from beets under running water; drain beets on paper towels. Cut beets into julienne strips; place in shallow glass or plastic dish.

3. Shake oil, vinegar, mustard and sugar in tightly covered container. Pour over beets. Cover and refrigerate at least 2 hours but no longer than 12 hours. Let stand at room temperature 30 minutes before preparing salad.

4. Arrange beets on 4 salad plates. Top with arugula and cheese. Drizzle with remaining oil mixture if desired. Sprinkle with walnuts. Serve immediately.

4 servings.

1 Serving: Calories 255 (Calories from Fat 180); Fat 20g (Saturated 6g); Cholesterol 20mg; Sodium 250mg; Carbohydrate 15g (Dietary Fiber 3g); Protein 7g
% Daily Value: Vitamin A 22%; Vitamin C 14%; Calcium 12%; Iron 8%
Diet Exchanges: 3 Vegetable, 4 Fat

BETTY'S TIPS

☺ Simplify
Substitute a 16-ounce can of julienne beets for the cooked fresh beets. Marinate as directed in step 3.

☺ Did You Know?
Beets range in color from the common deep garnet to white and gold. Although any color beet can be used in this salad, marinate each color separately because beets have a tendency to "bleed."

☺ Variation
Chévre is a white goat's milk cheese with a mildly tart flavor. If you prefer a slightly more assertive flavor, try a blue cheese such as Gorgonzola or Roquefort.

Beet and Arugula Salad

Betty... MAKES IT EASY

Italian Salad with Parmesan Fans

Prep: 20 min   Bake: 6 min

> Parmesan Fans (below)
> 1 bag (5 ounces) spring mix salad greens or 6 cups assorted greens
> ¼ cup Italian dressing
> ⅓ cup red or green pistachio nuts, coarsely chopped

1. Make Parmesan Fans.

2. Toss salad greens and dressing in medium bowl. Arrange greens on 6 salad plates; sprinkle with nuts. Place fans upright in salad.

6 servings.

Parmesan Fans

> 6 wonton wrappers (3½-inch square)
> 1 tablespoon Italian dressing
> 2 teaspoons grated Parmesan cheese

Heat oven to 350°. Place wonton wrappers on cutting board. Cut each wrapper into ⅜- to ½-inch strips to within ½ inch of bottom. Make 2 or 3 pleats in the same direction on bottom edge of each wrapper to form fan base; spread strips gently to form fan shape. Carefully transfer fans to cookie sheet. Brush with dressing; sprinkle with cheese. Bake 4 to 6 minutes or until light brown. Cool completely. Fans can be made up to 2 days ahead of time and stored in a tightly covered container at room temperature.

1 Serving: Calories 120 (Calories from Fat 80); Fat 9g (Saturated 1g); Cholesterol 5mg; Sodium 190mg; Carbohydrate 8g (Dietary Fiber 1g); Protein 3g
% Daily Value: Vitamin A 14%; Vitamin C 8%; Calcium 4%; Iron 4%
Diet Exchanges: 2 Vegetable, 1½ Fat

Cut wrapper into ⅜- to ½-inch strips to within ½ inch of bottom.

Make 2 or 3 pleats in the same direction on bottom edge of wrapper.

Italian Salad with Parmesan Fans

Wild Rice and Currant Salad

Prep: 20 min   Cook: 20 min

1 package (6¼ ounces) fast-cooking long-grain and wild rice mix

2 medium carrots, chopped (1 cup)

1 medium bell pepper, chopped (1 cup)

1 medium stalk celery, chopped (½ cup)

⅔ cup currants or raisins

2 tablespoons soy sauce

2 tablespoons water

2 teaspoons sugar

2 teaspoons cider vinegar

⅓ cup dry-roasted peanuts

Bibb lettuce leaves, if desired

1. Cook rice mix as directed on package. Spread rice evenly in thin layer on large cookie sheet. Let stand 10 to 12 minutes, stirring occasionally, until cool.

2. Mix carrots, bell pepper, celery and currants in large bowl. Mix soy sauce, water, sugar and vinegar in small bowl until sugar is dissolved.

3. Add rice and soy sauce mixture to carrot mixture. Gently toss until coated. Add peanuts; gently toss. Serve salad on lettuce leaves.

8 servings.

1 Serving: Calories 130 (Calories from Fat 45); Fat 5g (Saturated 1g); Cholesterol 5mg; Sodium 280mg; Carbohydrate 20g (Dietary Fiber 2g); Protein 3g
% Daily Value: Vitamin A 58%; Vitamin C 26%; Calcium 2%; Iron 4%
Diet Exchanges: ½ Starch, 1 Vegetable, ½ Fruit, 1 Fat

BETTY'S TIPS

⊕ **Do-Ahead**
You can make this salad the day before. Cover and refrigerate up to 24 hours. Just before serving, toss with peanuts.

⊕ **Extra Special**
Add a festive holiday finish to this salad with carrot stars. To make, thinly slice carrot. Cut slices into star shapes using a small canapé or cookie cutter.

Wild Rice and Currant Salad

Crowd Pleasers

Big-Batch Dishes for Larger Gatherings

Southwestern Turkey (page 195)

Big Batch Cheese Garlic Biscuits (page 206)

Impossibly Easy Chicken and Broccoli Pie

Prep: 15 min   Bake: 47 min   Stand: 5 min

2   packages (10 ounces each) frozen chopped broccoli, thawed and drained
3   cups shredded Cheddar cheese (12 ounces)
2   cups cut-up cooked chicken
1   large onion, chopped (1 cup)
1   cup Original Bisquick
2   cups milk
1   teaspoon salt
½   teaspoon pepper
4   eggs

1. Heat oven to 400°. Grease bottom and sides of rectangular baking dish, 13 × 9 × 2 inches, with shortening. Sprinkle broccoli, 2 cups of the cheese, the chicken and onion in baking dish.

2. Stir remaining ingredients until blended. Pour over chicken mixture.

3. Bake uncovered 40 to 45 minutes or until knife inserted in center comes out clean. Sprinkle with remaining 1 cup cheese. Bake 1 to 2 minutes or until cheese is melted. Let stand 5 minutes before cutting.

12 to 14 servings.

1 Serving: Calories 300 (Calories from Fat 160); Fat 18g (Saturated 9g); Cholesterol 150mg; Sodium 700mg; Carbohydrate 14g (Dietary Fiber 2g); Protein 23g
% Daily Value: Vitamin A 28%; Vitamin C 18%; Calcium 30%; Iron 8%
Diet Exchanges: ½ Starch, 3 Medium-Fat Meat, 1 Vegetable, 1 Fat

BETTY'S TIPS

☺ Substitution
Two cups of cut-up cooked turkey or ham instead of the chicken would also work well. Keep this recipe in mind for using up leftovers from your Thanksgiving turkey!

☺ Time-Saver
Thaw the frozen broccoli in the refrigerator up to 24 hours ahead of time.

☺ Serve-With
Purchase cut-up deli fruits for a salad, and let everyone enjoy a top-your-own ice-cream sundae for dessert.

Chicken and Vegetable Bake

Prep: 14 min   Bake: 30 min

2   cans (10¾ ounces each) condensed cream of chicken and mushroom soup
1   can (10¾ ounces) condensed chicken broth
4   cups cut-up cooked chicken
1   bag (1 pound) frozen mixed vegetables, thawed and drained
2   cups Original Bisquick
1½   cups milk
½   teaspoon poultry seasoning

1. Heat oven to 375° (350° for glass baking dish). Heat soup, broth, chicken and vegetables to boiling in 3-quart saucepan, stirring constantly. Boil and stir 1 minute. Spread in ungreased rectangular pan, 13 × 9 × 2 inches.

2. Stir together remaining ingredients. Pour over chicken mixture.

3. Bake uncovered about 30 minutes or until light brown.

10 servings.

1 Serving: Calories 285 (Calories from Fat 110); Fat 12g (Saturated 4g); Cholesterol 55mg; Sodium 1040mg; Carbohydrate 24g (Dietary Fiber 2g); Protein 22g
% Daily Value: Vitamin A 32%; Vitamin C 12%; Calcium 10%; Iron 10%
Diet Exchanges: 1½ Starch, 2 Medium-Fat Meat, 1 Vegetable

BETTY'S TIPS

☺ Success Hint
This recipe is perfect for a casual Friday night supper with neighbors. It's also quick to throw together at the last minute for unexpected company, and the ingredients are easy to keep on hand for emergency meals. You can quickly thaw frozen cut-up cooked chicken in the microwave, or use four 10-ounce cans of chunk chicken, drained.

☺ Serve-With
Serve this hearty pie with purchased Caesar salad. For a quick dessert, drizzle caramel ice-cream topping over apple slices.

Chicken and Vegetable Bake

Impossibly Easy Chicken and Broccoli Pie

Southwestern Turkey

Southwestern Turkey

Prep: 20 min   Bake: 3 hr 45 min   Stand: 15 min

12- to 14- pound turkey

8 to 10   fresh sage leaves

Slow Cooker Chorizo, Pecan and Cheddar Stuffing (page 204) or Old-Fashioned Bread Stuffing (page 204), if desired

⅓   cup butter or margarine, melted

1   teaspoon chili powder

1   teaspoon ground cumin

1 or 2   chipotle chilies in adobo sauce (from 7-ounce can), finely chopped

1. Heat oven to 325°. Starting at the back opening of the turkey, gently separate skin from turkey breast, using fingers. Place sage leaves under skin of turkey.

2. Prepare stuffing; do not cook. Fill wishbone area with stuffing first. Fasten neck skin to back with skewer. Fold wings across back with tips touching. Fill body cavity lightly with stuffing. (Do not pack—stuffing will expand while baking.) Tuck drumsticks under band of skin at tail, or tie together with heavy string, then tie to tail. Place turkey, breast side up, on rack in shallow roasting pan.

3. Heat butter, chili powder, cumin and chilies until butter is melted. Brush turkey with 2 tablespoons of the butter mixture. Insert meat thermometer so tip is in the thickest part of inside thigh muscle and does not touch bone.

4. Bake uncovered 3 hours to 3 hours 45 minutes, brushing occasionally with remaining butter mixture, until thermometer reads 180° and juice of turkey is no longer pink when center of thigh is cut. When turkey begins to turn golden, cover loosely with aluminum foil. When done, remove turkey from oven and let stand 15 minutes for easier carving. Garnish with whole chilies and additional sage leaves if desired.

5. Meanwhile, skim fat from drippings. Pour just the drippings into 1-quart saucepan; heat to boiling. Serve with turkey.

12 to 15 servings.

1 Serving: Calories 415 (Calories from Fat 190); Fat 21g (Saturated 8g); Cholesterol 165mg; Sodium 190mg; Carbohydrate 1g (Dietary Fiber 0g); Protein 56g
% Daily Value: Vitamin A 4%; Vitamin C 0%; Calcium 4%; Iron 14%
Diet Exchanges: 7¼ Lean Meat

Oven-Roasted Turkey Breast

Prep: 15 min   Bake: 2 hr 30 min   Stand: 15 min

4½- to 5 pound whole turkey breast
½ cup butter or margarine, melted
¼ cup dry white wine or apple juice
2 tablespoons chopped fresh or 1½ teaspoons dried thyme leaves
1 teaspoon salt
1 teaspoon paprika
2 cloves garlic, finely chopped
2 teaspoons cornstarch
2 tablespoons cold water

1. Heat oven to 325°. Place turkey, skin side up, on rack in large shallow roasting pan. Insert ovenproof meat thermometer so tip is in thickest part of meat and does not touch bone. Bake uncovered 1 hour.

2. Mix butter, wine, thyme, salt, paprika and garlic. Brush turkey with half of the butter mixture. Bake 30 minutes; brush with remaining butter mixture. Bake about 1 hour longer or until thermometer reads 180° and juice of turkey is no longer pink when center is cut.

3. Remove turkey from oven and let stand 15 minutes for easier carving.

4. Meanwhile, pour pan drippings into measuring cup; skim fat from drippings. Add enough water to drippings to measure 2 cups. Heat drippings to boiling in 1-quart saucepan. Mix cornstarch and cold water; stir into drippings. Boil and stir 1 minute. Serve with turkey.

8 to 10 servings.

1 Serving: Calories 420 (Calories from Fat 225); Fat 25g (Saturated 11g); Cholesterol 165mg; Sodium 480mg; Carbohydrate 1g (Dietary Fiber 0g); Protein 48g
% Daily Value: Vitamin A 10%; Vitamin C 0%; Calcium 2%; Iron 8%
Diet Exchanges: 7 Lean Meat, 1 Fat

BETTY'S TIPS

❂ Success Hint
Carving the turkey will be easier if you let the bird stand for about 15 minutes before cutting. This resting period allows the meat to become more firm, so carving smooth, uniform slices is easier.

❂ Extra Special
Garnish with small whole apples and fresh herbs, such as thyme or sage.

Oven-Roasted Turkey Breast

Saucy Smoked Turkey and Biscuits

Prep: 10 min   Cook: 15 min   Bake: 30 min

1   bag (1 pound) frozen whole kernel corn, thawed and drained
2   medium stalks celery, chopped (1 cup)
1   large onion, chopped (1 cup)
2   cans (10¾ ounces each) condensed chicken gumbo soup
1   cup water
3   tablespoons Original Bisquick
4   cups cut-up smoked (cooked) turkey
3⅓   cups Original Bisquick
1   cup milk

1. Heat oven to 375°. Heat corn, celery, onion and soup to boiling in 5-quart Dutch oven, stirring constantly. Stir together water and 3 tablespoons Bisquick; stir into soup mixture. Boil and stir 1 minute; remove from heat. Stir in turkey. Pour into ungreased rectangular pan, 13 × 9 × 2 inches.

2. Stir 3⅓ cups Bisquick and the milk until soft dough forms. Drop dough by 30 teaspoonfuls onto chicken mixture.

3. Bake uncovered 24 to 30 minutes or until biscuits are golden brown.

12 servings.

1 Serving: Calories 315 (Calories from Fat 110); Fat 12g (Saturated 3g); Cholesterol 45mg; Sodium 920mg; Carbohydrate 35g (Dietary Fiber 2g); Protein 19g
% Daily Value: Vitamin A 6%; Vitamin C 2%; Calcium 10%; Iron 12%
Diet Exchanges: 2 Starch, 1½ Medium-Fat Meat, 1 Vegetable, ½ Fat

BETTY'S TIPS

⚙ **Substitution**
You can use condensed cream of chicken vegetable soup instead of the chicken gumbo.

Fully cooked ham can be substituted for the smoked turkey.

⚙ **Variation**
Jazz up the flavor by adding a few drops of red pepper sauce with the turkey mixture.

⚙ **Special Touch**
Serve this saucy recipe in colorful rimmed salad bowls or soup bowls. The turkey and biscuits mixture will be easy to eat, and the bowls are a nice change from dinner plates.

Saucy Smoked Turkey and Biscuits

Philly Beef and Cheese Sandwich

Quick Cheeseburger Bake

Philly Beef and Cheese Sandwich

Prep: 15 min   Bake: 45 min   Stand: 5 min

- 1 medium bell pepper, cut into strips
- 1 medium onion, thinly sliced
- 4 cups Original Bisquick
- 2 cups milk
- 2 tablespoons mayonnaise or salad dressing
- 2 eggs
- 1/2 pound thinly sliced cooked roast beef
- 1/2 pound sliced Swiss cheese

1. Heat oven to 350°. Grease bottom and sides of rectangular baking dish, 13 × 9 × 2 inches, with shortening. Spray 10-inch skillet with cooking spray; heat over medium-high heat. Cook bell pepper and onion in skillet, stirring occasionally, until tender; remove from heat.

2. Stir together Bisquick, milk, mayonnaise and eggs. Pour half of the batter into baking dish. Top with half of the beef, the bell pepper mixture and three-fourths of the cheese. Top with remaining beef. Pour remaining batter over beef.

3. Bake uncovered 35 to 45 minutes or until golden brown. Top with remaining cheese. Let stand 5 minutes before cutting.

8 to 10 servings.

1 Serving: Calories 500 (Calories from Fat 235); Fat 26g (Saturated 10g); Cholesterol 110mg; Sodium 1010mg; Carbohydrate 43g (Dietary Fiber 1g); Protein 24g
% Daily Value: Vitamin A 10%; Vitamin C 12%; Calcium 46%; Iron 16%
Diet Exchanges: 3 Starch, 2 High-Fat Meat, 1/2 Fat

BETTY'S TIPS

☺ Did You Know?
This sandwich is an easy version of the original Philadelphia Cheese Steak, named for the city that is thought to have created the sandwich in the 1930s. It consisted of an Italian or French roll topped with thinly sliced beef and cheese (usually American) and sometimes sautéed onions.

Quick Cheeseburger Bake

Prep: 14 min   Bake: 35 min

- 1 1/2 pounds ground beef
- 1 1/4 cups chopped onions
- 1 can (10 3/4 ounces) condensed Cheddar cheese soup
- 1 1/4 cups frozen mixed vegetables, if desired
- 1/2 cup milk
- 2 1/3 cups Original Bisquick
- 2/3 cup water
- 1 1/3 cups shredded Cheddar cheese

1. Heat oven to 375°. Generously grease bottom and sides of jelly roll pan, 15 1/2 × 10 1/2 × 1 inch, with shortening. Cook beef and onions in 12-inch skillet over medium heat, stirring occasionally, until beef is brown; drain. Stir in soup, vegetables and milk.

2. Stir Bisquick and water in medium bowl until moistened. Spread evenly in pan. Spread beef mixture over batter. Sprinkle with cheese.

3. Bake uncovered 35 minutes.

16 to 20 servings.

1 Serving: Calories 225 (Calories from Fat 115); Fat 13g (Saturated 6g); Cholesterol 35mg; Sodium 500mg; Carbohydrate 14g (Dietary Fiber 0g); Protein 13g
% Daily Value: Vitamin A 10%; Vitamin C 0%; Calcium 10%; Iron 8%
Diet Exchanges: 1 Starch, 1 1/2 High-Fat Meat

BETTY'S TIPS

☺ Substitution
If your kids aren't fond of onions, replace the onions with 1 1/2 cups of sliced fresh mushrooms or leave them out completely.

☺ Serve-With
While the Cheeseburger Bake is in the oven, put together a simple fresh-vegetable tray and add a purchased dip. For dessert, top brownie squares with butter pecan or butter brickle ice cream and drizzle with chocolate sauce. An easy meal with lots of crowd appeal!

Speedy Lasagna Supper

Prep: 20 min   Bake: 47 min   Stand: 5 min

2 pounds ground beef

1 cup small curd creamed cottage cheese

½ cup grated Parmesan cheese

3 cups shredded mozzarella cheese (12 ounces)

1 tablespoon Italian seasoning

1 can (12 ounces) tomato paste

1⅓ cups Original Bisquick

2 cups milk

1 teaspoon salt

½ teaspoon pepper

4 eggs

1. Heat oven to 400°. Grease bottom and sides of rectangular baking dish, 13 × 9 × 2 inches, with shortening. Cook beef in 10-inch skillet over medium heat, stirring occasionally, until brown; drain.

2. Layer cottage cheese and Parmesan cheese in baking dish. Mix beef, 2 cups of the mozzarella cheese, the Italian seasoning and tomato paste; spoon evenly over cheeses. Stir remaining ingredients until blended. Pour over beef mixture.

3. Bake uncovered 40 to 45 minutes or until knife inserted in center comes out clean. Sprinkle with remaining 1 cup mozzarella cheese. Bake 1 to 2 minutes or until cheese is melted. Let stand 5 minutes before cutting.

12 to 14 servings.

1 Serving: Calories 385 (Calories from Fat 200); Fat 22g (Saturated 10g); Cholesterol 140mg; Sodium 980mg; Carbohydrate 17g (Dietary Fiber 1g); Protein 31g
% Daily Value: Vitamin A 22%; Vitamin C 10%; Calcium 36%; Iron 14%
Diet Exchanges: 1 Starch, 4 Medium-Fat Meat

BETTY'S TIPS

☺ **Substitution**
Italian sausage would add an extra flavor punch to this recipe. Use 1 pound of bulk mild or hot Italian sausage instead of 1 pound of the ground beef.

☺ **Serve-With**
If you have spaghetti sauce on hand, quickly pop it in the microwave to heat, and serve it with this tasty lasagna.

☺ **Variation**
This lasagna is a natural kid pleaser. Sneak in some shredded carrots for a nutrition boost!

Speedy Lasagna Supper

Thick-Crust Pizza

Prep: 16 min   Bake: 20 min

3 cups Original Bisquick

⅔ cup very hot water

2 tablespoons vegetable oil

1¼ cups pizza or spaghetti sauce

2 to 2½ cups favorite pizza toppings (sliced Canadian-style bacon, pepperoni, mushrooms, green onions, ripe olives)

1½ cups shredded mozzarella cheese (6 ounces)

1. Move oven rack to lowest position. Heat oven to 425°. Mix Bisquick, water and oil until dough forms; beat vigorously 20 strokes. Let stand 8 minutes.

2. Grease bottom and sides of jelly roll pan, 15½ × 10½ × 1 inch, or cookie sheet with shortening. Press dough in bottom and up sides of pan, using hands dipped in Bisquick. Or press into 13 × 10-inch rectangle on cookie sheet; pinch edges to form ¾-inch rim. Spread pizza sauce over dough; top with pizza toppings. Sprinkle with cheese.

3. Bake 15 to 20 minutes or until crust is brown and cheese is melted.

10 servings.

1 Serving: Calories 270 (Calories from Fat 125); Fat 14g (Saturated 4g); Cholesterol 15mg; Sodium 960mg; Carbohydrate 26g (Dietary Fiber 1g); Protein 11g
% Daily Value: Vitamin A 6%; Vitamin C 6%; Calcium 20%; Iron 8%
Diet Exchanges: 1 Starch, 1 High-Fat Meat, 2 Vegetable, 1 Fat

BETTY'S TIPS

☼ Success Hint

After you grease the jelly roll pan or cookie sheet, sprinkle the pan with cornmeal for a crispier crust.

Need another pizza? Prepare a second pizza while the first one bakes. Your family and friends can devour the first pizza, then the other one will be piping hot from the oven, ready for second helpings.

Thick-Crust Pizza

Sausage Chili Bake

Sausage Chili Bake

Prep: 11 min   Bake: 40 min

1 pound smoked sausage, cut into ½ -inch slices
1 small onion, chopped (¼ cup)
1 teaspoon garlic salt
1 to 2 tablespoons chili powder
1 can (14½ ounces) stewed tomatoes, undrained
1 can (15 to 16 ounces) kidney beans, undrained
2 cups Original Bisquick
½ cup cornmeal
1 cup milk
2 eggs

1. Heat oven to 350°. Spray 10-inch skillet with cooking spray; heat over medium-high heat. Cook sausage and onion in skillet 4 to 5 minutes, stirring occasionally, until onion is tender. Spoon into ungreased rectangular baking dish, 13 × 9 × 2 inches. Stir in garlic salt, chili powder, tomatoes and beans.

2. Stir remaining ingredients until blended. Pour over sausage mixture.

3. Bake uncovered 35 to 40 minutes or until crust is light golden brown.

8 to 10 servings.

1 Serving: Calories 425 (Calories from Fat 200); Fat 22g (Saturated 8g); Cholesterol 0mg; Sodium 1430mg; Carbohydrate 45g (Dietary Fiber 5g); Protein 17g
% Daily Value: Vitamin A 12%; Vitamin C 6%; Calcium 14%; Iron 22%
Diet Exchanges: 3 Starch, 1 High-Fat Meat, 2 Fat

BETTY'S TIPS

☺ Substitution

A 14½-ounce can of Italian- or Cajun-style stewed tomatoes would also add great flavor to this recipe.

One pound of ground beef, cooked and drained, can be substituted for the smoked sausage.

☺ Success Hint

Does 1 to 2 tablespoons seem like a lot of chili powder to you? When made with 2 tablespoons, this recipe is very flavorful but not too strong because the chili powder blends with the other ingredients.

— Low Fat —

Sweet and Spicy Rubbed Ham

Prep: 10 min   Bake 1 hr 30 min   Stand: 15 min

6- to 8 pound fully cooked smoked bone-in ham
½ cup packed brown sugar
⅓ cup maple-flavored syrup
½ teaspoon ground mustard
⅛ teaspoon ground cinnamon
⅛ teaspoon ground ginger
⅛ teaspoon ground cloves
Dash of ground nutmeg

1. Heat oven to 325°. Line shallow roasting pan with aluminum foil. Place ham, cut side down, on rack in pan. Insert ovenproof meat thermometer in thickest part of ham. Bake uncovered about 1 hour 30 minutes or until thermometer reads 135° to 140°.

2. While ham is baking, mix remaining ingredients. Brush over ham during last 30 minutes of baking.

3. Cover ham loosely with aluminum foil and let stand 10 to 15 minutes for easier carving.

20 servings.

1 Serving: Calories 130 (Calories from Fat 35); Fat 4g (Saturated 1g); Cholesterol 35mg; Sodium 800mg; Carbohydrate 10g (Dietary Fiber 0g); Protein 14g
% Daily Value: Vitamin A 0%; Vitamin C 0%; Calcium 0%; Iron 6%
Diet Exchanges: 2 Very Lean Meat, ½ Fruit, ½ Fat

Sweet and Spicy Rubbed Ham

Slow Cooker Chorizo, Pecan and Cheddar Stuffing

Prep: 15 min   Cook: 3 hr 30 min

- 1 pound chorizo sausage, casing removed and crumbled, or bulk chorizo sausage
- 1 large onion, chopped (1 cup)
- 3 medium stalks celery, sliced (1½ cups)
- 1 package (16 ounces) seasoned corn bread stuffing crumbs (5¾ cups)
- ⅓ cup butter or margarine, melted
- ½ teaspoon rubbed sage
- ¼ teaspoon pepper
- 2 cups chicken broth
- 1½ cups shredded sharp Cheddar cheese (6 ounces)
- 1 cup pecan halves, toasted

1. Cook sausage, onion and celery in 10-inch skillet over medium heat 8 to 10 minutes, stirring occasionally, until sausage is no longer pink; drain.

2. Place sausage mixture, stuffing, butter, sage and pepper in 4- to 5-quart slow cooker. Pour broth over mixture; toss to combine. Cover and cook on low heat setting 3 hours to 3 hours 30 minutes. Gently stir in cheese and pecans.

16 servings.

1 Serving: Calories 365 (Calories from Fat 215); Fat 24g (Saturated 9g); Cholesterol 45mg; Sodium 1080mg; Carbohydrate 25g (Dietary Fiber 2g); Protein 14g
% Daily Value: Vitamin A 14%; Vitamin C 0%; Calcium 8%; Iron 10%
Diet Exchanges: 1½ Starch, 1½ High-Fat Meat, 3 Fat

BETTY'S TIPS

☺ Substitution
Cooked chorizo can be substituted for the raw chorizo sausage. Decrease the cooking time in step 1 to 5 to 6 minutes or until onion and celery are crisp-tender.

☺ Variation
If desired, use this recipe to stuff **Southwestern Turkey** (page 195) or any 12- to 14-pound bird. After making the stuffing mixture, stuff and bake turkey as directed. The center of the stuffing must reach 165°.

Fruited Bread Stuffing

Prep: 15 min   Bake: 45 min

- 1 cup butter or margarine
- 2 large stalks celery (with leaves), chopped (1½ cups)
- ¾ cup finely chopped onion
- 9 cups soft bread cubes (about 15 slices bread)
- 1 cup diced orange sections or mandarin orange segments
- 1 cup chopped cooking apple
- 2 tablespoons chopped fresh or 1½ teaspoons dried sage leaves
- 1 tablespoon chopped fresh or 1 teaspoon dried thyme leaves
- 1½ teaspoons salt
- ½ teaspoon pepper

1. Heat oven to 325°. Grease bottom and side of 3-quart casserole or rectangular baking dish, 13 × 9 × 2 inches, with shortening.

2. Melt butter in 4-quart Dutch oven over medium-high heat. Cook celery and onion in butter, stirring occasionally, until tender; remove from heat.

3. Toss celery mixture and remaining ingredients. Spoon into casserole.

4. Cover and bake 30 minutes. Uncover and bake about 15 minutes longer or until heated through.

12 servings.

1 Serving: Calories 240 (Calories from Fat 155); Fat 17g (Saturated 10g); Cholesterol 40mg; Sodium 570mg; Carbohydrate 20g (Dietary Fiber 2g); Protein 3g
% Daily Value: Vitamin A 12%; Vitamin C 8%; Calcium 4%; Iron 6%
Diet Exchanges: 1 Starch, 3 Fat, ½ Fruit

BETTY'S TIPS

☺ Variation
You can also use this stuffing to stuff one 12- to 14- pound turkey. Prepare recipe as directed, but don't spoon into casserole. Stuff turkey just before baking.

For **Old-Fashioned Bread Stuffing,** omit the orange sections and apples.

Slow Cooker Chorizo, Pecan and Cheddar Stuffing

Fruited Bread Stuffing

Big Batch Cheese Garlic Biscuits

Prep: 10 min   Bake: 10 min per sheet

8   cups Original Bisquick

2⅔ cups milk

2   cups shredded Cheddar cheese (8 ounces)

1   cup butter or margarine, melted

1   teaspoon garlic powder

1. Heat oven to 450°. Stir Bisquick, milk and cheese until soft dough forms; beat 30 seconds.

2. Drop dough by 40 to 48 spoonfuls about 2 inches apart onto ungreased cookie sheet.

3. Bake 8 to 10 minutes or until golden brown. Mix butter and garlic powder; brush on warm biscuits before removing from cookie sheet. Serve warm.

40 to 48 biscuits.

1 Biscuit: Calories 165 (Calories from Fat 90); Fat 10g (Saturated 3g); Cholesterol 5mg; Sodium 440mg; Carbohydrate 15g (Dietary Fiber 0g); Protein 4g
% Daily Value: Vitamin A 6%; Vitamin C 0%; Calcium 8%; Iron 4%
Diet Exchanges: 1 Starch, 2 Fat

BETTY'S TIPS

⊕ **Success Hint**
You'll probably need to bake one cookie sheet at a time, for best baking results. Prepare the next sheet while the first one bakes. Refrigerate dough when not spooning it onto cookie sheets so the biscuits will be the best quality.

⊕ **Variation**
For **Plain Drop Biscuits,** omit the cheese, butter and garlic powder.

Big Batch Cheese Garlic Biscuits

Delightful Desserts

Irresistible Cakes, Pies, Tortes, and More

Chocolate Berry Cheesecake Dessert (page 211)

Peppermint Cream Brownie Torte (page 223)

Creamy Lemon Raspberry Dessert

Prep: 10 min Chill: 1 hr 5 min

Pretzel Crust (right)
1 can (14 ounces) sweetened condensed milk
½ cup lemon juice
1 package (4-serving size) lemon instant pudding and pie filling mix
1½ cups frozen (thawed) whipped topping
1 can (21 ounces) raspberry or strawberry pie filling

1. Make Pretzel Crust. Press crust mixture firmly on bottom of ungreased rectangular pan, 13 × 9 × 2 inches. Refrigerate while preparing filling.

2. Mix milk and lemon juice in large bowl until smooth. Beat in pudding mix (dry) with wire whisk or electric mixer on low speed 2 minutes. Refrigerate pudding mixture 5 minutes.

3. Fold whipped topping into pudding mixture. Pour over crust. Cover and refrigerate about 1 hour or until filling is firm.

4. To serve, cut into 4 rows by 3 rows. Top each serving with about 3 tablespoons pie filling. Store covered in refrigerator.

12 servings.

Pretzel Crust
1½ cups crushed pretzels
¼ cup sugar
½ cup butter or margarine, melted

Mix all ingredients.

1 Serving: Calories 365 (Calories from Fat 125); Fat 14g (Saturated 8g); Cholesterol 35mg; Sodium 360mg; Carbohydrate 56g (Dietary Fiber 1g); Protein 5g
% Daily Value: Vitamin A 8%; Vitamin C 2%; Calcium 14%; Iron 2%
Diet Exchanges: Not Recommended

BETTY'S TIPS

⊛ **Success Hint**
Pretzel sticks are hard to measure and too many are needed in the crust to count individually, so try this "unscientific" but handy little hint. Start with about 4 to 6 very full handfuls of pretzel sticks or twists, and crush more as needed.

⊛ **Extra Special**
Garnish this spectacular no-bake dessert with fresh raspberries and twists of lemon peel.

Creamy Lemon Raspberry Dessert

Maple Cream Brownie Dessert

Prep: 10 min   Bake: 30 min   Cool: 1 hr

1 package (1 pound 3.8 ounces) Betty Crocker fudge brownie mix

¼ cup water

½ cup vegetable oil

2 eggs

1 teaspoon maple extract

   Maple Cream Frosting (below)

4 bars (7.5 ounces each) chocolate-covered peanut and maple candy, coarsely chopped

¼ cup chocolate sundae or regular chocolate syrup

1. Heat oven to 350°. Grease bottom only of rectangular pan, 13 × 9 × 2 inches, with shortening. Make brownie mix as directed on package for fudgelike brownies, using water, oil and eggs and adding maple extract. Spread batter in pan. Bake as directed. Cool completely in pan on wire rack, about 1 hour.

2. Make Maple Cream Frosting; refrigerate. Spread frosting over cooled brownies. Cover and refrigerate until serving.

3. Cut dessert into 4 rows by 3 rows. Sprinkle each serving with chopped candy bars; drizzle with syrup. Store covered in refrigerator.

12 servings.

Maple Cream Frosting

2 cups frozen (thawed) whipped topping

2 teaspoons maple extract

Mix ingredients until well blended.

1 Serving: Calories 405 (Calories from Fat 170); Fat 19g (Saturated 5g); Cholesterol 35mg; Sodium 220mg; Carbohydrate 56g (Dietary Fiber 1g); Protein 4g
% Daily Value: Vitamin A 0%; Vitamin C 0%; Calcium 4%; Iron 6%
Diet Exchanges: Not Recommended

BETTY'S TIPS

☺ **Success Hint**
Chocolate sundae syrup is slightly thicker than regular chocolate syrup, so it clings better to the top of the brownies. Look for it in your supermarket next to the other ice-cream toppings. If sundae syrup is unavailable, the regular variety will work just fine.

☺ **Extra Special**
Another fun garnish for these maple-flavored squares are the little maple sugar candies shaped like maple leaves. Look for them in specialty candy shops.

Maple Cream Brownie Dessert

Hot Buttered Rum Cheesecake

Prep: 45 min   Bake: 1 hr 25 min   Cool: 1 hr   Chill: 12 hr

1 cup finely crushed shortbread cookies (about 10 cookies)

3 tablespoons packed brown sugar

2 tablespoons butter or margarine, melted

5 packages (8 ounces each) cream cheese, softened

1¼ cups granulated sugar

⅓ cup whipping (heavy) cream

1 tablespoon rum extract

¼ teaspoon ground cinnamon

⅛ teaspoon ground cloves

⅛ teaspoon ground nutmeg

3 eggs

1. Heat oven to 325°. Mix crushed cookies, brown sugar and butter. Press firmly in bottom of ungreased springform pan, 9 × 3 inches.

2. Beat cream cheese, granulated sugar, whipping cream, rum extract, cinnamon, cloves and nutmeg in large bowl with electric mixer on medium speed about 1 minute or until smooth. Beat in eggs on low speed until well blended. Pour over crust; smooth top.

3. Bake 1 hour 15 minutes to 1 hour 25 minutes. Turn off oven; leave cheesecake in oven 30 minutes. Remove from oven and cool in pan on wire rack away from drafts 30 minutes.

4. Without releasing or removing side of pan, run metal spatula carefully along side of cheesecake to loosen. Refrigerate uncovered about 3 hours or until chilled; cover and continue refrigerating at least 9 hours but no longer than 48 hours.

5. Run metal spatula along side of cheesecake to loosen again; remove side of pan. Store cheesecake covered in refrigerator.

16 to 20 servings.

1 Serving: Calories 545 (Calories from Fat 335); Fat 37g (Saturated 22g); Cholesterol 145mg; Sodium 320mg; Carbohydrate 45g (Dietary Fiber 0g); Protein 8g
% Daily Value: Vitamin A 28%; Vitamin C 0%; Calcium 8%; Iron 6%
Diet Exchanges: Not Recommended

BETTY'S TIPS

⊛ Success Hint
After baking, the cheesecake may not appear to be done; if a small area in the center seems soft, it will become firm as the cheesecake cools. Do not insert a knife to test for doneness because the hole could cause the cheesecake to crack.

⊛ Extra Special
Delicious by itself, this cheesecake is heavenly topped with **Divine Caramel Sauce** (page 238) or purchased caramel topping and garnished with toasted pecan halves.

Chocolate Berry Cheesecake Dessert

Prep: 15 min   Bake: 45 min   Chill: 2 hr
Photo on page 207

1   package Betty Crocker SuperMoist® chocolate fudge cake mix
½   cup butter or margarine, softened
2   packages (8 ounces each) cream cheese, softened
1   container (6 ounces) Yoplait® Original raspberry yogurt (⅔ cup)
1   tub Betty Crocker Rich & Creamy chocolate ready-to-spread frosting
3   eggs
1½ cups sliced strawberries
½   cup blueberries
1   can (21 ounces) strawberry pie filling

1. Heat oven to 325°. Grease bottom only of rectangular pan, 13 × 9 × 2 inches, with shortening.

2. Beat cake mix and butter in large bowl with electric mixer on low speed until crumbly; reserve 1 cup. Press remaining crumbly mixture, using floured fingers, in bottom of pan.

3. Beat cream cheese, yogurt and frosting in same bowl on medium speed until smooth. Beat in eggs until blended. Pour into pan. Sprinkle with reserved crumbly mixture.

4. Bake about 45 minutes or until center is set and dry to the touch. Refrigerate at least 2 hours until chilled. Just before serving, stir strawberries and blueberries into pie filling. Top each serving with berry mixture. Store covered in refrigerator.

15 servings.

1 Serving: Calories 485 (Calories from Fat 245); Fat 27g (Saturated 18g); Cholesterol 90mg; Sodium 410mg; Carbohydrate 58g (Dietary Fiber 3g); Protein 6g
% Daily Value: Vitamin A 14%; Vitamin C 16%; Calcium 8%; Iron 8%
Diet Exchanges: Not Recommended

BETTY'S TIPS

⊙ Time-Saver
You can soften the cream cheese in the microwave. Remove foil wrapper and place cream cheese in a microwavable bowl. Microwave uncovered on Medium (50%) 1 minute to 1 minute 30 seconds for an 8-ounce package of cream cheese.

⊙ Variation
Make a special Strawberry-Blueberry Topping. Stir 1½ cups sliced fresh strawberries and ½ cup blueberries into 1 can (21 ounces) strawberry pie filling.

Betty . . .
ON WHAT'S NEW

Creative Candles

Light up a 2-layer cake with these simple but special ideas from Betty.

FRUIT CANDLEHOLDERS

PICTURE FRAME CANDLEHOLDERS

SUPPLIES

Fresh fruit (such as strawberries, kumquats, starfruit, small Key limes, peach wedges or apricot wedges)

Skewer

Small birthday candles

Frosted 8- or 9-inch 2-layer cake

DIRECTIONS

1. Make a small hole in each piece of fruit with skewer.

2. Place a birthday candle into each piece of fruit.

3. Gently push fruits into cake frosting. Keep cake cool until ready to serve.

SUPPLIES

Picture of birthday child

Person-shaped or other child picture frame

Zigzag or other small birthday candles

Colored paper clips, thin rubber band or fun wire

Frosted 8- or 9-inch 2-layer cake

Small colored candies and gumdrops

DIRECTIONS

1. Place picture of child in frame.

2. Attach candle to each hand of the frame with a paper clip.

3. Place frame in center of cake. Arrange candies and gumdrops around frame.

LICORICE CANDLEHOLDERS

SUPPLIES

Fruit-filled licorice sticks

Small lightweight birthday candles

Frosted 8- or 9-inch 2-layer cake

DIRECTIONS

1. Cut licorice sticks to 3- to 3½-inch lengths. Loosely cover licorice sticks and let stand at room temperature 8 to 12 hours until stiffened.

2. Push candle into one end of each licorice stick about ⅛ inch deep or until secure, removing some filling if necessary.

3. Arrange licorice sticks on cake. (Licorice may bend on humid days.)

TEACUP CANDLE

SUPPLIES

Miniature or small teacup with saucer

Frosted 8- or 9-inch 2-layer cake

Small candle (can be floating candle)

Edible fresh flowers (such as pansies, begonias, nasturtiums, violets, roses, dianthus or carnations)

DIRECTIONS

1. Place teacup and saucer in middle of cake.

2. Place candle inside teacup (with small amount of water if floating candle).

3. Arrange flowers on cake. (Blow out candle soon after lighting.)

SPIRAL CANDLES

SUPPLIES

Thin sparkler candles (6½ × ⅛ inch)

Pencils

Flat mint or rainbow candy-coating wafers

Frosted 8- or 9-inch 2-layer cake

DIRECTIONS

1. Place candles in warm water until soft and pliable; wrap each candle around pencil.

2. Cool candles about 15 seconds; remove pencils.

3. Arrange candles and wafers on cake.

Mini Hot Chocolate Cakes

Chocolate Turtle Cake

Mini Hot Chocolate Cakes

Prep: 15 min   Bake: 13 min

- 5 ounces semisweet or bittersweet baking chocolate, chopped
- ½ cup plus 2 tablespoons butter or margarine
- 3 eggs
- 3 egg yolks
- 1½ cups powdered sugar
- ½ cup Gold Medal all-purpose flour
  Additional powdered sugar, if desired
- 1 can (21 ounces) cherry pie filling, if desired

1. Heat oven to 450°. Grease bottom and side of six 6-ounce custard cups with shortening. Melt chocolate and butter in 2-quart saucepan over low heat, stirring frequently. Cool slightly.

2. Beat eggs and egg yolks in large bowl with wire whisk or hand beater until well blended. Beat in 1½ cups powdered sugar. Beat in melted chocolate mixture and flour. Divide batter evenly among custard cups.

3. Bake 11 to 13 minutes or until sides are set and cakes feel soft when touched in center. Run small knife or metal spatula along sides of cakes to loosen. Immediately turn upside down onto individual plates; remove cups. Sprinkle with additional powdered sugar. Top with pie filling. Serve warm.

6 servings.

1 Serving: Calories 485 (Calories from Fat 260); Fat 29g (Saturated 17g); Cholesterol 160mg; Sodium 160mg; Carbohydrate 53g (Dietary Fiber 2g); Protein 5g
% Daily Value: Vitamin A 16%; Vitamin C 0%; Calcium 2%; Iron 8%
Diet Exchanges: Not Recommended

BETTY'S TIPS

❂ Success Hint

These cakes are meant to have a hot, flowing chocolate center that oozes out when you cut into them. Oven temperature and baking time are critical to the success of the recipe. Be sure to check at the minimum bake time. If the cakes are too soft or do not hold their shape, bake a minute or two longer. If the centers are too cakelike in texture, bake a few minutes less next time. ·

Chocolate Turtle Cake

Prep: 15 min   Cook: 10 min   Bake: 55 min   Cool: 1 hr

- 1 package Betty Crocker SuperMoist devil's food cake mix
- 1⅓ cups water
- ½ cup vegetable oil
- 3 eggs
- 1 bag (14 ounces) caramels
- ½ cup evaporated milk
- 1 cup chopped pecans
- 1 bag (6 ounces) semisweet chocolate chips (1 cup)
  Ice cream or whipped cream, if desired

1. Heat oven to 350°. Grease bottom and sides of rectangular pan, 13 × 9 × 2 inches, with shortening; lightly flour. Make cake mix as directed on package, using water, oil and eggs. Pour half of the batter into pan. Bake 25 minutes.

2. Meanwhile, heat caramels and milk in 1-quart saucepan over medium heat about 10 minutes, stirring frequently, until caramels are melted. Pour and spread caramel over warm cake in pan. Sprinkle with pecans and chocolate chips. Spread with remaining batter.

3. Bake 30 minutes. Run knife around side of pan to loosen cake. Cool completely, about 1 hour. Serve with ice cream. Store tightly covered at room temperature.

20 servings.

1 Serving: Calories 340 (Calories from Fat 155); Fat 17g (Saturated 5g); Cholesterol 35mg; Sodium 200mg; Carbohydrate 44g (Dietary Fiber 2g); Protein 4g
% Daily Value: Vitamin A 0%; Vitamin C 0%; Calcium 6%; Iron 8%
Diet Exchanges: Not Recommended

BETTY'S TIPS

❂ Time-Saver

Caramels can be melted in the microwave. Place caramels and milk in a 4-cup glass measuring cup. Microwave uncovered on High 2 minutes to 3 minutes 30 seconds, stirring once or twice.

❂ Special Touch

If you are serving this special cake with ice cream, make it extra special by drizzling chocolate and caramel syrups over the ice cream and sprinkling with a few additional chopped pecans.

Easy Red Velvet Cake

Prep: 15 min   Bake: 35 min   Cool: 1 hr

1 package Betty Crocker SuperMoist German chocolate cake mix
¾ cup buttermilk
¼ cup water
¼ cup vegetable oil
3 eggs
1 bottle (1 ounce) red food color
   Cooked White Frosting (below)

1. Heat oven to 350°. Grease bottom and sides of rectangular pan, 13 × 9 × 2 inches, with shortening.

2. Beat all ingredients except frosting in large bowl with electric mixer on low speed 30 seconds, scraping bowl occasionally. Beat on medium speed 1 minute, scraping bowl occasionally. Pour into pan.

3. Bake 30 to 35 minutes or until toothpick inserted in center comes out clean. Run knife around side of pan to loosen cake. Cool completely, about 1 hour. Frost with Cooked White Frosting.

12 servings.

Cooked White Frosting
1 cup milk
⅓ cup Gold Medal all-purpose flour
1 cup butter or margarine, softened
1 cup powdered sugar
1 teaspoon vanilla

Stir milk and flour in 2-quart saucepan until blended. Heat over medium heat until thickened. Cover and refrigerate about 15 minutes or until cool. Beat butter, powdered sugar and vanilla in medium bowl on medium speed until smooth. Gradually beat in flour mixture until blended.

1 Serving: Calories 435 (Calories from Fat 215); Fat 24g (Saturated 12g); Cholesterol 95mg; Sodium 450mg; Carbohydrate 50g (Dietary Fiber 0g); Protein 5g
% Daily Value: Vitamin A 14%; Vitamin C 0%; Calcium 8%; Iron 6%
Diet Exchanges: Not Recommended

BETTY'S TIPS

⊙ **Substitution**
SuperMoist milk chocolate cake mix can also be used for this recipe. If you don't have time to make the **Cooked White Frosting**, use Betty Crocker Rich & Creamy vanilla ready-to-spread frosting instead.

⊙ **Success Hint**
You will need the whole 1-ounce bottle of red food color to achieve the intense red color that is characteristic of this special cake.

Easy Red Velvet Cake

Better-than-Almost-Anything Cake

Prep: 10 min   Bake: 35 min   Cool: 15 min   Chill: 2 hr

1   package Betty Crocker SuperMoist German chocolate cake mix
1⅓   cups water
½   cup vegetable oil
3   eggs
1   can (14 ounces) sweetened condensed milk
1   jar (16 to 17 ounces) caramel, butterscotch or fudge topping
1   container (8 ounces) frozen whipped topping, thawed
1   bag (8 ounces) toffee chips or bits

1. Heat oven to 350°. Generously grease bottom only of rectangular pan, 13 × 9 × 2 inches, with shortening. Make cake mix as directed on package, using water, oil and eggs. Pour into pan. Bake 30 to 35 minutes or until toothpick inserted in center comes out clean. Cool 15 minutes.

2. Poke top of warm cake every ½ inch with handle of wooden spoon. Drizzle milk evenly over top of cake; let stand until milk has been absorbed into cake. Drizzle with caramel topping. Run knife around side of pan to loosen cake. Cover and refrigerate about 2 hours or until chilled.

3. Spread whipped topping over top of cake. Sprinkle with toffee chips. Store covered in refrigerator.

15 servings.

1 Serving: Calories 535 (Calories from Fat 190); Fat 21g (Saturated 9g); Cholesterol 60mg; Sodium 310mg; Carbohydrate 80g (Dietary Fiber 1g); Protein 7g
% Daily Value: Vitamin A 6%; Vitamin C 0%; Calcium 18%; Iron 4%
Diet Exchanges: Not Recommended

BETTY'S TIPS

⚙ **Success Hint**
The cake may stick to the wooden spoon handle while you're making holes in the cake, so occasionally wipe off the handle.

The caramel topping will be easier to drizzle if it has been kept at room temperature.

⚙ **Special Touch**
Instead of the toffee chips or bits, coarsely chop 5 bars (1.4 ounces each) chocolate-covered English toffee candy and sprinkle on top of the cake.

Better-than-Almost-Anything Cake

Betty... MAKES IT EASY

Peanut Caramel Candy Bar Cake

Prep: 15 min   Bake: 45 min   Cool: 1 hr 10 min   Chill: 2 hr

  ½ cup butter or margarine
  ¼ cup whipping (heavy) cream
  1 cup packed brown sugar
  ½ cup peanuts, coarsely chopped
  1 package Betty Crocker SuperMoist devil's food cake mix
  1⅓ cups water
  ½ cup vegetable oil
  3 eggs
  1 package Betty Crocker HomeStyle fluffy white frosting mix
  ½ cup boiling water
  4 bars (2.07 ounces each) chocolate-covered peanut, caramel and nougat candy, coarsely chopped

1. Heat oven to 325°. Mix butter, whipping cream and brown sugar in heavy 1½-quart saucepan. Cook over low heat, stirring occasionally, just until butter is melted. Pour into 2 ungreased round pans, 9 × 1½ inches. Sprinkle evenly with peanuts. Make cake mix as directed on package, using 1⅓ cups water, the oil and eggs. Carefully spoon batter over peanuts.

2. Bake 35 to 45 minutes or until toothpick inserted in center comes out clean. Cool 10 minutes. Run knife around side of pans to loosen cakes; remove from pans to wire rack, placing cakes peanut side up. Cool completely, about 1 hour.

3. Make frosting mix as directed on package, using boiling water. Fold in candy. Place 1 cake layer, peanut side up, on serving plate. Spread with half of the frosting mixture. Top with second layer, peanut side up. Spread top of cake with remaining frosting mixture. Cover and refrigerate at least 2 hours but no longer than 24 hours. Store covered in refrigerator.

Sprinkle peanuts evenly over caramel mixture.

Spread ½ of frosting over peanut side of cake layer.

12 servings.

1 Serving: Calories 810 (Calories from Fat 540); Fat 60g (Saturated 14g); Cholesterol 85mg; Sodium 470mg; Carbohydrate 89g (Dietary Fiber 2g); Protein 6g
% Daily Value: Vitamin A 8%; Vitamin C 0%; Calcium 10%; Iron 12%
Diet Exchanges: Not Recommended

Peanut Caramel Candy Bar Cake

Chocolate Ganache Cake

Prep: 25 min   Bake: 35 min   Cool: 1 hr 10 min   Chill: 1 hr

1 package Betty Crocker SuperMoist chocolate fudge cake mix

1⅓ cups water

½ cup vegetable oil

3 eggs

1 tub Betty Crocker Rich & Creamy chocolate ready-to-spread frosting

⅓ cup whipping (heavy) cream

½ cup semisweet chocolate chips

2 bars (1.4 ounces each) chocolate-covered English toffee candy, very coarsely chopped

1. Heat oven to 350°. Generously grease bottoms only of 2 round pans, 8 or 9 × 1½ inches, with shortening. Make cake mix as directed on package, using water, oil and eggs. Pour into pans.

2. Bake 30 to 35 minutes or until toothpick inserted in center comes out clean. Cool 10 minutes. Run knife around side of pans to loosen cakes; remove from pans to wire rack. Cool completely, about 1 hour.

3. Fill layers and frost side and top of cake with frosting. Heat whipping cream in 1-quart saucepan over medium heat until hot (do not boil); remove from heat. Stir in chocolate chips until melted and smooth. Let stand 5 minutes. Carefully pour chocolate mixture onto top center of cake; spread to edge, allowing some to drizzle down side. Garnish top of cake with toffee candy. Refrigerate about 1 hour or until chocolate is set. Store covered in refrigerator.

16 servings.

1 Serving: Calories 400 (Calories from Fat 190); Fat 21g (Saturated 11g); Cholesterol 50mg; Sodium 270mg; Carbohydrate 50g (Dietary Fiber 2g); Protein 4g
% Daily Value: Vitamin A 2%; Vitamin C 0%; Calcium 4%; Iron 6%
Diet Exchanges: Not Recommended

BETTY'S TIPS

☺ Success Hint

Ganache, the cream and chocolate mixture, is ready to use when it mounds slightly when dropped from a spoon. It will become firmer the longer it cools.

If you glaze the cake on a cooling rack with waxed paper under the rack, any extra drips of the ganache will fall onto the waxed paper. When the ganache hardens, you can easily and neatly transfer the cake to your serving plate.

☺ Variation

Stir 2 tablespoons freeze-dried or powdered instant coffee (dry) or 1 tablespoon grated orange peel into the cake batter.

Chocolate Ganache Cake

Chocolate Fantasy Cake

Prep: 1 hr Bake: 20 min Cool: 1 hr 10 min Chill: 2 hr

1 package Betty Crocker SuperMoist chocolate fudge cake mix
1⅓ cups water
⅓ cup vegetable oil
1 tablespoon prepared coffee or coffee liqueur
4 eggs
Chocolate Mocha Mousse (below)
Chocolate Whipped Cream Frosting (right)

1. Heat oven to 350°. Grease bottoms and sides of 3 round pans, 8 or 9 × 1½ inches, with shortening; lightly flour. Beat cake mix, water, oil, coffee and eggs in large bowl with electric mixer on low speed 1 minute, scraping bowl constantly. Pour into pans. (If baking only 2 pans at one time, refrigerate remaining batter until ready to use.) Bake about 20 minutes or until top springs back when touched lightly in center. Cool 10 minutes. Run knife around side of pans to loosen cakes; remove from pans to wire rack. Cool completely, about 1 hour.

2. Make Chocolate Mocha Mousse and Chocolate Whipped Cream Frosting.

3. Place 1 cake layer on plate; spread with half of the mousse. Repeat with second layer and remaining mousse. Top with remaining layer. Frost side and top of cake with frosting. Cover and refrigerate at least 2 hours before serving. Store covered in refrigerator.

16 servings.

Chocolate Mocha Mousse
¾ cup whipping (heavy) cream
2 tablespoons granulated sugar
⅓ cup prepared coffee or coffee liqueur
1 bag (6 ounces) semisweet chocolate chips (1 cup)
2 teaspoons vanilla

Place ¼ cup of the whipping cream, the sugar and the coffee in 2-quart saucepan. Cook over medium heat, stirring until sugar is dissolved and mixture simmers; remove from heat. Stir in chocolate chips until chips are melted. Stir in vanilla. Pour into large bowl; cool about 10 minutes. Beat remaining ½ cup whipping cream in chilled bowl on high speed just until soft peaks form. Fold whipped cream into chocolate mixture. Cover and refrigerate 30 minutes.

Chocolate Whipped Cream Frosting
1½ cups whipping (heavy) cream
1¼ cups powdered sugar
⅓ cup Dutch process baking cocoa
½ teaspoon vanilla

Beat all ingredients in chilled large bowl on high speed until soft peaks form.

1 Serving: Calories 390 (Calories from Fat 200); Fat 22g (Saturated 11g); Cholesterol 90mg; Sodium 330mg; Carbohydrate 46g (Dietary Fiber 2g); Protein 4g
% Daily Value: Vitamin A 8%; Vitamin C 0%; Calcium 6%; Iron 8%
Diet Exchanges: Not Recommended

BETTY'S TIPS

⊗ Substitution
You can use a 2.8-ounce package of chocolate or milk chocolate mousse mix instead of making **Chocolate Mocha Mousse**.

You can use a tub of Betty Crocker Whipped chocolate ready-to-spread frosting instead of making the chocolate frosting.

⊗ Success Hint
Use about 1½ cups of cake batter for each pan to be certain that all three layers are the same size.

⊗ Special Touch
Add chopped semisweet chocolate on top of the frosted cake.

Chocolate Fantasy Cake

Meringue-Swirled Chocolate Cake

Prep: 20 min   Bake: 1 hr 30 min   Cool: 1 hr 10 min

1   package Betty Crocker SuperMoist
    chocolate fudge cake mix
1⅓   cups water
½   cup vegetable oil
3   eggs
3   egg whites
¾   cup sugar

1. Heat oven to 325°. Generously grease bottom and side of springform pan, 9 × 3 inches, with shortening; lightly flour. Make batter for cake mix as directed on package, using water, oil and 3 eggs.

2. Beat 3 egg whites in medium bowl with electric mixer on high speed until soft peaks form. Beat in sugar, 1 tablespoon at a time; continue beating until stiff and glossy.

3. Spread two-thirds of the meringue up side of pan (do not spread on bottom of pan). Pour cake batter into pan; top with remaining meringue. Cut through meringue on top of cake and cake batter with tip of knife to swirl meringue through batter.

4. Bake about 1 hour 30 minutes or until toothpick inserted in center comes out clean. Cool 10 minutes on wire rack. Run metal spatula along side of cake to loosen; remove side of pan. Cool cake completely, about 1 hour. Store loosely covered at room temperature.

10 servings.

1 Serving: Calories 380 (Calories from Fat 135); Fat 15g (Saturated 3g); Cholesterol 65mg; Sodium 420mg; Carbohydrate 57g (Dietary Fiber 1g); Protein 5g
% Daily Value: Vitamin A 0%; Vitamin C 0%; Calcium 4%; Iron 6%
Diet Exchanges: Not Recommended

BETTY'S TIPS

☺ Success Hint
Egg whites will not beat up if even a trace of fat is present. Because egg yolks contain fat, not even the smallest amount of yolk can be in the whites. The beaters and bowl must also be clean and dry.

☺ Variation
If you don't have a springform pan, you can bake this cake in a greased and floured 13 × 9 × 2-inch rectangular pan for 40 to 45 minutes or until a toothpick inserted in the center comes out clean.

Meringue-Swirled Chocolate Cake

Peppermint Cream Brownie Torte

Prep: 30 min   Bake: 30 min   Cool: 1 hr
Photo on page 207

1   package (1 pound 6.5 ounces) Betty Crocker Original Supreme brownie mix (with chocolate syrup pouch)
¼   cup water
⅓   cup vegetable oil
2   eggs
    Peppermint Cream (below)
    Dark Chocolate Ganache (right)
10 to 12   hard peppermint candies, coarsely crushed
    Chocolate Trees (right), if desired

1. Heat oven to 350°. Line rectangular pan, 13 × 9 × 2 inches, with 17 × 12-inch piece of aluminum foil. Grease bottom only of foil with shortening. Make brownie mix as directed on package for fudgelike brownies, using water, oil and eggs. Spread batter in pan. Bake as directed. Cool completely on wire rack, about 1 hour.

2. Make Peppermint Cream and Dark Chocolate Ganache. Remove brownies from pan, using foil to lift. Cut brownies crosswise to make 3 equal rectangles. Trim sides if desired.

3. To assemble torte, place 1 brownie rectangle on serving platter; spread with ⅔ cup Peppermint Cream. Top with second brownie rectangle; spread with Dark Chocolate Ganache. Top with third brownie rectangle; spread with remaining cream. Refrigerate uncovered until serving.

4. Just before serving, sprinkle with candies and arrange Chocolate Trees on top. Store covered in refrigerator.

9 servings.

Peppermint Cream
½   cup whipping (heavy) cream
½   package (8-ounce size) cream cheese, softened
¼   cup powdered sugar
½   teaspoon peppermint extract

Beat whipping cream in medium bowl with electric mixer on high speed until soft peaks form; set aside. Beat remaining ingredients in medium bowl on low speed until blended; beat on medium speed until smooth. Fold whipped cream into cream cheese mixture.

Dark Chocolate Ganache
¼   cup whipping (heavy) cream
½   cup semisweet chocolate chips

Heat whipping cream in 1-quart saucepan over low heat until hot but not boiling; remove from heat. Stir in chocolate chips until melted. Let stand at room temperature about one hour or until slightly thickened.

Chocolate Trees
1   cup semisweet chocolate chips
1   teaspoon shortening

1. Place a piece of cooking parchment or waxed paper on a cookie sheet. Draw 1½- to 2-inch tree outlines or trace around 2-inch tree-shaped cookie cutter, leaving ½ inch space between trees. Center toothpick at bottom of and ½ inch into each tree outline.

2. Heat chocolate chips and shortening in 1-quart saucepan over low heat, stirring constantly, until chips are melted. Pour chocolate into decorating bag fitted with plain tip or resealable plastic bag; snip one corner.

3. Starting at top of each tree outline, pipe chocolate over tree and end of toothpick within tree; fill center with random, squiggly lines. Refrigerate until chocolate hardens. Gently remove trees from paper; refrigerate until serving.

1 Serving: Calories 540 (Calories from Fat 235); Fat 26g (Saturated 11g); Cholesterol 85mg; Sodium 300mg; Carbohydrate 70g (Dietary Fiber 0g); Protein 6g
% Daily Value: Vitamin A 10%; Vitamin C 0%; Calcium 6%; Iron 6%
Diet Exchanges: Not Recommended

BETTY'S TIPS
✪ Extra Special
For a sparkling finish, sprinkle white coarse sugar crystals (decorating sugar) over the top of the torte.

Betty... MAKES IT EASY

Chocolate Chip Swirl Cake

Prep: 15 min   Bake: 40 min   Cool: 1 hr

1	package Betty Crocker SuperMoist white cake mix
1¼	cups water
⅓	cup vegetable oil
3	egg whites
¾	cup miniature semisweet chocolate chips
¼	cup chocolate-flavored syrup
1	tub Betty Crocker Rich & Creamy vanilla ready-to-spread frosting
	Additional chocolate-flavored syrup, if desired

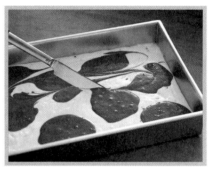

Cut through batters with spatula or knife in S-shaped curves in one continuous motion.

1. Heat oven to 350°. Generously grease bottom only of rectangular pan, 13 × 9 × 2 inches, with shortening. Make cake mix as directed on package, using water, oil and egg whites. Stir in ½ cup of the chocolate chips. Reserve 1 cup of the batter. Pour remaining batter into pan.

2. Stir ¼ cup chocolate syrup into reserved batter. Drop by generous tablespoonfuls randomly in 6 to 8 mounds onto batter in pan. Cut through batters with spatula or knife in S-shaped curves in one continuous motion. Turn pan ¼ turn, and repeat cutting for swirled design.

Turn pan ¼ turn, and repeat cutting for swirled design.

3. Bake about 40 minutes or until cake springs back when touched in center. Run knife around side of pan to loosen cake. Cool completely, about 1 hour. Stir remaining ¼ cup chocolate chips into frosting. Frost top of cake with frosting; drizzle with additional chocolate syrup.

15 servings.

1 Serving: Calories 370 (Calories from Fat 135); Fat 15g (Saturated 7g); Cholesterol 0mg; Sodium 250mg; Carbohydrate 57g (Dietary Fiber 1g); Protein 3g
% Daily Value: Vitamin A 0%; Vitamin C 0%; Calcium 4%; Iron 4%
Diet Exchanges: Not Recommended

Chocolate Chip Swirl Cake

Strawberries and Cream Cake

Prep: 15 min   Bake: 35 min   Cool: 1 hr

1   package Betty Crocker SuperMoist white cake mix
1   package (0.14 ounce) strawberry-flavored unsweetened soft drink mix
¾   cup water
3   eggs (including yolks)
1   package (10 ounces) frozen sliced strawberries, thawed and undrained
    Whipped Cream Cheese Frosting (below)

1. Heat oven to 350°. Grease bottom only of rectangular pan, 13 × 9 × 2 inches, with shortening; lightly flour.

2. Beat cake mix, drink mix (dry), water, eggs and strawberries in large bowl with electric mixer on low speed 30 seconds. Beat on medium speed 2 minutes. Pour into pan.

3. Bake 30 to 35 minutes or until toothpick inserted in center comes out clean. Run knife around side of pan to loosen cake. Cool completely, about 1 hour. Frost with Whipped Cream Cheese Frosting. Store covered in refrigerator.

15 servings.

Whipped Cream Cheese Frosting
1   package (3 ounces) cream cheese, softened
1   tablespoon milk
2   cups whipping (heavy) cream
⅔   cup powdered sugar

Beat cream cheese and milk in chilled large bowl on low speed until smooth. Beat in whipping cream and powdered sugar on high speed, scraping bowl occasionally, until soft peaks form.

1 Serving: Calories 405 (Calories from Fat 145); Fat 16g (Saturated 9g); Cholesterol 85mg; Sodium 530mg; Carbohydrate 62g (Dietary Fiber 1g); Protein 4g
% Daily Value: Vitamin A 10%; Vitamin C 6%; Calcium 8%; Iron 8%
Diet Exchanges: Not Recommended

BETTY'S TIPS

⊙ **Success Hint**
There's no mistake: no vegetable oil is added to this cake. Use whole eggs in this recipe instead of the egg whites called for in the package directions.

You can use either fully sweetened or reduced-sugar strawberries in this recipe.

⊙ **Special Touch**
Make a patchwork design on top of this cake. Visually divide the cake into serving pieces, and place strawberries on half of the servings. Whole, halved, diagonal cut and strawberry fans all would work well. Add a few washed strawberry leaves for variety.

Strawberries and Cream Cake

Raspberry Poke Cake

Prep: 10 min   Bake: 33 min   Cool: 1 hr   Chill: 2 hr

1 package Betty Crocker SuperMoist white cake mix

1¼ cups water

⅓ cup vegetable oil

3 egg whites

1 package (4-serving size) raspberry-flavored gelatin

1 cup boiling water

½ cup cold water

1 container (8 ounces) frozen whipped topping, thawed (3 cups)

Fresh raspberries, if desired

1. Heat oven to 350°. Grease bottom only of rectangular pan, 13 × 9 × 2 inches, with shortening. Make cake mix as directed on package, using water, oil and egg whites. Pour into pan.

2. Bake 28 to 33 minutes or until toothpick inserted in center comes out clean. Cool completely, about 1 hour.

3. Pierce cake all over with fork. Stir gelatin and boiling water in small bowl until smooth; stir in cold water. Pour over cake. Run knife around side of pan to loosen cake. Refrigerate 2 hours. Frost with whipped topping; garnish with raspberries. Store covered in refrigerator.

12 servings.

1 Serving: Calories 300 (Calories from Fat 115); Fat 13g (Saturated 3g); Cholesterol 10mg; Sodium 300mg; Carbohydrate 42g (Dietary Fiber 0g); Protein 4g
% Daily Value: Vitamin A 2%; Vitamin C 0%; Calcium 4%; Iron 4%
Diet Exchanges: Not Recommended

BETTY'S TIPS

۞ Substitution
Any flavor of gelatin that you like can be used for this recipe. Try strawberry gelatin and garnish the cake with strawberries, or experiment with strawberry-banana, strawberry-kiwi or sparkling berry gelatin.

Raspberry Poke Cake

Strawberry Yogurt Cake

Lemon Orange Cake

Lemon Orange Cake

Prep: 25 min   Bake: 32 min   Cool: 1 hr 10 min   Chill: 1 hr

1   package Betty Crocker SuperMoist white cake mix
1¼ cups orange juice
⅓   cup vegetable oil
3   egg whites
1   can (15¾ ounces) lemon pie filling
1   tub Betty Crocker Whipped fluffy white ready-to-spread frosting
    Grated orange peel, if desired

1. Heat oven to 350°. Grease bottoms and sides of 2 round pans, 8 or 9 × 1½ inches, with shortening; lightly flour. Beat cake mix, orange juice, oil and egg whites in large bowl with electric mixer on low speed 30 seconds. Beat on medium speed 2 minutes, scraping bowl constantly. Pour into pans.

2. Bake 8-inch rounds 27 to 32 minutes, 9-inch rounds 23 to 28 minutes, or until toothpick inserted in center comes out clean. Cool 10 minutes. Run knife around side of pans to loosen cakes; remove from pans to wire rack. Cool completely, about 1 hour.

3. Cut each cake layer horizontally in half to make 2 layers. Fill layers with generous ½ cup pie filling. Frost side and top of cake with frosting. Garnish with orange peel. Refrigerate about 1 hour or until chilled. Store covered in refrigerator.

16 servings.

1 Serving: Calories 300 (Calories from Fat 100); Fat 11g (Saturated 4g); Cholesterol 0mg; Sodium 230mg; Carbohydrate 48g (Dietary Fiber 0g); Protein 2g
% Daily Value: Vitamin A 0%; Vitamin C 6%; Calcium 2%; Iron 4%
Diet Exchanges: Not Recommended

BETTY'S TIPS

☺ **Success Hint**
To split cake rounds evenly, mark side of cake with toothpicks and cut with a long, thin knife.

☺ **Special Touch**
For an extra-special cake, add a fragrant mound of yellow and orange rose petals to the top of the cake. Just discard before eating.

Strawberry Yogurt Cake

Prep: 20 min   Bake: 35 min   Cool: 1 hr 10 min

1   package Betty Crocker SuperMoist white cake mix
¾   cup water
⅓   cup vegetable oil
3   egg whites
1   container (6 ounces) Yoplait Original strawberry yogurt (⅔ cup)
1   tub Betty Crocker Whipped vanilla ready-to-spread frosting
1   quart (4 cups) strawberries, whole or halved

1. Heat oven to 350°. Generously grease bottoms and sides of 2 round pans, 8 or 9 × 1½ inches, with shortening. Beat cake mix, water, oil, egg whites and yogurt in large bowl with electric mixer on low speed 30 seconds. Beat on medium speed 2 minutes. Pour into pans.

2. Bake 30 to 35 minutes or until toothpick inserted in center comes out clean. Cool 10 minutes. Run knife around side of pans to loosen cakes; remove from pans to wire rack. Cool completely, about 1 hour.

3. Place 1 cake layer on plate. Spread with ⅓ cup frosting almost to edge. Cut about 10 strawberries into ¼-inch slices; arrange on frosted layer. Top with second layer. Frost side and top of cake with remaining frosting. Garnish with remaining strawberries. Store loosely covered in refrigerator.

16 servings.

1 Serving: Calories 290 (Calories from Fat 100); Fat 11g (Saturated 5g); Cholesterol 0mg; Sodium 230mg; Carbohydrate 46g (Dietary Fiber 1g); Protein 3g
% Daily Value: Vitamin A 0%; Vitamin C 6%; Calcium 4%; Iron 4%
Diet Exchanges: 1 Starch, 2 Fruit, 2 Fat

BETTY'S TIPS

☺ **Success Tip**
If strawberries are cut in half, some juice will appear on frosting—so add halved strawberries at serving time.

☺ **Variation**
For greater portability, make cake as directed using a greased and floured rectangular pan, 13 × 9 × 2 inches, and bake 35 to 40 minutes. Cool completely in pan. Spread frosting over top of cake. Garnish with 1 pint (2 cups) of strawberries.

Neapolitan Cake

Prep: 25 min   Bake: 50 min   Cool: 1 hr 30 min

1 package Betty Crocker SuperMoist white cake mix
1 cup water
¼ cup vegetable oil
3 eggs
½ teaspoon peppermint extract
12 drops red food color
⅓ cup chocolate-flavored syrup
Chocolate Glaze (below)

1. Heat oven to 350°. Grease 12-cup Bundt cake pan with shortening; lightly flour. Make cake mix as directed on package, using water, oil and eggs.

2. Pour about 1⅔ cups batter into pan. Pour 1⅔ cups batter into small bowl; stir in peppermint extract and food color. Carefully pour pink batter over white batter in pan. Stir chocolate syrup into remaining batter. Carefully pour chocolate batter over pink batter.

3. Bake 45 to 50 minutes or until toothpick inserted in center of cake comes out clean. Cool 10 minutes; turn upside down onto wire rack and remove pan. Cool completely, 1 hour 20 minutes. Spread with Chocolate Glaze, allowing some to drizzle down side.

16 servings.

Chocolate Glaze

¾ cup semisweet chocolate chips
3 tablespoons butter or margarine
3 tablespoons corn syrup
2 to 3 teaspoons hot water

Heat all ingredients except water in 1-quart saucepan over low heat, stirring frequently, until chocolate chips are melted. Cool about 10 minutes. Stir in hot water, 1 teaspoon at a time, until consistency of thick syrup.

1 Serving: Calories 265 (Calories from Fat 110); Fat 12g (Saturated 5g); Cholesterol 45mg; Sodium 260mg; Carbohydrate 37g (Dietary Fiber 1g); Protein 3g
% Daily Value: Vitamin A 2%; Vitamin C 0%; Calcium 2%; Iron 6%
Diet Exchanges: 1 Starch, 1½ Fruit, 2 Fat

BETTY'S TIPS

☺ Time-Saver

To microwave **Chocolate Glaze**, place chocolate chips, butter and corn syrup in 2-cup microwavable measure. Microwave uncovered on Medium (50%) 1 to 2 minutes or until chocolate can be stirred smooth. Cool about 10 minutes. Stir in hot water, 1 teaspoon at a time, until consistency of thick syrup.

☺ Variation

Would you like an almond flavor for this cake instead of peppermint? Use ¼ teaspoon almond extract instead of the peppermint extract.

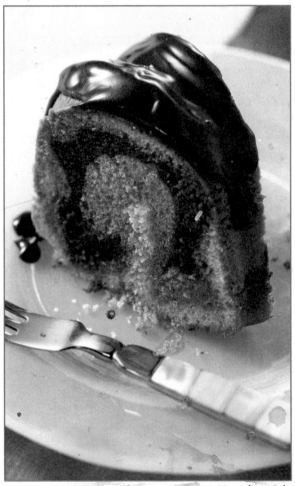

Neapolitan Cake

Luscious Mandarin Orange Cake

Prep: 10 min   Bake: 35 min   Cool: 1 hr

1 package Betty Crocker SuperMoist yellow cake mix

½ cup vegetable oil

½ cup chopped walnuts

4 eggs

1 can (11 ounces) mandarin orange segments, undrained

Pineapple Frosting (below)

1 package (4-serving size) vanilla instant pudding and pie filling mix

1 cup frozen (thawed) whipped topping

Stir together pineapple and pudding mix (dry). Gently stir in whipped topping.

1. Heat oven to 350°. Grease bottom only of rectangular pan, 13 × 9 × 2 inches, with shortening; lightly flour.

2. Beat cake mix, oil, walnuts, eggs and orange segments in large bowl with electric mixer on low speed 2 minutes (do not overbeat). Pour into pan.

3. Bake 30 to 35 minutes or until toothpick inserted in center comes out clean. Run knife around side of pan to loosen cake. Cool completely, about 1 hour. Frost with Pineapple Frosting. Store tightly covered in refrigerator.

20 servings.

Pineapple Frosting

1 can (20 ounces) crushed pineapple, undrained

1 Serving: Calories 240 (Calories from Fat 100); Fat 11g (Saturated 2g); Cholesterol 45mg; Sodium 250mg; Carbohydrate 33g (Dietary Fiber 1g); Protein 3g
% Daily Value: Vitamin A 2%; Vitamin C 6%; Calcium 6%; Iron 4%
Diet Exchanges: 1 Starch, 1 Fruit, 2 Fat

BETTY'S TIPS

✪ Variation

You can add a burst of orange flavor to the frosting. Stir in ½ to 1 teaspoon grated orange peel with the pineapple and pudding mix.

✪ Special Touch

Garnish this sensational cake with curly strips of orange peel. Or sprinkle with toasted coconut to enhance the tropical flavors of the cake and frosting.

Luscious Mandarin Orange Cake

Cherry Cassata

Prep: 25 min   Chill: 2 hr 45 min

- ⅓ cup currants or raisins
- 1 can (16½ ounces) pitted dark sweet cherries, drained and syrup reserved
- 1 container (15 ounces) ricotta cheese
- ½ cup frozen (thawed) whipped topping
- 6 tablespoons sweet Marsala wine or orange juice
- 1 loaf (16 ounces) pound cake
- 1 bag (12 ounces) semisweet chocolate chips (2 cups)
- 1 cup firm butter or margarine, cut into pieces

1. Place currants and 3 tablespoons of reserved cherry syrup in small bowl; reserve ½ cup cherry syrup. Let stand about 15 minutes or until currants are softened; drain. Coarsely chop cherries; set aside.

2. Place ricotta cheese, whipped topping and 3 tablespoons of the wine in food processor or blender. Cover and process until smooth. Transfer to medium bowl; fold in cherries and currants.

3. Cut pound cake horizontally into 3 layers. Place bottom layer on serving dish. Spread with half of the ricotta mixture. Add middle cake layer. Spread with remaining ricotta mixture. Add top cake layer. Cover with plastic wrap and refrigerate about 2 hours or until ricotta mixture is firm.

4. Melt chocolate chips in 2-quart saucepan over low heat, stirring frequently. Stir in remaining 3 tablespoons wine and reserved ½ cup cherry syrup until smooth; remove from heat. Beat in butter, a few pieces at a time, using wire whisk, until melted. Refrigerate about 45 minutes or until thick enough to spread. Spread chocolate mixture over top and sides of dessert. Store covered in refrigerator.

16 servings.

1 Serving: Calories 430 (Calories from Fat 260); Fat 29g (Saturated 16g); Cholesterol 75mg; Sodium 140mg; Carbohydrate 38g (Dietary Fiber 2g); Protein 6g
% Daily Value: Vitamin A 12%; Vitamin C 2%; Calcium 10%; Iron 8%
Diet Exchanges: Not Recommended

BETTY'S TIPS

✿ **Extra Special**
Dress up this yummy dessert with a dusting of powdered sugar.

✿ **Did You Know?**
A cassata is a traditional Italian dessert made up of layers of liqueur-soaked cake, ricotta cheese, candied fruit and chocolate.

Cherry Cassata

Ultimate Carrot Cake

Prep: 20 min   Bake: 45 min   Cool: 1 hr 10 min

1 package Betty Crocker SuperMoist carrot cake mix

½ cup water

½ cup vegetable oil

4 eggs

1 can (8 ounces) crushed pineapple in juice, undrained

½ cup chopped nuts

½ cup shredded coconut

½ cup raisins

Cream Cheese Frosting (below)

1. Heat oven to 350°. Grease bottoms only of 2 round pans, 8 or 9 × 1½ inches, with shortening; lightly flour.

2. Beat cake mix, water, oil, eggs and pineapple in large bowl with electric mixer on low speed 30 seconds. Beat on medium speed 2 minutes. Stir in nuts, coconut and raisins. Pour into pans.

3. Bake 8-inch rounds 40 to 45 minutes, 9-inch rounds 28 to 32 minutes, or until toothpick inserted in center comes out clean. Cool 10 minutes. Run knife around side of pans to loosen cakes; remove from pans to wire rack. Cool completely, about 1 hour. Fill layers and frost side and top of cake with Cream Cheese Frosting. Store covered in refrigerator.

12 servings.

Cream Cheese Frosting

1 package (8 ounces) cream cheese, softened

¼ cup butter or margarine, softened

2 to 3 teaspoons milk

1 teaspoon vanilla

4 cups powdered sugar

Beat cream cheese, butter, milk and vanilla in medium bowl on low speed until smooth. Gradually beat in powdered sugar, 1 cup at a time, on low speed until smooth and spreadable.

1 Serving: Calories 470 (Calories from Fat 290); Fat 32g (Saturated 11g); Cholesterol 1010mg; Sodium 400mg; Carbohydrate 40g (Dietary Fiber 1g); Protein 6g
% Daily Value: Vitamin A 10%; Vitamin C 2%; Calcium 2%; Iron 4%
Diet Exchanges: Not Recommended

BETTY'S TIPS

⊕ Substitution
You can use 1 tub of Betty Crocker Rich & Creamy cream cheese frosting instead of making your own frosting.

⊕ Success Hint
To cut easily, use a thin nonserrated knife.

⊕ Variation
You can add extra carrots to this cake. Omit the water, and add ¾ cup finely shredded carrots. Decrease the bake time for 8-inch pans to about 35 minutes (bake time for 9-inch pans remains the same).

Ultimate Carrot Cake

Pound Cake with Fruit Salsa

Prep: 15 min   Bake: 40 min   Cool: 1 hr 10 min

1 package Betty Crocker SuperMoist yellow cake mix

1 cup milk

1 package (3 ounces) cream cheese, softened

1 teaspoon vanilla

3 eggs
   Powdered sugar, if desired
   Fruit Salsa (below)

1. Heat oven to 350°. Generously grease 12-cup Bundt cake pan with shortening; lightly flour.

2. Beat cake mix (dry), milk, cream cheese, vanilla and eggs in medium bowl with electric mixer on low speed 1 minute, scraping bowl constantly. Beat 2 minutes longer. Pour into pan.

3. Bake 35 to 40 minutes or until toothpick inserted in center comes out clean. Cool 10 minutes; turn up-side down onto wire rack or heatproof serving plate and remove pan. Cool completely, about 1 hour. Make Fruit Salsa. Place cake on serving plate; sprinkle with powdered sugar. Serve with salsa.

16 servings.

Fruit Salsa

1⅓ cups large chunks peeled kiwifruit (2 medium)

1 cup chopped orange sections (2 medium)

1 cup sliced strawberries

2 tablespoons lime juice

4 teaspoons sugar

½ teaspoon ground ginger or 1 teaspoon finely chopped gingerroot, if desired

Mix ingredients in large bowl. Cover and refrigerate about 1 hour or until chilled.

1 Serving: Calories 190 (Calories from Fat 55); Fat 6g (Saturated 3g); Cholesterol 35mg; Sodium 240mg; Carbohydrate 32g (Dietary Fiber 1g); Protein 3g
% Daily Value: Vitamin A 4%; Vitamin C 20%; Calcium 10%; Iron 4%
Diet Exchanges: 1 Starch, 1 Fruit, 1 Fat

BETTY'S TIPS

⊕ **Substitution**

You can substitute SuperMoist lemon cake mix for the yellow cake mix; omit the vanilla and increase the first beat time to 2 minutes.

⊕ **Serve-With**

Leftover cake? Make a **Pound Cake Trifle:** Cut the cake into large cubes, and place them in a large glass or plastic bowl. Sprinkle with a little orange-flavored liqueur or orange juice, cover with plastic wrap and refrigerate about 2 hours. Layer cake, whipped cream and fresh fruit in goblets. Cover and refrigerate at least 1 hour before serving.

Pound Cake with Fruit Salsa

Piña Colada Cake

Prep: 25 min Bake: 35 min Cool: 1 hr 10 min

1 package Betty Crocker SuperMoist yellow cake mix

1¼ cups water

⅓ cup vegetable oil

3 eggs

1 can (8 ounces) crushed pineapple in juice, well drained and juice reserved

1 teaspoon rum extract

1 package Betty Crocker HomeStyle fluffy white frosting mix

1 teaspoon rum extract

¼ cup flaked coconut, toasted

1. Heat oven to 350°. Grease bottoms and sides of 2 round pans, 8 or 9 × 1½ inches, with shortening; lightly flour. Beat cake mix, water, oil, eggs, pineapple and 1 teaspoon rum extract in large bowl with electric mixer on low speed 30 seconds, scraping bowl constantly, until moistened. Beat on medium speed 2 minutes, scraping bowl occasionally. Pour into pans.

2. Bake 30 to 35 minutes or until cakes spring back when touched lightly in center. Cool 10 minutes. Run knife around side of pans to loosen cakes; remove from pans to wire rack. Cool completely, about 1 hour.

3. Add enough water to reserved pineapple juice to measure ½ cup; heat to boiling. Make frosting mix as directed on package, using pineapple juice mixture for the boiling water called for in package directions. Beat 1 teaspoon rum extract into frosting on low speed. Fill cake layers with about ⅔ cup frosting. Frost side and top of cake with remaining frosting. Sprinkle top and sides with coconut. Store loosely covered at room temperature.

12 servings.

1 Serving: Calories 595 (Calories from Fat 380); Fat 42g (Saturated 3g); Cholesterol 55mg; Sodium 300mg; Carbohydrate 51g (Dietary Fiber 0g); Protein 3g
% Daily Value: Vitamin A 2%; Vitamin C 2%; Calcium 8%; Iron 4%
Diet Exchanges: Not Recommended

BETTY'S TIPS

⊗ Success Hint
To toast coconut, spread coconut in an ungreased shallow pan and bake uncovered at 350° for 5 to 7 minutes, stirring occasionally, until golden brown. Or sprinkle in an ungreased heavy skillet and cook over medium-low heat 6 to 14 minutes, stirring frequently until browning begins, then stirring constantly until golden brown.

⊗ Variation
This cake can be made with SuperMoist butter recipe yellow cake mix, substituting ½ cup butter or margarine, softened, for the vegetable oil.

Piña Colada Cake

Banana Toffee Picnic Cake

Prep: 10 min   Bake: 40 min   Cool: 1 hr

- 1 package Betty Crocker SuperMoist yellow cake mix
- 1 cup mashed very ripe bananas (2 medium)
- ⅓ cup water
- ⅓ cup vegetable oil
- 3 eggs
- 1 teaspoon almond extract
- ½ cup almond brickle chips

1. Heat oven to 350°. Grease bottom and sides of rectangular pan, 13 × 9 × 2 inches, with shortening; lightly flour.

2. Beat cake mix, bananas, water, oil, eggs and almond extract in large bowl with electric mixer on low speed 30 seconds. Beat on medium speed 2 minutes. Pour into pan. Sprinkle brickle chips evenly over batter.

3. Bake 35 to 40 minutes or until cake springs back when touched lightly in center. Run knife around side of pan to loosen cake. Cool completely, about 1 hour.

12 servings.

1 Serving: Calories 315 (Calories from Fat 125); Fat 14g (Saturated 4g); Cholesterol 60mg; Sodium 310mg; Carbohydrate 45g (Dietary Fiber 1g); Protein 3g
% Daily Value: Vitamin A 2%; Vitamin C 0%; Calcium 11%; Iron 4%
Diet Exchanges: Not Recommended

BETTY'S TIPS

Success Hint
Measure the amount of mashed bananas carefully. Using too much banana makes the cake sink and have a gummy texture.

Special Touch
Bananas and chocolate is a great flavor combination. You can frost this moist, tasty cake with Betty Crocker Rich & Creamy chocolate frosting. This cake also makes a great banana split dessert. Split each serving of cake horizontally in half, add your favorite ice cream on the bottom half, top with top of cake and drizzle with chocolate and caramel toppings. Add a maraschino cherry with a stem if you like.

Frosty Coffee Almond Pie

Prep: 15 min   Freeze: 3 hr 15 min   Stand: 10 min

- 18 creme-filled chocolate sandwich cookies, finely crushed
- 3 tablespoons butter or margarine, melted
- 1 quart coffee ice cream, slightly softened
- ½ cup sliced almonds, toasted
- 1 cup hot fudge sauce, warmed

1. Mix crushed cookies and butter until well blended. Press on bottom and up side of ungreased pie plate, 9 × 1¼ inches. Freeze about 15 minutes or until firm.

2. Carefully spread ice cream evenly in crust. Sprinkle with almonds. Freeze about 3 hours or until firm.

3. Remove pie from freezer about 10 minutes before serving. Serve with hot fudge sauce. Store covered in freezer.

8 servings.

1 Serving: Calories 470 (Calories from Fat 215); Fat 24g (Saturated 10g); Cholesterol 35mg; Sodium 360mg; Carbohydrate 60g (Dietary Fiber 4g); Protein 7g
% Daily Value: Vitamin A 10%; Vitamin C 0%; Calcium 12%; Iron 12%
Diet Exchanges: Not Recommended

BETTY'S TIPS

☺ Substitution
Have fun picking the ice cream flavor for this special treat. You can use chocolate, vanilla, strawberry or any flavor that you like.

☺ Success Hint
To quickly soften ice cream, microwave on High 15 to 30 seconds.

☺ Simplify
Use a purchased chocolate crumb crust instead of making your own crust.

Banana Toffee Picnic Cake

Frosty Coffee Almond Pie

Betty ... ON BASICS

Divine Caramel Sauce

Prep: 5 min   Cook: 35 min   Cool: 30 min

    2 cups sugar
   ¾ cup butter or margarine
    2 cups whipping (heavy) cream
    1 cup light corn syrup
      Dash of salt
    1 teaspoon vanilla

Stir until sugar is dissolved and mixture is light caramel colored.

1. Heat all ingredients except vanilla to boiling in heavy 4-quart Dutch oven over medium heat, stirring constantly; reduce heat slightly.

2. Boil about 30 minutes, stirring frequently, until sugar is dissolved and mixture is light caramel colored.

3. Stir in vanilla. Cool about 30 minutes. Serve warm. Store covered in refrigerator up to 2 months. Reheat slightly before serving if desired.

4 cups sauce.

1 Tablespoon: Calories 75 (Calories from Fat 35); Fat 4g (Saturated 3g); Cholesterol 15mg; Sodium 25mg; Carbohydrate 10g (Dietary Fiber 0g); Protein 0g
% Daily Value: Vitamin A 2%; Vitamin C 0%; Calcium 0%; Iron 0%
Diet Exchanges: ½ Fruit, 1 Fat

Peanut Brittle Bread Pudding

Prep: 20 min   Bake: 30 min

Divine Caramel Sauce (opposite page) or
purchased caramel topping, if desired

4   cups soft bread cubes (6 to 7 slices
    bread)

½   cup coarsely broken peanut brittle

1   egg

1   cup milk

½   cup packed brown sugar

¼   cup butter or margarine, melted
    Whipped cream, if desired

1. Prepare Divine Caramel Sauce.

2. Heat oven to 350°. Grease bottom and side of 1-
quart casserole with shortening. Place 2 cups of the
bread cubes in casserole. Sprinkle with half of the
peanut brittle; repeat with remaining bread cubes
and peanut brittle.

3. Beat egg in small bowl. Stir in milk, brown sugar
and butter. Pour over bread mixture.

4. Bake uncovered 25 to 30 minutes or until golden
brown. Serve with caramel sauce and whipped cream.

6 servings.

1 Serving: Calories 285 (Calories from Fat 115); Fat 13g (Saturated 6g);
Cholesterol 60mg; Sodium 240mg; Carbohydrate 38g (Dietary Fiber
1g); Protein 5g
% Daily Value: Vitamin A 8%; Vitamin C 0%; Calcium 8%; Iron 6%
Diet Exchanges: 2 Starch, ½ Fruit, 2 Fat

BETTY'S TIPS

✿ Do-Ahead
You can prepare this dessert up to 24 hours ahead of
time. Follow directions through step 2; cover and refrigerate
until ready to bake.

Peanut Brittle Bread Pudding

Praline Puffs

Praline Puffs

Prep: 30 min   Bake: 40 min   Cool: 1 hr

1 cup water

½ cup butter or margarine

¾ cup Gold Medal all-purpose flour

½ cup pecan halves, toasted and coarsely ground or finely chopped

4 eggs

Brittle Spears, if desired (below)

Praline Cream Filling (right)

¾ cup Divine Caramel Sauce (page 238) or purchased caramel topping

Chopped pecans, if desired

1. Heat oven to 400°. Heat water and butter to rolling boil in 2-quart saucepan. Stir in flour and ground pecans. Stir vigorously over low heat about 1 minute or until mixture forms a ball; remove from heat. Beat in eggs all at once with spoon; continue beating until smooth.

2. Drop dough by scant ¼ cupfuls about 3 inches apart onto ungreased cookie sheet. Bake 35 to 40 minutes or until puffed and golden. Cool 1 hour away from draft. Meanwhile make Brittle Spears.

3. Prepare Praline Cream Filling. Cut off tops of puffs with sharp knife; pull out any soft dough. Fill puffs with cream filling; replace tops. Serve immediately, or cover and refrigerate up to 3 hours. Just before serving, drizzle with Divine Caramel Sauce and sprinkle with chopped pecans. Garnish with Brittle Spears.

12 servings.

Brittle Spears

Heat oven to 200°. Butter sheet of aluminum foil on large cookie sheet; keep warm in oven. Heat 1 cup sugar, ¼ cup water and 2 tablespoons corn syrup to boiling in heavy 8-inch skillet over medium heat, stirring constantly, until sugar is melted and light golden brown, about 6 minutes. Quickly pour onto foil, tilting cookie sheet to spread until syrup is very thin. (If syrup hardens too quickly, warm in 400° oven until warm enough to spread.) Cool on cookie sheet on wire rack until completely hard. Score brittle with sharp knife into uneven pieces; carefully break apart. (Brittle Spears can be tightly covered and stored at room temperature up to 3 days.)

Praline Cream Filling

1½ cups whipping (heavy) cream

¼ cup Divine Caramel Sauce (page 238) or purchased caramel topping

15 oval-shaped hard caramel candies, unwrapped and crushed

Beat whipping cream and Divine Caramel Sauce in chilled large bowl with electric mixer on high speed until stiff. Fold in crushed candies.

1 Serving: Calories 380 (Calories from Fat 250); Fat 28g (Saturated 15g); Cholesterol 145mg; Sodium 115mg; Carbohydrate 29g (Dietary Fiber 1g); Protein 4g
% Daily Value: Vitamin A 18%; Vitamin C 0%; Calcium 4%; Iron 4%
Diet Exchanges: Not Recommended

BETTY'S TIPS

☻ **Success Hint**

To toast nuts, bake uncovered in ungreased shallow pan in 350° oven about 10 minutes, stirring occasionally, until golden brown. Or cook in ungreased heavy skillet over medium-low heat 5 to 7 minutes, stirring frequently until browning begins, then stirring constantly until golden brown.

☻ **Simplify**

Forgo the **Praline Cream Filling** and fill puffs with frozen (thawed) whipped topping. Serve with a purchased caramel or butterscotch topping.

Nutty Squash Pie

Prep: 15 min   Bake: 1 hr 10 min   Cool: 2 hr

Nut Cookie Crust (below)
1 cup cooled mashed cooked squash
2 eggs
¾ cup packed brown sugar
1 teaspoon ground cinnamon
½ teaspoon salt
¼ teaspoon ground cloves
¼ teaspoon ground ginger
¼ teaspoon ground nutmeg
1 can (12 ounces) evaporated milk

1. Heat oven to 425°. Make Nut Cookie Crust. Press crust mixture on bottom and side of ungreased deep-dish pie plate, 9 × 1½ inches, or regular pie plate, 9 × 1¼ inches, building up ½-inch edge (high edge is necessary to prevent filling from running over).

2. Beat eggs slightly in large bowl. Stir in remaining ingredients except milk until smooth. Gradually stir in milk. Pour into crust. Cover edge with 2- to 3-inch strip of aluminum foil to prevent excessive browning.

3. Bake 15 minutes. Reduce oven temperature to 350°. Bake 45 to 55 minutes longer or until knife inserted near center comes out clean. Cool completely on wire rack, about 2 hours. Store covered in refrigerator.

8 servings.

Nut Cookie Crust
½ cup butter or margarine, softened
⅓ cup packed brown sugar
1¼ cups Gold Medal all-purpose flour
½ cup chopped nuts
½ teaspoon vanilla
¼ teaspoon salt
¼ teaspoon baking soda

Mix butter and brown sugar in large bowl. Stir in remaining ingredients just until crumbly.

1 Serving: Calories 400 (Calories from Fat 170); Fat 19g (Saturated 15g); Cholesterol 40mg; Sodium 400mg; Carbohydrate 53g (Dietary Fiber 2g); Protein 6g
% Daily Value: Vitamin A 30%; Vitamin C 2%; Calcium 18%; Iron 12%
Diet Exchanges: Not Recommended

BETTY'S TIPS

❂ **Substitution**
You can substitute mashed cooked sweet potatoes or pumpkin for the squash.

❂ **Extra Special**
Crown this pie with **Brown Sugar Whipped Cream.** To make, beat 1 cup whipping (heavy) cream and 3 tablespoons packed brown sugar in chilled small bowl with electric mixer on high speed until stiff.

Sprinkle ground cinnamon lightly over each serving—plate and all.

Nutty Squash Pie

Sweet Somethings

Tempting Truffles, Cookies, Bars, and Cupcakes

Raspberry Truffle Cups (page 253)

White Chocolate Chunk Cranberry Cookies (page 269)

Fruit Bruschetta

Prep: 10 min   Broil: 5 min

1   package (10.75 ounces) frozen pound cake
     loaf, cut into fourteen ½-inch slices

⅔   cup soft cream cheese with strawberries,
     raspberries or pineapple

1   can (11 ounces) mandarin orange segments,
     well drained

     Assorted bite-size pieces fresh fruit
     (kiwifruit, strawberry, raspberry, pear, apple)

     Chocolate-flavored syrup, if desired

     Toasted coconut or sliced almonds, if
     desired

1. Set oven control to broil. Place pound cake slices on
rack in broiler pan. Broil with tops 4 to 5 inches from
heat 3 to 5 minutes, turning once, until light golden
brown.

2. Spread each slice with about 2 teaspoons cream
cheese. Cut slices diagonally in half to make 28
pieces. Top with orange segments and desired fruit.
Drizzle with syrup; sprinkle with coconut. Arrange on
serving platter.

28 servings.

1 Serving: Calories 70 (Calories from Fat 23); Fat 4g (Saturated 2g);
Cholesterol 15mg; Sodium 20mg; Carbohydrate 9g (Dietary Fiber 1g);
Protein 1g
% Daily Value: Vitamin A 2%; Vitamin C 20%; Calcium 0%; Iron 2%
Diet Exchanges: 1 Fruit

BETTY'S TIPS

⊙ **Substitution**
You can drizzle the fruit with caramel ice-cream topping
instead of the chocolate syrup.

⊙ **Do-Ahead**
Toast the pound cake up to a day ahead of time. You can
assemble the bruschetta up to 4 hours before your party.
Cover and refrigerate until serving time.

Chocolate-Dipped Fruit Wreath

Prep: 20 min   Chill: 30 min

1   bag (6 ounces) semisweet chocolate chips
     (1 cup)

1   tablespoon shortening

6   cups assorted fresh fruit pieces (whole
     strawberries, grapes, mandarin orange
     segments, cherries)

     Fresh mint leaves and/or fresh rosemary
     stems

1. Line jelly roll pan, 15½ × 10½ × 1 inch, with waxed
paper. Heat chocolate chips and shortening in 1-
quart saucepan over low heat, stirring frequently,
until smooth; remove from heat.

2. Dip half of each piece of fruit into chocolate. Place
in pan.

3. Refrigerate uncovered about 30 minutes or until
chocolate is firm. Arrange fruit on plate in wreath
shape. Garnish with mint.

4 dozen confections.

1 Confection: Calories 25 (Calories from Fat 10); Fat 1g (Saturated 1g);
Cholesterol 0mg; Sodium 0mg; Carbohydrate 5g (Dietary Fiber 1g);
Protein 0g
% Daily Value: Vitamin A 0%; Vitamin C 8%; Calcium 0%; Iron 0%
Diet Exchanges: Free Food

BETTY'S TIPS

⊙ **Substitution**
Use 6 ounces vanilla milk chips (1 cup) for the chocolate
chips.

⊙ **Do-Ahead**
You can dip the fruit into chocolate up to 6 hours ahead of
time. Store uncovered in the refrigerator until chocolate is
set, then cover loosely.

⊙ **Special Touch**
Garnish with an orange peel bow sprinkled with sugar. Use
a channel knife (available in kitchen stores) to remove the
peel in one strip and form the strip into a bow.

Chocolate-Dipped Fruit Wreath

Fruit Bruschetta

Peachy Fruit Pizza

Prep: 20 min   Bake: 40 min   Cool: 1 hr

1   package Betty Crocker SuperMoist yellow cake mix
½   cup butter or margarine, slightly softened
¼   cup packed brown sugar
1   teaspoon ground cinnamon
1   cup sour cream
1   egg
1   can (29 ounces) sliced peaches, drained and patted dry
½   cup finely chopped nuts, if desired
    Cinnamon Glaze (below)

1. Heat oven to 350°. Mix cake mix (dry), butter, brown sugar and cinnamon with spoon in large bowl until crumbly. Reserve 1 cup of crumbly mixture. Press remaining crumbly mixture on bottom and side of ungreased 12-inch pizza pan or on bottom only of ungreased rectangular pan, 13 × 9 × 2 inches.

2. Beat sour cream and egg with spoon until blended; carefully spread over crumbly mixture. Top with peaches. Sprinkle with reserved crumbly mixture and nuts.

3. Bake 35 to 40 minutes or until topping is light golden brown and set in the center. Cool completely, about 1 hour. Drizzle with Cinnamon Glaze. Store covered in refrigerator.

12 servings.

Cinnamon Glaze
½   cup powdered sugar
⅛ to ¼   teaspoon ground cinnamon
2   teaspoons milk

Stir all ingredients until consistency of thick syrup, adding additional milk, 1 teaspoon at a time, if necessary.

1 Serving: Calories 350 (Calories from Fat 135); Fat 15g (Saturated 8g); Cholesterol 50mg; Sodium 340mg; Carbohydrate 53g (Dietary Fiber 1g); Protein 2g
% Daily Value: Vitamin A 18%; Vitamin C 2%; Calcium 10%; Iron 6%
Diet Exchanges: Not Recommended

BETTY'S TIPS

⊙ **Serve-With**
Add a scoop of vanilla, butter pecan or dulce de leche ice cream to make this dessert extra special.

⊙ **Variation**
Make a **Fresh Apple Pizza** during the fall when local apple orchards offer a wonderful selection. Use 2 medium apples, thinly sliced, instead of the peaches. Good choices of baking apples include Cortland, Crispin, Golden Delicious, Ida Red, Jonagold, Newtown Pippin, Paula Red and Rome.

Peachy Fruit Pizza

Low Fat

Chocolate-Dipped Confections

Prep: 15 min   Cook: 5 min   Chill: 30 min

1 bag (6 ounces) semisweet chocolate chips (1 cup)

1 tablespoon shortening

Assorted dippers (dried apricots, strawberries, maraschino cherries, pretzels, small cookies, pound cake cubes)

Betty Crocker colored sugar or decors, if desired

1. Line jelly roll pan, 15½ × 10½ × 1 inch, with waxed paper. Heat chocolate chips and shortening in 1-quart heavy saucepan over low heat, stirring frequently, until smooth; remove from heat.

2. Dip any of the assorted dippers ¾ of the way into chocolate; sprinkle with sugar. Place on waxed paper in pan.

3. Refrigerate uncovered about 30 minutes or until chocolate is firm.

3 to 4 dozen confections.

1 Confection: Calories 35 (Calories from Fat 20); Fat 2g (Saturated 1g); Cholesterol 0mg; Sodium 25mg; Carbohydrate 5g (Dietary Fiber 0g); Protein 0g
% Daily Value: Vitamin A 0%; Vitamin C 0%; Calcium 0%; Iron 0%
Diet Exchanges: ½ Fruit

BETTY'S TIPS

⊕ Variation

Use 6 ounces vanilla-flavored candy coating (almond bark), cut up, for the chocolate chips.

⊕ Extra Special

Dip into melted chocolate chips, then drizzle with melted vanilla-flavored candy coating or sprinkle with crushed candies.

Chocolate-Dipped Confections

Betty...
MAKES IT EASY

Strawberry Santas

Prep: 30 min

1	package (8 ounces) cream cheese, softened
½	cup marshmallow creme
12	large strawberries
12	fresh or canned pineapple chunks (1-inch pieces)
12	frilled toothpicks
24	miniature semisweet chocolate chips

Thread strawberry piece, pineapple chunk and remaining strawberry piece onto toothpick.

1. Beat cream cheese and marshmallow creme in medium bowl with electric mixer on high speed until fluffy. Place cream cheese mixture in decorating bag fitted with #17 star tip or in resealable plastic food bag.

2. Cut strawberries crosswise in half. Thread strawberry piece, pineapple chunk and remaining strawberry piece onto toothpick; press chocolate chips into pineapple for eyes. Pipe cream cheese mixture onto strawberry "hat" to form fur trim and onto pineapple to form beard. (If using bag, snip corner of bag to pipe cream cheese.) Cover and refrigerate no longer than 2 hours. Serve on white chocolate-covered creme-filled chocolate sandwich cookies.

12 Santas.

Pipe cream cheese mixture on to form fur trim and beard.

1 Santa: Calories 95 (Calories from Fat 65); Fat 7g (Saturated 4g); Cholesterol 20mg; Sodium 60mg; Carbohydrate 7g (Dietary Fiber 1g); Protein 2g
% Daily Value: Vitamin A 6%; Vitamin C 20%; Calcium 2%; Iron 2%
Diet Exchanges: ½ Fruit, 1 Fat

Strawberry Santas

Key Lime Mini-Tarts

Prep: 10 min   Chill: 1 hr

1   can (14 ounces) sweetened condensed
    milk

½   cup Key lime juice

1   container (8 ounces) frozen whipped
    topping, thawed

4   packages (2.1 ounces each) frozen mini fillo
    dough shells

    Raspberries, if desired

1. Beat milk and lime juice in large bowl with electric
   mixer on medium speed until smooth and thickened.
   Fold in whipped topping.

2. Spoon heaping teaspoonful lime mixture into each
   fillo shell. Cover and refrigerate tarts at least 1 hour
   or until set but no longer than 24 hours. Garnish
   with raspberries.

60 mini-tarts.

1 Mini-Tart: Calories 45 (Calories from Fat 10); Fat 1g (Saturated 1g);
Cholesterol 5mg; Sodium 25mg; Carbohydrate 8g (Dietary Fiber 0g);
Protein 1g
% Daily Value: Vitamin A 0%; Vitamin C 0%; Calcium 2%; Iron 0%
Diet Exchanges: ½ Starch

BETTY'S TIPS

⊗ **Substitution**

If you don't have Key lime juice, substitute ½ cup of regular
lime juice. You'll need about 2 limes.

⊗ **Success Hint**

There is no need to thaw the fillo dough shells ahead of
time. Just remove them from the freezer when you are ready
to fill them, and they will thaw in the refrigerator.

If you are serving fewer people, you can easily reduce this
recipe by half. Use ½ cup sweetened condensed milk, ¼ cup
lime juice and ½ cup frozen (thawed) whipped topping.

⊗ **Special Touch**

Add 3 drops of green food color to the lime mixture, if desired.

Key Lime Mini-Tarts

Chocolate Truffle Brownie Cups

Prep: 15 min   Bake: 22 min   Cool: 40 min   Stand: 15 min

1 package (19.8 ounces) Betty Crocker fudge brownie mix

¼ cup water

½ cup vegetable oil

2 eggs

⅔ cup whipping (heavy) cream

6 ounces semisweet baking chocolate, chopped

Chocolate sprinkles, if desired

1. Heat oven to 350°. Place miniature paper baking cup in each of 48 small muffin cups, 1¾ × 1 inch.

2. Stir brownie mix, water, oil and eggs until well blended. Fill muffin cups about ¾ full (about 1 tablespoon each) with batter. Bake 20 to 22 minutes or until toothpick inserted into edge of muffin comes out clean. Cool 10 minutes before removing from pan. Cool completely, about 30 minutes.

3. Heat whipping cream in 1-quart saucepan over low heat just until hot but not boiling; remove from heat. Stir in chocolate until melted. Let stand about 15 minutes or until mixture coats spoon. (It will become firmer the longer it cools.) Spoon about 2 teaspoons chocolate mixture over each brownie. Sprinkle with chocolate sprinkles.

48 brownie cups.

1 Brownie Cup: Calories 80 (Calories from Fat 45); Fat 5g (Saturated 2g); Cholesterol 15mg; Sodium 5mg; Carbohydrate 9g (Dietary Fiber 1g); Protein 1g
% Daily Value: Vitamin A 0%; Vitamin C 0%; Calcium 0%; Iron 2%
Diet Exchanges: ½ Starch, 1 Fat

BETTY'S TIPS

☺ Variation
Add ½ teaspoon peppermint extract to the brownie batter. Sprinkle crushed peppermint candies over the chocolate glaze.

☺ Success Hint
If you have only 1 muffin pan, bake 12 brownie cups at a time, letting the remaining batter stand at room temperature.

☺ Do-Ahead
Bake and freeze unfrosted brownie cups for up to 1 month. Thaw brownie cups at room temperature before spooning glaze over them.

Chocolate Truffle Brownie Cups

Raspberry Truffle Cups

Mini Candy Bar Cupcakes

Raspberry Truffle Cups

Prep: 30 min   Chill: 1 hr 5 min

- 6 ounces vanilla-flavored candy coating (almond bark), cut up
- 6 ounces semisweet baking chocolate, cut up
- 2 tablespoons butter or margarine, cut into pieces
- ⅓ cup whipping (heavy) cream
- 2 tablespoons raspberry liqueur
- 24 raspberries

1. Melt candy coating as directed on package. Spread 1 teaspoon coating evenly in bottoms and up sides of 24 miniature paper candy cups. Let stand until hardened.

2. Melt chocolate in heavy 2-quart saucepan over low heat, stirring constantly; remove from heat. Stir in remaining ingredients except raspberries. Refrigerate about 35 minutes, stirring frequently, until mixture is thickened and mounds when dropped from a spoon.

3. Place raspberry in each candy-coated cup. Spoon chocolate mixture into decorating bag with star tip. Pipe mixture into candy-coated cups over raspberry. Place cups on cookie sheet. Refrigerate about 30 minutes or until chocolate mixture is firm. Peel paper from cups before serving, if desired. Store tightly covered in refrigerator.

24 candies.

1 Candy: Calories 105 (Calories from Fat 65); Fat 7g (Saturated 4g); Cholesterol 5mg; Sodium 15mg; Carbohydrate 9g (Dietary Fiber 0g); Protein 1g
% Daily Value: Vitamin A 2%; Vitamin C 0%; Calcium 2%; Iron 2%
Diet Exchanges: ½ Starch, 1½ Fat

BETTY'S TIPS

✪ Variation
For **Cherry Truffle Cups,** substitute cherry liqueur for the raspberry liqueur and 24 candied cherry halves for the raspberries.

For **Crème de Menthe Truffle Cups,** add ¼ cup finely ground almonds to the chocolate mixture and substitute crème de menthe for the raspberry liqueur.

Mini Candy Bar Cupcakes

Prep: 20 min   Bake: 15 min per pan   Cool: 30 min

- 5 bars (2.1 ounces each) chocolate-covered crispy peanut-butter candy
- 1 package Betty Crocker SuperMoist white cake mix
- 1¼ cups water
- ⅓ cup vegetable oil
- 3 egg whites
- 1 tub Betty Crocker Whipped milk chocolate ready-to-spread frosting

1. Heat oven to 350°. Line small muffin cups, 1¾ × 1 inch, with small paper baking cups. Finely chop enough candy to equal ¾ cup (about 1½ bars).

2. Make cake mix as directed on package, using water, oil and egg whites. Beat in chopped candy on low speed just until blended. Divide batter evenly among muffin cups (⅔ full). Refrigerate any remaining cake batter until ready to use.

3. Bake 13 to 15 minutes or until cupcakes spring back when touched lightly in center. Remove from pan to wire rack. Cool completely, about 30 minutes. Frost cupcakes with frosting. Coarsely chop remaining candy. Place candy pieces on frosting, pressing down slightly. Store cupcakes loosely covered at room temperature.

Makes 72 cupcakes.

1 Cupcake: Calories 85 (Calories from Fat 35); Fat 4g (Saturated 2g); Cholesterol 0mg; Sodium 65mg; Carbohydrate 11g (Dietary Fiber 0g); Protein 1g
% Daily Value: Vitamin A 0%; Vitamin C 0%; Calcium 0%; Iron 0%
Diet Exchanges: 1 Starch, ½ Fat

BETTY'S TIPS

✪ Success Hint
The candy bars will be easier to chop if chilled in the refrigerator about 1 hour.

✪ Variation
You can make 24 regular-size cupcakes if you like. Use medium muffin cups, 2½ × 1¼ inches, and either line with paper baking cups or grease and flour. Bake for 18 to 23 minutes.

Caramel Pecan Cheesecake Bites

Prep: 15 min   Bake: 45 min   Stand: 30 min   Chill: 2 hr

Graham Cracker Crust (below)

3 packages (8 ounces each) cream cheese, softened

⅔ cup granulated sugar

1 teaspoon vanilla

¼ cup whipping (heavy) cream

3 eggs

½ cup pecan halves, coarsely chopped

1 tablespoon butter or margarine, softened

1 tablespoon packed brown sugar

⅓ cup caramel topping

1. Heat oven to 325°. Make Graham Cracker Crust.

2. Beat cream cheese in large bowl with electric mixer on medium speed until smooth. Gradually beat in granulated sugar and the vanilla until smooth. Beat in whipping cream. Beat in eggs, one at a time. Pour over crust. Stir pecans, butter, brown sugar and caramel topping until mixed; drop evenly over cheesecake.

3. Bake 30 to 35 minutes or until set and light golden brown around edges. Let stand 30 minutes to cool. Cover and refrigerate at least 2 hours but no longer than 48 hours. Cut cheesecake with 1¼-inch round cookie cutter; place on serving plate. Drizzle with additional caramel topping if desired.

70 bites.

Graham Cracker Crust

1½ cups graham cracker crumbs

¼ cup sugar

¼ cup butter or margarine, melted

Line rectangular pan, 15½ × 10½ × 1 inch, with aluminum foil. Mix all ingredients. Press in bottom of pan, using fork. Bake 8 to 10 minutes; cool.

1 Bite: Calories 95 (Calories from Fat 45); Fat 5g (Saturated 3g); Cholesterol 20mg; Sodium 105mg; Carbohydrate 11g (Dietary Fiber 0g); Protein 2g
% Daily Value: Vitamin A 2%; Vitamin C 0%; Calcium 0%; Iron 4%
Diet Exchanges: ½ Starch, 1 Fat

BETTY'S TIPS

⊙ **Success Hint**
After cutting a few of the cheesecake rounds, wipe off the cookie cutter with a paper towel.

⊙ **Variation**
You can also cut the cheesecake into squares instead of rounds.

Caramel Pecan Cheesecake Bites

Frosted Cupcake Cones

Prep: 20 min   Bake: 25 min per pan   Cool: 1 hr

1   package Betty Crocker SuperMoist cake mix (any flavor)
     Water, oil and eggs called for on cake mix package
30 to 36   flat-bottom ice-cream cones
1   tub Betty Crocker Whipped frosting (any flavor)
     Decorations, if desired

1. Heat oven to 350°. Make cake batter as directed on package, using water, oil and eggs.

2. Fill each cone about half full of batter. Stand cones in muffin pan.

3. Bake 20 to 25 minutes or until toothpick carefully inserted in center comes out clean. Cool completely, about 1 hour. Frost with frosting and decorate. Store loosely covered.

30 to 36 cupcake cones.

1 Cone: Calories 165 (Calories from Fat 65); Fat 7g (Saturated 2g); Cholesterol 15mg; Sodium 120mg; Carbohydrate 25g (Dietary Fiber 0g); Protein 1g
% Daily Value: Vitamin A 0%; Vitamin C 0%; Calcium 2%; Iron 0%
Diet Exchanges: ½ Starch, 1 Fruit, 1½ Fat

BETTY'S TIPS

☺ Special Touch
The cake bakes right inside the cone! Just decorate and enjoy. You can use miniature chocolate chips, colored candy sprinkles or assorted candies for decorations.

Kids love bugs and butterflies. Create some exciting "creatures" on the top of these fun cupcakes using small cookies or licorice candies for bodies, mini candy-coated chocolate candies for eyes and small pieces of licorice for legs and antennae.

Frosted Cupcake Cones

Betty...
MAKES IT EASY

Cream Cheese Cupcakes

Prep: 30 min   Bake: 25 min per pan   Cool: 1 hr

2	packages (3 ounces each) cream cheese, softened
1/3	cup sugar
1	egg
1	bag (6 ounces) semisweet chocolate chips (1 cup)
1	package Betty Crocker SuperMoist devil's food cake mix
1 1/3	cups water
1/2	cup vegetable oil
3	eggs
1 1/2	ounces cream cheese, softened
4	teaspoons sugar

Place small plastic bag in glass. Spoon cream cheese mixture into corner of bag. Snip about 1/8 inch off corner.

1. Heat oven to 350°. Place paper baking cup in each of 24 medium muffin cups, 2 1/2 × 1 1/4 inches. Beat 2 packages cream cheese, 1/3 cup sugar and 1 egg in medium bowl with electric mixer on medium speed until smooth. Stir in chocolate chips; set aside.

2. Make cake mix as directed on package, using water, oil and 3 eggs. Divide batter among cups. Top each with 1 tablespoon cream cheese mixture (mixture will sink into batter).

3. Beat 1 1/2 ounces cream cheese and 4 tablespoons sugar with spoon until smooth. Spoon into corner of small plastic bag. Snip about 1/8 inch off corner of bag. Squeeze mixture onto batter in a small design to decorate tops of cupcakes.

Before baking, squeeze mixture onto batter in design of your choice.

4. Bake 20 to 25 minutes or until tops spring back when touched lightly. Cool 10 minutes; remove from pan to wire rack. Cool completely, about 50 minutes.

24 cupcakes.

1 Cupcake: Calories 295 (Calories from Fat 145); Fat 16g (Saturated 8g); Cholesterol 45mg; Sodium 190mg; Carbohydrate 36g (Dietary Fiber 1g); Protein 3g
% Daily Value: Vitamin A 2%; Vitamin C 0%; Calcium 4%; Iron 6%
Diet Exchanges: 1 1/2 Starch, 1 Fruit, 3 Fat

Cream Cheese Cupcakes

Grasshopper Bars

Prep: 15 min   Bake: 30 min   Cool: 15 min   Chill: 3 hr 15 min

- 1 cup granulated sugar
- ½ cup butter or margarine, softened
- 1 teaspoon vanilla
- 2 eggs
- ⅔ cup Gold Medal all-purpose flour
- ½ cup baking cocoa
- ½ teaspoon baking powder
- ½ teaspoon salt
- 3 cups powdered sugar
- ⅓ cup butter or margarine, softened
- 2 tablespoons green crème de menthe
- 2 tablespoons white crème de cacao
- 1½ ounces unsweetened baking chocolate

1. Heat oven to 350°. Grease square pan, 8 × 8 × 2 inches. Beat granulated sugar, ½ cup butter, the vanilla and eggs in medium bowl with electric mixer on medium speed, or stir with spoon, until smooth. Stir in flour, cocoa, baking powder and salt. Spread in pan.

2. Bake 25 to 30 minutes or until toothpick inserted in center comes out clean; cool 15 minutes. Mix remaining ingredients except chocolate; spread over brownies. Refrigerate 15 minutes.

3. Melt chocolate over low heat; spread evenly over powdered sugar mixture. Refrigerate at least 3 hours. For bars, cut into 5 rows by 5 rows.

25 bars.

1 Bar: Calories 160 (Calories from Fat 70); Fat 8g (Saturated 5g); Cholesterol 35mg; Sodium 105mg; Carbohydrate 22g (Dietary Fiber 1g); Protein 1g
% Daily Value: Vitamin A 4%; Vitamin C 0%; Calcium 0%; Iron 0%
Diet Exchanges: ½ Starch, 1 Fruit, 1½ Fat

BETTY'S TIPS

✪ Substitution
You can substitute ¼ cup milk plus ½ teaspoon peppermint extract for the liqueurs.

✪ Extra Special
Cut bars into triangles for a new shape on your holiday tray. Or use deep cookie cutters in festive shapes. Spray cookie cutters with cooking spray for easier cutting.

Triple-Chocolate Cherry Bars

Prep: 10 min   Bake: 30 min   Cool: 1 hr

- 1 package Betty Crocker SuperMoist chocolate fudge cake mix
- 1 can (21 ounces) cherry pie filling
- 2 eggs, beaten
- ½ bag (12-ounce size) miniature semisweet chocolate chips (1 cup)
- 1 tub Betty Crocker Whipped chocolate ready-to-spread frosting

1. Heat oven to 350°. Grease bottom and sides of jelly roll pan, 15½ × 10½ × 1 inch, with shortening; lightly flour.

2. Mix cake mix (dry), pie filling, eggs and chocolate chips in large bowl with spoon. Pour into pan.

3. Bake 20 to 30 minutes or until toothpick inserted in center comes out clean. Cool completely, about 1 hour. Frost with frosting. Cut into 8 rows by 6 rows.

48 bars.

1 Bar: Calories 110 (Calories from Fat 35); Fat 4g (Saturated 2g); Cholesterol 10mg; Sodium 80mg; Carbohydrate 18g (Dietary Fiber 1g); Protein 1g
% Daily Value: Vitamin A 0%; Vitamin C 0%; Calcium 0%; Iron 2%
Diet Exchanges: ½ Starch, ½ Fruit, 1 Fat

BETTY'S TIPS

✪ Success Hint
Shiny metal pans are preferred for making bars. They reflect the heat away from the bars, preventing the crust from getting too brown and dark. Dark nonstick and glass baking pans should be used following the manufacturer's directions, usually reducing the oven temperature 25°. Be careful when cutting bars in nonstick pans, or you may scratch the surface. Use a plastic knife to avoid this problem.

✪ Variation
Make **Triple Chocolate Strawberry Bars** by using strawberry pie filling instead of the cherry.

Grasshopper Bars

Triple-Chocolate Cherry Bars

Rocky Road Bars

Prep: 15 min   Bake: 35 min   Cool: 1 hr

- 1 package Betty Crocker SuperMoist chocolate fudge cake mix
- ½ cup butter or margarine, melted
- ⅓ cup water
- ¼ cup packed brown sugar
- 2 eggs
- 1 cup chopped nuts
- 3 cups miniature marshmallows
- ½ cup candy-coated chocolate candies
- ⅓ cup Betty Crocker Rich & Creamy chocolate ready-to-spread frosting

1. Heat oven to 350°. Grease bottom and sides of rectangular pan, 13 × 9 × 2 inches, with shortening. Mix half of the cake mix (dry), the butter, water, brown sugar and eggs in large bowl with spoon until smooth (some dry mix will remain). Stir in remaining cake mix and the nuts. Spread in pan.

2. Bake 20 minutes; sprinkle with marshmallows. Bake 10 to 15 minutes longer or until marshmallows are puffed and golden. Immediately sprinkle with candies. Microwave frosting in microwavable bowl uncovered on High 15 seconds. Drizzle over bars. Cool completely, about 1 hour. For bars, cut into 6 rows by 4 rows.

24 bars.

1 Bar: Calories 210 (Calories from Fat 90); Fat 10g (Saturated 4g); Cholesterol 30mg; Sodium 200mg; Carbohydrate 28g (Dietary Fiber 0g); Protein 2g
% Daily Value: Vitamin A 2%; Vitamin C 0%; Calcium 2%; Iron 4%
Diet Exchanges: 1 Starch, 1 Fruit, 1½ Fat

BETTY'S TIPS

⊗ **Substitution**
You can use SuperMoist devil's food cake mix instead of the chocolate fudge cake mix.

⊗ **Success Hint**
For easier cutting, use a plastic knife dipped in hot water.
Line baking pans with aluminum foil for super-quick cleanup.

Rocky Road Bars

German Chocolate Bars

Prep: 15 min   Bake: 40 min   Cool: 1 hr   Chill: 2 hr

⅔ cup butter or margarine, softened

1 package Betty Crocker SuperMoist German chocolate cake mix

1 tub Betty Crocker Rich & Creamy coconut pecan ready-to-spread frosting

1 bag (6 ounces) semisweet chocolate chips (1 cup)

¼ cup milk

1. Heat oven to 350°. Lightly grease bottom and sides of rectangular pan, 13 × 9 × 2 inches, with shortening. Cut butter into cake mix (dry) in medium bowl, using pastry blender or crisscrossing 2 knives, until crumbly. Press half of the mixture (2½ cups) in bottom of pan. Bake 10 minutes.

2. Carefully spread frosting over baked layer; sprinkle evenly with chocolate chips. Stir milk into remaining cake mixture. Drop by teaspoonfuls onto chocolate chips.

3. Bake 25 to 30 minutes or until cake portion is slightly dry to the touch. Cool completely, about 1 hour.

Cover and refrigerate about 2 hours or until firm. Cut into 8 rows by 6 rows. Store covered in refrigerator.

48 bars.

1 Bar: Calories 135 (Calories from Fat 70); Fat 8g (Saturated 4g); Cholesterol 15mg; Sodium 100mg; Carbohydrate 15g (Dietary Fiber 0g); Protein 1g
% Daily Value: Vitamin A 2%; Vitamin C 0%; Calcium 2%; Iron 2%
Diet Exchanges: ½ Starch, ½ Fruit, 1½ Fat

BETTY'S TIPS

☺ Variation
For a deliciously easy dessert, place 2 bars on individual serving plates. Top with canned whipped cream and grated milk chocolate from a candy bar.

☺ Special Touch
Pack 'em for a picnic! These mouthwatering bars are a great change of pace from the standard brownies typically brought on picnics. Take them right in the pan.

German Chocolate Bars

Carrot Raisin Bars

Prep: 10 min   Bake: 20 min   Cool: 1 hr

1   package Betty Crocker SuperMoist carrot cake mix
½   cup vegetable oil
¼   cup water
2   eggs
¾   cup raisins
½   cup chopped nuts
1   tub Betty Crocker Rich & Creamy cream cheese frosting

1. Heat oven to 350°. Grease bottom and sides of jelly roll pan, 15½ × 10½ × 1 inch, with shortening; lightly flour.

2. Mix cake mix (dry), oil, water and eggs in large bowl with spoon. Stir in raisins and nuts. Spread evenly in pan.

3. Bake 15 to 20 minutes or until bars spring back when touched lightly in center. Cool completely, about 1 hour. Frost with frosting. Cut into 8 rows by 6 rows.

48 bars.

1 Bar: Calories 115 (Calories from Fat 45); Fat 5g (Saturated 1g); Cholesterol 10mg; Sodium 9mg; Carbohydrate 17g (Dietary Fiber 0g); Protein 1g
% Daily Value: Vitamin A 2%; Vitamin C 0%; Calcium 2%; Iron 2%
Diet Exchanges: 1 Starch, ½ Fruit, 1 Fat

BETTY'S TIPS

⊕ **Substitution**
Use orange juice instead of the water to give these bars a nice flavor boost. Make your own cream cheese frosting using the recipe on page 233.

⊕ **Special Touch**
Add a cinnamon design. Dip small cookie cutters into cinnamon, and press lightly into frosting.
Or sprinkle chopped walnuts onto frosted bars.

Pecan Pie Squares

Prep: 15 min   Bake: 45 min   Cool: 1 hr

3   cups Gold Medal all-purpose flour
¾   cup butter or margarine, softened
⅓   cup sugar
½   teaspoon salt
     Pecan Filling (below)

1. Heat oven to 350°. Grease jelly roll pan, 15½ × 10½ × 1 inch. Beat flour, butter, sugar and salt in large bowl with electric mixer on low speed until crumbly (mixture will be dry). Press firmly in pan. Bake about 20 minutes or until light golden brown.

2. Make Pecan Filling. Pour filling over baked layer; spread evenly. Bake about 25 minutes or until filling is set. Cool completely, about 1 hour. For squares, cut into 10 rows by 6 rows.

60 squares.

Pecan Filling
4   eggs, slightly beaten
1½   cups sugar
1½   cups corn syrup
3   tablespoons butter or margarine, melted
1½   teaspoons vanilla
2½   cups chopped pecans

Mix all ingredients except pecans in large bowl until well blended. Stir in pecans.

1 Square: Calories 140 (Calories from Fat 65); Fat 7g (Saturated 2g); Cholesterol 20mg; Sodium 55mg; Carbohydrate 18g (Dietary Fiber 0g); Protein 1g
% Daily Value: Vitamin A 2%; Vitamin C 0%; Calcium 0%; Iron 2%
Diet Exchanges: ½ Starch, ½ Fruit, 1½ Fat

BETTY'S TIPS

⊕ **Substitution**
Walnut Pie Squares are just as delicious and are made by substituting walnuts for the pecans.

⊕ **Special Touch**
Enjoy a real Southern-style taste treat—the flavor of pecan pie without having to roll out the dough! For an extra-special treat, dip the squares into melted semisweet chocolate chips.

⊕ **Variation**
Cut into triangles instead of squares.

Pecan Pie Squares

Carrot Raisin Bars

Caramel Bars

Lemon Cheesecake Bars

Lemon Cheesecake Bars

Prep: 15 min   Bake: 25 min   Cool: 1 hr   Chill: 3 hr

- 1   package Betty Crocker SuperMoist lemon cake mix
- ⅓   cup butter or margarine, softened
- 3   eggs
- 1   package (8 ounces) cream cheese, softened
- 1   cup powdered sugar
- 2   teaspoons grated lemon peel
- 2   tablespoons lemon juice

1. Heat oven to 350°. Beat cake mix (dry), butter and 1 of the eggs in large bowl with electric mixer on low speed until crumbly. Press in bottom of ungreased rectangular pan, 13 × 9 × 2 inches.

2. Beat cream cheese in medium bowl on medium speed until smooth. Gradually beat in powdered sugar on low speed. Stir in lemon peel and lemon juice until smooth. Reserve ½ cup; refrigerate. Beat remaining 2 eggs into remaining cream cheese mixture on medium speed until blended. Spread over cake mixture.

3. Bake about 25 minutes or until set. Cool completely, about 1 hour. Spread with reserved cream cheese mixture. Refrigerate about 3 hours or until firm. For bars, cut into 8 rows by 6 rows. Store covered in refrigerator.

48 bars.

1 Bar: Calories 85 (Calories from Fat 35); Fat 4g (Saturated 2g); Cholesterol 20mg; Sodium 95mg; Carbohydrate 11g (Dietary Fiber 0g); Protein 1g
% Daily Value: Vitamin A 2%; Vitamin C 0%; Calcium 2%; Iron 2%
Diet Exchanges: ½ Starch, ½ Fruit, ½ Fat

BETTY'S TIPS

✪ Success Hint

How many lemons do you need for this recipe? One lemon will be fine. One medium lemon yields 1½ to 3 teaspoons of grated peel and 2 to 3 tablespoons of lemon juice.

Bake bars in the exact pan size called for in a recipe. Bars baked in a pan that is too large will overbake and be hard. Those baked in a pan that's too small can be doughy in the center and hard on the edges.

✪ Special Touch

These bars will look extra special if each piece is garnished with a curl of lemon peel.

Caramel Bars

Prep: 15 min   Bake: 22 min   Cool: 20 min   Chill: 2 hr

- 1   cup packed brown sugar
- 1   cup butter or margarine, softened
- 1½ teaspoons vanilla
- 1   egg
- 2   cups Gold Medal all-purpose flour
- ½   cup light corn syrup
- 2   tablespoons butter or margarine
- 1   cup butterscotch-flavored chips
- 1½ to 2   cups assorted candies and nuts (such as candy-coated chocolate candies and salted peanuts)

1. Heat oven to 350°. Mix brown sugar, 1 cup butter, the vanilla and egg in large bowl. Stir in flour. Press evenly in bottom of ungreased rectangular pan, 13 × 9 × 2 inches. Bake 20 to 22 minutes or until light brown. Cool 20 minutes.

2. Heat corn syrup, 2 tablespoons butter and the butterscotch chips in 1-quart saucepan over medium heat, stirring constantly, until chips are melted; remove from heat. Cool 10 minutes.

3. Spread butterscotch mixture over baked layer. Sprinkle half the bars with candies and remaining half with nuts; gently press into butterscotch mixture. Cover and refrigerate at least 2 hours until butterscotch mixture is firm. For bars, cut into 6 rows by 6 rows.

36 bars.

1 Bar: Calories 185 (Calories from Fat 90); Fat 10g (Saturated 6g); Cholesterol 20mg; Sodium 70mg; Carbohydrate 22g (Dietary Fiber 1g); Protein 2g
% Daily Value: Vitamin A 4%; Vitamin C 0%; Calcium 2%; Iron 2%
Diet Exchanges: 1 Starch, ½ Fruit, 2 Fat

BETTY'S TIPS

✪ Success Hint

To make smoother cuts, spray knife with cooking spray before cutting bars.

✪ Variation

Use your favorite assortment of colorful candies and nuts!

Betty... MAKES IT EASY

Rolled Sugar Cookies

Prep: 45 min   Bake: 7 min per sheet   Cool: 1 min

Paint colors on freshly iced, glazed or frosted cookies, using a fine-tip brush.

- 1 package Betty Crocker SuperMoist white cake mix
- ½ cup shortening
- ⅓ cup butter or margarine, softened
- 1 teaspoon vanilla, almond extract or lemon extract
- 1 egg
- Sugar
- 1 cup Betty Crocker Rich & Creamy vanilla ready-to-spread frosting
- Food colors

1. Heat oven to 375°. Beat half of the cake mix (dry), the shortening, butter, vanilla and egg in large bowl with electric mixer on medium speed until smooth, or mix with spoon. Stir in remaining cake mix.

2. Divide dough into 4 equal parts. Roll each part ⅛ inch thick on lightly floured cloth-covered surface with cloth-covered rolling pin. Cut into desired shapes; sprinkle with sugar. Place 2 inches apart on ungreased cookie sheet.

3. Bake 5 to 7 minutes or until light brown. Cool 1 minute; remove from cookie sheet to wire rack. Microwave frosting in microwavable bowl uncovered on High 20 to 30 seconds or until melted; stir. Frost cookies. Stir together small amounts of water and food color. Paint colors on freshly frosted cookies, using fine-tip brush, then swirl colors with brush or toothpick to create marbled designs. Dry completely before storing.

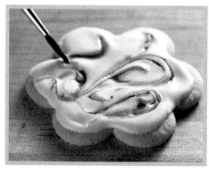

Swirl colors with a brush or toothpick to create marbled designs.

About 4 dozen 2½-inch cookies.

1 Cookie: Calories 120 (Calories from Fat 55); Fat 6g (Saturated 3g); Cholesterol 10mg; Sodium 85mg; Carbohydrate 15g (Dietary Fiber 0g); Protein 1g
% Daily Value: Vitamin A 0%; Vitamin C 0%; Calcium 2%; Iron 0%
Diet Exchanges: ½ Starch, ½ Fruit, 1 Fat

Rolled Sugar Cookies

Munchy Chocolate Cookies

Prep: 10 min   Bake: 10 min per sheet

1   package Betty Crocker SuperMoist devil's food cake mix

⅓   cup vegetable oil

2   eggs

Granulated sugar

1. Heat oven to 350°. Mix cake mix (dry), oil and eggs in large bowl with spoon until dough forms (some dry mix will remain).

2. Shape dough into 1-inch balls; roll in sugar. Place about 2 inches apart on ungreased cookie sheet.

3. Bake 8 to 10 minutes or until set. Remove from cookie sheet to wire rack.

About 4 dozen cookies.

1 Cookie: Calories 60 (Calories from Fat 20); Fat 2g (Saturated 1g); Cholesterol 10mg; Sodium 80mg; Carbohydrate 10g (Dietary Fiber 0g); Protein 0g
% Daily Value: Vitamin A 0%; Vitamin C 0%; Calcium 0%; Iron 0%
Diet Exchanges: ½ Starch, ½ Fat

BETTY'S TIPS

✪ Substitution
SuperMoist chocolate fudge cake mix can be used instead of the devil's food cake mix.

✪ Success Hint
The tops of these cookies look crinkled, and they have a soft, chewy texture.

✪ Variation
For **Kissed Crinkles,** roll cookie balls in powdered sugar. Bake as directed, then immediately press a milk chocolate kiss or white chocolate kiss with milk chocolate stripes in the center of each cookie.

Munchy Chocolate Cookies

White Chocolate Chunk Cranberry Cookies

Prep: 15 min   Bake: 12 min per sheet   Cool: 32 min

⅔ cup packed brown sugar

½ cup granulated sugar

½ cup butter or margarine

⅔ cup shortening

1 teaspoon vanilla

1 teaspoon finely shredded orange peel

1 egg

2¼ cups Gold Medal all-purpose flour

1 teaspoon baking soda

¼ teaspoon salt

⅔ cup dried cranberries

1 package (6 ounces) white baking bars (white chocolate), cut into ¼- to ½-inch chunks

White Chocolate Glaze (below)

1. Heat oven to 350°. Beat sugars, butter, shortening, vanilla, orange peel and egg in large bowl with electric mixer on medium speed until light and fluffy, or mix with spoon. Stir in flour, baking soda and salt. Stir in cranberries and white baking bar chunks. Drop by rounded teaspoonfuls about 2 inches apart onto ungreased cookie sheet.

2. Bake 10 to 12 minutes or until light brown. Cool 1 to 2 minutes; remove from cookie sheet to wire rack. Cool completely, about 30 minutes. Drizzle with White Chocolate Glaze.

About 5½ dozen cookies.

White Chocolate Glaze

1 package (6 ounces) white baking bars (white chocolate), chopped

2 teaspoons shortening

Place ingredients in 2-cup microwavable measuring cup or deep bowl. Microwave uncovered on High 45 seconds; stir.

1 Cookie: Calories 90 (Calories from Fat 45); Fat 5g (Saturated 2g); Cholesterol 10mg; Sodium 45mg; Carbohydrate 11g (Dietary Fiber 0g); Protein 1g
% Daily Value: Vitamin A 0%; Vitamin C 0%; Calcium 0%; Iron 0%
Diet Exchanges: 1 Fruit, 1 Fat

BETTY'S TIPS

☺ **Substitution**
For **White Chocolate Chunk Macadamia Cookies,** omit the orange peel and cranberries and stir in a 3½-ounce jar of macadamia nuts, coarsely chopped.

☺ **Special Touch**
Instead of drizzling the glaze over the cookies, dip half of each cookie into the glaze.

White Chocolate Chunk Cranberry Cookies

Betty... MAKES IT EASY

Luscious Chocolate Truffles

Prep: 20 min   Chill: 25 min   Freeze: 30 min

1   bag (12 ounces) semisweet chocolate chips (2 cups)
2   tablespoons butter or margarine
¼   cup whipping (heavy) cream
2   tablespoons liqueur (almond, cherry, coffee, hazelnut, Irish cream, orange, raspberry, etc.), if desired
1   tablespoon shortening
    Finely chopped nuts, if desired
    Finely chopped dried apricots, if desired
    White baking bar, chopped, if desired

Drop mixture by teaspoonfuls onto cookie sheet.

1. Line cookie sheet with aluminum foil or parchment paper. Melt 1 cup of the chocolate chips in heavy 2-quart saucepan over low heat, stirring constantly; remove from heat. Stir in butter. Stir in whipping cream and liqueur. Refrigerate 10 to 15 minutes, stirring frequently, just until thick enough to hold a shape.

2. Drop mixture by teaspoonfuls onto cookie sheet. Shape into balls. (If mixture is too sticky, refrigerate until firm enough to shape.) Freeze 30 minutes.

3. Heat shortening and remaining 1 cup chocolate chips over low heat, stirring constantly, until chocolate is melted and mixture is smooth; remove from heat. Dip truffles, one at a time, into chocolate. Return to cookie sheet. Immediately sprinkle nuts and apricots over some of the truffles. Refrigerate 10 minutes or until coating is set.

Using a fork, dip truffles into chocolate.

4. Heat baking bar over low heat, stirring constantly, until melted. Drizzle over some of the truffles. Refrigerate just until set. Store in airtight container in refrigerator. Remove truffles from refrigerator about 30 minutes before serving; serve at room temperature.

About 15 truffles.

1 Truffle: Calories 145 (Calories from Fat 90); Fat 10g (Saturated 6g); Cholesterol 10mg; Sodium 15mg; Carbohydrate 14g (Dietary Fiber 1g); Protein 1g
% Daily Value: Vitamin A 2%; Vitamin C 0%; Calcium 0%; Iron 4%
Diet Exchanges: 1 Fruit, 2 Fat

Luscious Chocolate Truffles

White Chocolate Cherry Crunch

Almond Caramel Corn

White Chocolate Cherry Crunch

Prep: 10 min   Cook: 5 min   Stand: 1 hr

2 cups Corn Chex® cereal
2 cups tiny fish-shaped pretzels
2 cups dry-roasted peanuts
1 cup miniature marshmallows
1 package (3 ounces) dried cherries (⅔ cup)
1 bag (12 ounces) white baking chips (2 cups)
¼ cup half-and-half
½ teaspoon almond extract

1. Toss cereal, pretzels, peanuts, marshmallows and cherries in large bowl.

2. Heat baking chips and half-and-half in 2-quart saucepan over low heat, stirring frequently, until chips are melted. Stir in almond extract.

3. Pour melted mixture over dry ingredients. Toss gently until dry ingredients are coated. Drop mixture by tablespoonfuls onto waxed paper. Let stand about 1 hour or until set. Store loosely covered up to 1 week.

About 16 servings (½ cup each).

½ Cup: Calories 70 (Calories from Fat 35); Fat 4g (Saturated 1g); Cholesterol 0mg; Sodium 50mg; Carbohydrate 8g (Dietary Fiber 1g); Protein 2g
% Daily Value: Vitamin A 0%; Vitamin C 0%; Calcium 2%; Iron 2%
Diet Exchanges: ½ Starch, ½ Fat

BETTY'S TIPS

☺ Substitution
You can use 12 ounces vanilla-flavored candy coating (almond bark), chopped, instead of the white baking chips. Omit half-and-half, and melt coating as directed on package.

☺ Special Touch
Drop mixture into paper candy cups, and let stand until set.

Almond Caramel Corn

Prep: 20 min   Bake: 1 hr   Cool: 30 min

12 cups popped popcorn
3 cups unblanched whole almonds
1 cup packed brown sugar
½ cup butter or margarine
¼ cup light corn syrup
½ teaspoon salt
½ teaspoon baking soda

1. Heat oven to 200°. Place popcorn and almonds in very large roasting pan or divide popcorn mixture between 2 ungreased rectangular pans, 13 × 9 × 2 inches.

2. Heat brown sugar, butter, corn syrup and salt in 2-quart saucepan over medium heat, stirring occasionally, until bubbly around edges. Continue cooking 5 minutes without stirring; remove from heat. Stir in baking soda until foamy.

3. Pour sugar mixture over popcorn; toss until evenly coated. Bake 1 hour, stirring every 15 minutes. Spread on aluminum foil or cooking parchment paper. Cool completely, about 30 minutes. Store tightly covered.

About 30 servings (½ cup each).

½ Cup: Calories 170 (Calories from Fat 110); Fat 12g (Saturated 3g); Cholesterol 10mg; Sodium 90mg; Carbohydrate 15g (Dietary Fiber 2g); Protein 3g
% Daily Value: Vitamin A 2%; Vitamin C 0%; Calcium 4%; Iron 4%
Diet Exchanges: 1 Starch, 2 Fat

BETTY'S TIPS

☺ Variation
For **Oven Caramel Corn,** increase popcorn to 15 cups and omit the almonds.

☺ Substitution
You can use pecan or walnut halves instead of the almonds.

Rich Chocolate Fudge

Prep: 10 min   Chill: 1 hr 30 min

  1   can (14 ounces) sweetened condensed milk
  1   bag (12 ounces) semisweet chocolate chips
       (2 cups)
  1   ounce unsweetened baking chocolate,
       chopped, if desired
 1½ cups chopped nuts, if desired
  1   teaspoon vanilla

1. Grease bottom and sides of square pan, 8 × 8 × 2 inches, with butter.

2. Heat milk, chocolate chips and unsweetened chocolate in 2-quart saucepan over low heat, stirring constantly, until chocolate is melted and mixture is smooth; remove from heat.

3. Quickly stir in nuts and vanilla. Spread in pan. Refrigerate about 1 hour 30 minutes or until firm. Cut into 1-inch squares.

64 candies.

1 Candy: Calories 55 (Calories from Fat 20); Fat 2g (Saturated 1g); Cholesterol 5mg; Sodium 10mg; Carbohydrate 8g (Dietary Fiber 0g); Protein 1g
% Daily Value: Vitamin A 0%; Vitamin C 0%; Calcium 2%; Iron 0%
Diet Exchanges: ½ Starch, ½ Fat

BETTY'S TIPS

⊙ Success Hint

For a deeper, richer chocolate flavor, be sure to add the unsweetened baking chocolate.

Line the pan with aluminum foil for super-quick cleanup and for lifting the fudge out of the pan so you can cut it evenly.

Rich Chocolate Fudge

Company's Coming!

Impressive Ideas for Entertaining

Baked Chicken and Rice with Autumn Vegetables (page 129)

Nutty Squash Pie (page 242)

Searching for fresh, new ideas to add some zip to your next party or get-together? Well, look no further! Family and friends will rave when you serve these fun and creative menus. From an elegant dinner party, to a seafood feast, to a sunny gathering in the garden, you'll find the perfect combination of delicious dishes to wow all your guests. As an added extra, menus also include suggestions for side dishes or beverages that you can easily find in your supermarket or prepare without a recipe.

Elegant Dinner Party

Brie in Puff Pastry with Cranberry Sauce
(page 46)

Tomato-Lentil Soup (page 70)

Pork Tenderloin with Roasted Vegetables
(page 138)

Mixed greens with your favorite vinaigrette

Hot Buttered Rum Cheesecake (page 210)

Wine or sparkling water and coffee

Birthday Party for Kids

Cheesy Chicken Strips (page 121)
Pizza Burgers (page 85)
Carrot sticks
Frosted Cupcake Cones (page 255)
Chocolate Chip Swirl Cake (page 224)
Fruit punch and chocolate milk

Girls' Slumber Party
(evening & morning menus)

Thick-Crust Pizza (page 201)
Rocky Road Bars (page 260)
Rolled Sugar Cookies (page 266)
Chocolate milk
Blueberry Pancakes with Maple Cranberry Syrup (page 7)
Orange juice

Fall Harvest Meal

Baked Chicken and Rice with Autumn Vegetables (page 129)
Beet and Arugula Salad (page 187)
Sweet Potato Biscuits (page 27)
Nutty Squash Pie (page 242)
Hot apple cider with cinnamon sticks

Warm Winter Supper

Home-Style Turkey and Potato Bake (page 129)
Mesclun with vinegar-and-oil dressing
Glazed Carrots (page 172)
Peanut Brittle Bread Pudding (page 239)
Wine or seltzer

Spring Is Here

Fruit cocktail
Spring Vegetable Fettuccine (page 96)
Lemon Basil Muffins (page 23)
Lemon Orange Cake (page 229)
Iced tea with lemon slices

Summer Fun

Denver Deviled Eggs (page 55)
Garlic and Mustard Burgers (page 162)
Smoky Cheddar Potatoes (page 147)
Coleslaw
Strawberry Yogurt Cake (page 229)

Dessert Party

Chocolate-Dipped Confections (page 247)
Caramel Pecan Cheesecake Bites (page 254)
Chocolate Ganache Cake (page 220)
Gourmet coffee

Gift Basket

Apple Cheddar Muffins (page 21)
Savory Sweet Potato Pan Bread (page 343)
Almond Caramel Corn (page 273)
Rich Chocolate Fudge (page 274)
White Chocolate Chunk Cranberry Cookies (page 269)
Individual packs of gourmet instant cocoa and coffee

Sunday Brunch

Smoked Salmon and Cream Cheese Omelet (page 13)
Hash Brown Potato Brunch Bake (page 18)
Spinach Cheese Bread (page 34)
Fresh fruit salad
Orange juice and coffee

Movie Night

Caribbean Shrimp (page 66)
Cincinnati Chili (page 80)
Air-popped popcorn
German Chocolate Bars (page 261)
Assorted soft drinks

Friendly Get-Together

Timesaving Tortellini (page 102)
Caesar salad
Mini Rosemary Garlic Breads (page 28)
Frosty Coffee Almond Pie (page 236)

Kaffeeklatsch

Easy Caramel Sticky Rolls (page 2)
Apple Kuchen Coffee Cake (page 2)
Lemon Cheesecake Bars (page 265)
Coffee and hot tea

Italian Buffet

Manicotti (page 133)

Mexican Chicken Sour Cream Lasagna (page 126)

Pine Tree Parmesan Breadsticks (page 30)

Your favorite tossed salad

Fruit Bruschetta (page 244)

Wine or sparkling cider

Espresso or cappucino

Oscar Night

Portabella and Brie Appetizer Pizza (page 66)

Winter Fruit Kabobs with
Peach Glaze (page 55)

Roasted-Vegetable Lasagna (page 109)

Chocolate Truffle Brownie Cups (page 251)

Seafood Sampler

Salmon Crostini (page 52)

Shrimp Bisque (page 75)

Bow-Ties with Salmon
and Tarragon Mustard Sauce (page 98)

Mesclun with olive oil vinaigrette

Sorbet parfaits

White wine or club soda

Lotsa Company

Southwestern Turkey (page 195)

Slow Cooker Chorizo, Pecan and Cheddar
Stuffing (page 204)

Steamed mixed vegetables

Mixed greens with balsamic vinaigrette

Big Batch Cheese Garlic Biscuits (page 206)

Nutty Squash Pie (page 242)

Better-than-Almost-Anything Cake (page 217)

Assorted wines and soft drinks

Garden Gathering

Olive Tapenade on Cucumber Stars (page 49)

Pear and Rosemary Foccaccia with Fontina Cheese
(page 38)

Tomato-Basil Soup with Garlic Croutons (page 70)

Garden Medley Salad (page 184)

Fresh strawberries and kiwifruit

Champagne and sparkling grape juice

helpful **nutrition** and **cooking** information

nutrition guidelines

We provide nutrition information for each recipe that includes calories, fat, cholesterol, sodium, carbohydrate, fiber and protein. Individual food choices can be based on this information.

Recommended intake for a daily diet of 2,000 calories as set by the Food and Drug Administration		
Total Fat	Less than 65g
Saturated Fat	Less than 20g
Cholesterol	Less than 300mg
Sodium	Less than 2,400mg
Total Carbohydrate	300g
Dietary Fiber	25g

criteria used for calculating nutrition information

- The first ingredient was used wherever a choice is given (such as ⅓ cup sour cream or plain yogurt).
- The first ingredient amount was used wherever a range is given (such as 3- to 3½-pound cut-up broiler-fryer chicken).
- The first serving number was used wherever a range is given (such as 4 to 6 servings).
- "If desired" ingredients and recipe variations were not included (such as sprinkle with brown sugar, if desired).
- Only the amount of a marinade or frying oil that is estimated to be absorbed by the food during preparation or cooking was calculated.

ingredients used in recipe testing and nutrition calculations

- Ingredients used for testing represent those that the majority of consumers use in their homes: large eggs, 2% milk, 80%-lean ground beef, canned ready-to-use chicken broth and vegetable oil spread containing not less than 65 percent fat.

- Fat-free, low-fat or low-sodium products were not used, unless otherwise indicated.

- Solid vegetable shortening (not butter, margarine, nonstick cooking sprays or vegetable oil spread as they can cause sticking problems) was used to grease pans, unless otherwise indicated.

equipment used in recipe testing

We use equipment for testing that the majority of consumers use in their homes. If a specific piece of equipment (such as a wire whisk) is necessary for recipe success, it is listed in the recipe.

- Cookware and bakeware without nonstick coatings were used, unless otherwise indicated.

- No dark-colored, black or insulated bakeware was used.

- When a pan is specified in a recipe, a metal pan was used; a baking dish or pie plate means ovenproof glass was used.

- An electric hand mixer was used for mixing only when mixer speeds are specified in the recipe directions. When a mixer speed is not given, a spoon or fork was used.

cooking terms glossary

Beat: Mix ingredients vigorously with spoon, fork, wire whisk, hand beater or electric mixer until smooth and uniform.

Boil: Heat liquid until bubbles rise continuously and break on the surface and steam is given off. For rolling boil, the bubbles form rapidly.

Chop: Cut into coarse or fine irregular pieces with a knife, food chopper, blender or food processor.

Cube: Cut into squares ½ inch or larger.

Dice: Cut into squares smaller than ½ inch.

Grate: Cut into tiny particles using small rough holes of grater (citrus peel or chocolate).

Grease: Rub the inside surface of a pan with shortening, using pastry brush, piece of waxed paper or paper towel, to prevent food from sticking during baking (as for some casseroles).

Julienne: Cut into thin, matchlike strips, using knife or food processor (vegetables, fruits, meats).

Mix: Combine ingredients in any way that distributes them evenly.

Sauté: Cook foods in hot oil or margarine over medium-high heat with frequent tossing and turning motion.

Shred: Cut into long thin pieces by rubbing food across the holes of a shredder, as for cheese, or by using a knife to slice very thinly, as for cabbage.

Simmer: Cook in liquid just below the boiling point on top of the stove; usually after reducing heat from a boil. Bubbles will rise slowly and break just below the surface.

Stir: Mix ingredients until uniform consistency. Stir once in a while for stirring occasionally, often for stirring frequently and continuously for stirring constantly.

Toss: Tumble ingredients (such as green salad) lightly with a lifting motion, usually to coat evenly or mix with another food.

metric conversion chart

Volume

U.S. Units	Canadian Metric	Australian Metric
¼ teaspoon	1 mL	1 ml
½ teaspoon	2 mL	2 ml
1 teaspoon	5 mL	5 ml
1 tablespoon	15 mL	20 ml
¼ cup	50 mL	60 ml
⅓ cup	75 mL	80 ml
½ cup	125 mL	125 ml
⅔ cup	150 mL	170 ml
¾ cup	175 mL	190 ml
1 cup	250 mL	250 ml
1 quart	1 liter	1 liter
1½ quarts	1.5 liters	1.5 liters
2 quarts	2 liters	2 liters
2½ quarts	2.5 liters	2.5 liters
3 quarts	3 liters	3 liters
4 quarts	4 liters	4 liters

Weight

U.S. Units	Canadian Metric	Australian Metric
1 ounce	30 grams	30 grams
2 ounces	55 grams	60 grams
3 ounces	85 grams	90 grams
4 ounces (¼ pound)	115 grams	125 grams
8 ounces (½ pound)	225 grams	225 grams
16 ounces (1 pound)	455 grams	500 grams
1 pound	455 grams	½ kilogram

Measurements

Inches	Centimeters
1	2.5
2	5.0
3	7.5
4	10.0
5	12.5
6	15.0
7	17.5
8	20.5
9	23.0
10	25.5
11	28.0
12	30.5
13	33.0

Temperatures

Fahrenheit	Celsius
32°	0°
212°	100°
250°	120°
275°	140°
300°	150°
325°	160°
350°	180°
375°	190°
400°	200°
425°	220°
450°	230°
475°	240°
500°	260°

Note: The recipes in this cookbook have not been developed or tested using metric measures. When converting recipes to metric, some variations in quality may be noted.

Index

Underscored page references indicate Betty's Tips and tables. **Boldface** references indicate photographs.